# Two Shores of Zen

# Two Shores of Zen

## *An American Monk's Japan*

---

*Jiryu Mark Rutschman-Byler*

An incomplete but final draft for the wide Sangha.

www.ShoresOfZen.com
www.lulu.com/ShoresOfZen

Portions of earlier drafts of this work have appeared in the literary magazine *Puerto del Sol* and in *Turning Wheel: The Journal of Socially Engaged Buddhism*; reflections stemming from it have appeared in *San Francisco Zen Center's Sangha-E* and in *Buddhadharma: The Practitioner's Quarterly*.

ISBN: 978-0-557-16821-7

Copyright © 2009 by Jiryu Mark Rutschman-Byler.

All rights reserved.

*to Seido Lee deBarros & Tangen Harada Roshi—
one side of two coins*

# CONTENTS

| | | |
|---|---|---|
| Preface | | 1 |
| 1 | The Simple Life | 8 |
| 2 | No Zen in the West | 18 |
| 3 | Home Leaving | 37 |
| 4 | Deluded About Enlightenment | 48 |
| 5 | The Temple Priest | 69 |
| 6 | Notes from an A-Bomb Tour | 79 |
| 7 | Days of Work, and a Day of No Work and Good Eating | 82 |
| 8 | Do Not Call Winter the Beginning of Spring | 95 |
| 9 | Spring | 118 |
| 10 | Breaking Through | 133 |
| 11 | No Coming, No Going | 152 |
| 12 | Three Days After Money | 158 |
| 13 | Homecoming | 171 |
| Epilogue | | 177 |

*To minimize undue narrative complications, to blur the identities of real people involved, and to acknowledge the unrealiability of my memory and perception, most names and places have been altered, and details of some events have been fictionalized.*

# Preface

*Sou to omou kedo, sou dewanai kamoshirenai.*

Japanese saying, roughly, "I think so, but I doubt it."

Back and forth monks travel, weaving new threads into the tapestry that strains to span the eastern, western shores of Zen. The shuttle clicks again, and I lead myself back to Japan, tour its landscape in me. Exploring the coasts of this private Japan, it reflects, breaks, and refracts like Dogen-Zenji's endlessly opening oceans and mountains—increasing and blossoming, awakening at inquiry. These words, then, provisionally sketch some edges of experience, the shores at the limit of my eye of practice. They mark the borders of what is unwritten, like a penciled shoreline that excludes both land and ocean.

When he said goodbye to me, my American Zen teacher told me that after being in Japanese temples for a while, I should come back and tell people about it. A year and a half later, I came back. This half-sewn patchwork cannot possibly be what he had in mind, but I offer it as a gesture towards his request.

He knew of course that I could not share Japan, but just myself. People say things like, "For the first eight years, don't ask any questions," and "No one could *begin* to understand Japanese Zen in less than five years," and they are right, in my view. I leave expositions of Japanese Zen, then, to the people who have mastered it, and of American Zen, for that matter, to those who understand it, and I offer only my misunderstandings. I offer only myself, myself at the meeting of two Zens—the life on my island, washed by eastern, western currents.

○ ○ ○ ○

Many of you reading this now have inquired after or read versions of the project that inadvertently began upon my return from Japan in 2004. Initially a batch of simple stories that I thought might be of interest to my friends in the American Sangha, the writing soon ballooned into a full scale manuscript that has taken many forms and consumed many hours likely better spent less productively. Encouragement early on in the project led me to pursue publication. To that end, the focus shifted from a simple telling of my adventures in Japan into an attempt (likely doomed, as I will detail below) to compare Japanese and American Zen, holding up each to illuminate and reflect the other.

Two or three years ago I distilled the incomplete manuscript into a book proposal which has since met with cold to lukewarm responses from the publishing world. Most recently, Shambhala Publications expressed a real interest, but after a year of conversation and further revision, they declined to take on the project. It seems unlikely to me that a mainstream press would see a readership where even the Buddhist press could not (Wisdom Publications also passed on an early draft back around 2005). So, despite some of your encouragements to the contrary, I have for now set aside my efforts to refine and formally publish *Two Shores of Zen*. Out of respect for the hard work I've put into it, though, and to make good on my original intention to share my stories of Japan with the Sangha, I've chosen to make this latest draft available through print-on-demand self-publishing at *lulu.com*.

In the absence of a traditional publisher, and frankly because my heart has moved on from this project, I will not subject it to another round of editing, however necessary or beneficial it might be. I will not take the time to revise the completed chapters to my satisfaction, much less to add relevant chapters. I will not smooth out lingering structural inconsistencies, nor deepen the characters, nor surface more completely the American Zen context, nor update the piece with my current provisional Dharma understanding, nor wrap my conclusions into an easy to digest moral. "Unfinished" is no longer a temporary state but rather the permanent nature of the project—an abandoned work.

○ ○ ○ ○

A further inadequacy which I will only address by confessing is more fundamental to my story, which despite my better judgment purports to contrast orthodox Japanese Zen with its American Zen departures. Unfortunately, I arrived too late to tell this story, and to the wrong place—orthodox Zen, if it ever existed, is in the eyes of many already lost in Japan. I don't here refer to those traditionalists who lament the gradual decay that Zen monasticism has endured over the last century or two, although they too might reject the orthodoxy of contemporary Japanese Zen. Instead, I refer to the analysis of Buddhist scholars, notably Robert Sharf of U.C. Berkeley, who argue that the Zen I experienced in Japan was a Zen already influenced by Western philosophical and spiritual values. Sharf precisely documents a historical web through which Western assumptions about the meaning of Buddhism (based largely on William James and Paul Carus) were taken up in the early and mid-twentieth century by mainstream Japanese Buddhists and philosophers. As a result, the understanding of and obsession with individual enlightenment experience which I encountered in Japan does not necessarily represent traditional Asian Buddhism but may in fact result from the influence of and accommodation to modern Western values.

I, then, was a Western monk not-so-surprisingly drawn to a purportedly traditional Japanese temple that in fact had already been reshaped in a Western mold. Naturally I felt at home there, and naturally I accepted its biases and orientation. All of us practicing at Bukkokuji (the main source for the "Gendoji" of this book) understood that we were at a marginal temple—we understood it as a super-orthodox temple, recreating the fierce ancestral monastic effort in contrast to the laxity of the mainstream Japanese temple system. Perhaps more accurately, though, we were marginal in the sense of cutting edge, a product of a feedback loop that within the last century has injected Western cultural and spiritual values into a Japanese redefinition of Zen. Thus key aspects of the "Japanese Zen" described in this book may owe as much to Western culture as does the American Zen I attempt to compare it too, leaving "genuine" Japanese Zen more or less overlooked.

Bukkokuji, a nominally Soto Zen temple, is in fact much closer in lineage, doctrine, and practice to the independent Zen sect known as "Sanbokyodan," founded in 1954 by Yasutani Hakuun Roshi.

Sanbokyodan more than any other Zen sect has stripped away the scriptural, ritual, and monastic contexts of traditional Zen (no less important in Rinzai than Soto) and teaches a pivotal *kensho* experience as the core and culmination of Zen training. As Sharf also describes, the individual experience-oriented, narrowly focused, and essentializing movement of Sanbokyodan not coincidentally developed in close contact with, if not outright response to, Western students. It remains a largely non-Japanese movement. While most of the practitioners at Bukkokuji do not see themselves as affiliated with Sanbokyodan, the abbot Harada Tangen Roshi trained alongside Yasutani Roshi, and both received Dharma Transmission from the same teacher, Harada Daiun Roshi. Though Sanbokyodan was formally founded by his disciple, Harada Daiun Roshi laid the foundations for Sanbokyodan's eventual independence from the traditional Zen sects by integrating Soto and Rinzai elements, strongly emphasizing kensho, and disproportionately attracting lay and foreign disciples.

Thus my story of leaving a California Zen that under-emphasizes individual enlightenment breakthrough, a Zen that doesn't value personal meditative experience, for a Japanese form that highly values individual achievement, is fundamentally backwards. My disillusion with what I understood to be the Japanese style, and my return to a more communal and holistic approach, is also the opposite of what it seems. My return to American Zen, a Zen aiming beyond personal pure experience and towards a broader, holistic, transpersonal maturity, may in fact be closer to traditional Asian Buddhism. The American Zen I returned to is perhaps one that has developed beyond its fixation with personal experience and towards an actually more authentic understanding of what Buddhism is and offers. And the ostensibly Japanese Zen that I left may in fact be a Zen that is frozen in a Western preconception already to some extent outgrown in American Zen, a view of individual achievement wherein the defining element of the religious life is a heroic spiritual experience.

A premise of this book, then, falls apart. It attempts a straightforward comparison of poles too complex and divergent: a Western version of Japanese Soto Zen, and a Japanese version of (Western-influenced) Sanbokyodan Zen. I might instead have focused my writing about Japan on my rich experience at Hokyoji, a formal, mainstream Soto Zen *sodo* in Echizen, where I spent about three months training. Comparing my experience there to my life in American Soto Zen might well have proven more fruitful. However, just as my intention to practice traditional Soto Zen in Japan was derailed at the moment I met the powerfully charismatic Harada Tangen Roshi, so too as I recount my story the images with the strongest resonance are from my Sanbokyodan foray rather than my admittedly more brief Soto Zen monastic experience.

Incidentally, I have tried clumsily to amalgamate the two temples, Hokyoji and Bukkokuji—a decision which I hope does not too deeply undermine my account. The resulting Gendoji temple is a temple that one would in fact not encounter in Japan—nowhere would such a diverse group of kensho-hungry practitioners interact with the very strictest of hierarchal and ceremonial observances designed to train professional Japanese clergy for a life of ritual service. These are two distinct streams of modern Zen, and though narrative cohesion seemed to demand it, I regret the distortions which result from combining them. Gendoji is thus best seen as a fictionalized frame for a variety of experiences that I wanted to recount without undue digressions.

I confess these complications not to dismiss completely my own story—the issues at play have been real, the coming of age has been real, the insights and struggles very real—but rather to problematize the many layers of cultural stereotypes that I have no doubt unintentionally reinforced. The fact is that in our twenty-first century world, cross-cultural dualities do not hold up as neatly as they perhaps have in the past. Cross-cultural is no longer a straightforward meeting of two clearly distinct and independent cultures, but more a mash, a mass of inter-relationships, of interdependence and mutual influence. It is ironic that I gloss over this in my account, as my whole life has expressed this same cultural tangle: I was born in Argentina to Latin American parents, themselves children of North American missionaries of a European denomination, and as an adult I have dedicated myself to a North American version of an Indian, Chinese, and Japanese world-view in a United States whose culture is itself increasingly diverse and inexorably tangled. I apologize then, not for the cultural ambiguity of these so-called "two shores," but for their reduction into two discreet shores at all. To assert two independently existing, self-sufficient shores is both factually incorrect and decidedly anti-Zen. I apologize for not celebrating cultural confusion, the chaotic interpenetration of our one life on this planet in all its impenetrable entwinings, and instead dividing it all-too-neatly into pre-fabricated and insidious cultural and religious stereotypes.

I go forward, then, only because it seems too late to go back. I offer this story with a humility that borders on shame, in the dim hope that, for all of its problems and simplifications, it may somehow, sometime, bring some benefit to someone somewhere.

o o o o

Though it accords no honor to be acknowledged here, in preface to this patchwork draft, still I would be remiss not to name at least a few of the people whose editorial, material, and spiritual support over the years of my fiddling with this manuscript have sustained and encouraged me more than they know.

Dave Rutschman, my brother in blood and in Dharma, has from the start offered tremendous encouragement, carefully reading and commenting on more than one draft and insisting throughout, for better or for worse, that I not throw the whole thing away. I am indebted to Rev. Catherine Gammon for wielding Manjushri's sword (regrettably too little heeded) in her suggested revisions to the earliest drafts. Merrill Collett took precious free time from a practice period at Green Gulch Farm to read and help polish the excerpts and proposal; his warm, quiet, and steady enthusiasm gave me real hope in the manuscript's merit.

Writing anything longer than haiku while living at a Zen temple East or West is virtually impossible, and I have imposed upon the generosity of a few people who opened their homes to me when I found a stray month or two to dedicate to this writing. To Helen Appell I am grateful for quiet, well-lit weeks in Tiburon; and to Henry Frummer for freely offering his home to me, at the time virtually a stranger. My parents, David Rutschman and Marjory Byler, welcomed and nourished me as always during periods of work on this project. Without their support I would never have made it to this earth, much less to Japan, much less back from Japan. Where would I be without them? My love and gratitude to them is immense and under-expressed.

I am grateful to the many people at Tassajara, Green Gulch Farm, and the San Francisco Zen Center who have taken the time to read or listen to versions of the manuscript, and particularly to those whose enthusiastic responses spurred me to see it through to an albeit clumsy end. Of these many dear Dharma friends, Prudence Simon and Henry Frummer stand out in my mind as the project's most exuberant fans—a great blessing on dark, doubting days.

I also appreciate Taigen Dan Leighton and David Chadwick for their encouragement and support.

This project could never have come to fruition without the loving attention of my wife Sara, who has known just when to tolerate my late nights of writing and just when to cut off the power and demand that I get to bed and start taking care of myself.

From the start I have dedicated this endeavor to my ordination teacher, Seido Lee deBarros—who has and continues to reveal to me my own life—and to my teacher in Japan, the peerless living Buddha Harada Tangen.

To all of you, to the many more known and unmentioned, and further to the countless unknown and unmentioned, I offer my deep gratitude.

Knees, forehead, palms.


*Jiryu Mark Rutschman-Byler*
*Green Gulch Farm / Green Dragon Temple*
*October, 2009*

# 1   The Simple Life

Here at Gendoji Zen Temple is a monk whose ears are deformed, whose hands are swollen and blistered. Shoryu-san. Compact, Japanese. It is July, sweltering. I have been in Japan for three weeks, at Gendoji for two. Everything is compact and intense. The monk's hands are swollen and deformed from the cold. Sweltering Fukui province summer.

Shoryu-san helps me get to the doctor. I figured we would drive, but when I meet him in the parking lot outside the main temple gate, he pulls two rickety, dump-salvaged bikes out of the shed.

"Bike OK?" he asks. My foot throbs. He expects me to bike to the doctor?

Shoryu-san glances at me, gets on his bike, and starts riding. I follow him, pedaling harder with one foot than the other in a sort of bike-limp, zipping with him around farmhouses and rice paddies toward the narrow highway past which our town of Maibara grows denser, less rural.

Three days ago I slipped on a rock in hot rain while dashing through the temple courtyard on my way to meet the abbot, the pudgy, compact, and intense saint who sits in a narrow room behind the altar of the ceremony hall, ringing his bell while Japanese disciples and we American Zen refugees, all equally desperate for the True Way, file in one by one to meet him, shouting or whispering or pounding the ground, enacting our understanding and our longing, meeting his.

I didn't really notice the fall—I just got back up and dived through the ceremony hall doors, cutting into the waiting line for the *dokusan* interview just in front of a slower Japanese layman, Mr. Tanaka. Whatever the wisdom of racing to see the teacher, it does get the heart-rate up, the body out of the mind. To be fair, some people walk, and some even linger in the meditation hall, waiting a while for the line to wind down. Our kind abbot, "Roshi-sama," as we call him, using reverently redundant honorifics to mean something like "Reverend Venerable Master," doesn't seem to care either way—when I get there first in line, he just meets me. When I'm at the end of the line, he just meets me.

*Just here...* I whispered in the interview line, oblivious to the pain in my foot, exhaling deeply, overflowing with an edgy concentration born of anxiety and devotion. My moment was coming again, my moment to prove myself to Roshi-sama, to show myself, to reveal the depth of my meditation, the depth of my being, my understanding. If I could bring myself, he would recognize me. If he could recognize me, he would say a turning word that would meld with the chord of my meditation, propel me into the clear sky of enlightenment. To bring myself fully, I could not prepare. That much I knew. To prepare myself, I could only sit *here, just here*, in line in the *seiza* position, shins against the hardwood floor, releasing even the subtle prayer that my presence of mind would extend to the dokusan room.

In response to the maddening, prolonged clash of Roshi-sama's hand bell, the monk ahead of me in the waiting line clanged two cacophonous strikes on the bell that hung from a low stand in front of him. The robe-draped, glossy-headed Japanese monk then rose and glided through the ceremony hall toward the dokusan room with a grace like silk slipping from a lacquer table, a grace I'd yet to see even the most senior Western monks embody. The line advanced one place. Now I sat at the bell. I lifted the mallet in a cold, sweaty hand, and with the other I stabilized the bell stand. *Just here*, I whispered in impossible preparation. I felt the worn-down wooden handle of the mallet resting in my fingers, heard the gentle dance of rain on rocks, roof, and moss, felt the heat build and crawl under my layers of robes, my belly slowly rising, slowly falling. *Just here.*

Roshi-sama's hand bell erupted again from deep in the inner chamber concealed by the altar—my own hand shot forth—*clang! clang!*—

and I pushed up my body, clumsy and stiff from long hours of meditation, and hobbled through the ceremony hall toward the interview room where perhaps today, in the soft and electric stillness of our meeting, the nature of things might be laid bare. If only I could bring myself fully. *Just here.* I didn't notice the drops of blood my injured foot left on the hardwood floor.

I pushed through a curtain and entered into the dim, womb-like room through the left side, just as the monk before me backed respectfully out through the right. I dropped my head and knees to the ground in a full bow, then scurried to the straw *tatami* mat in front of Roshi-sama and sat kneeling in seiza.

Roshi-sama sat beneath the portrait of his gaunt and imposing late master, referred to in hushed tones as "Rodaishi," the religious honorific of which even "Roshi" is a mere abbreviation. His robes rested loosely around him, draping his full-lotus crossed legs. He was completely still. His short *kyosaku*, or "encouragement stick," lay flat in front of him, vibrating with potential. Though I had only met him a few times in dokusan, I knew already that in the space of my momentary hesitation or pretense the stick would snap against my shoulder, its force rippling through my body not in punishment but in insistent love.

His eyes were cast down, nearly closed. His shoulders hung relaxed and drooped slightly forward, in a breech of good Zen posture to which old age and enlightened reputation entitled him. His stillness sat like a great abyss before me. His warmth, too, was palpable: what he wanted for me, so passionately, so unreservedly, was just that I awaken to the great joy of my true life.

"My name is *Jiryu*—Compassionate Dragon. My practice is *shikantaza*—just sitting," I pronounced, as is the formula. We name our practice at the start of each dokusan, to recall our practice but also to remind him where we are coming from, since his disciples, although all technically part of the Soto Zen school, practice one of three styles of meditation. Some practice with the koan "*mu*," keeping the sound close to themselves at all times; others practice counting or following their breath; still others, like myself, practice shikantaza.

"Shikantaza," Roshi-sama repeated, the word lingering and echoing in his stillness. He raised his head slightly and glanced at me through his barely open eyes.

"All beings are Buddha," he said, almost in a whisper. "All beings have true Buddha wisdom, fulfilled Buddha virtue. So only shikantaza. Only nothing grasp. Nothing bring. Only…" he let his belly-full of air deflate, demonstrating. No muscle was tense in his body, no strain showed on his face—he seemed completely absorbed in the wide and warm oneness of things. He sat in total present ease, inactive, with no planning, no calculating, no seeking. But I knew that the moment something arose, response would flash through him. I had seen it already: a bird calls, a student falters, and he would call back, leap up, his tremendous energy instantly activated.

"Shikantaza not here," he insisted in elementary English, pointing to his head. "Not here," he continued, pointing to his heart. "Only point here!" He drove his fist into his lower belly, the energy center that the Japanese call *hara*.

I have spent the last several years in an American Zen temple that by our standards is strict and intense, but my training, I am finding, seems moot here. I have labored for years to open out my meditation—which is, after all "just sitting"—away from reliance on heavy-handed internal or external concentration objects, and toward a more subtle, broad, open awareness. Roshi-sama is said to be a master of this wide practice of shikantaza, the objectless meditation characteristic of the Soto school. But he insists, again and again, weeping at my deafness, shouting at my stubbornness, that hara focus is precisely shikantaza. That it makes no sense makes it no less inspiring; it is his presence, not his words, that I believe.

"No grasping—only point here." He rested his fist on his belly. I had nothing to say. Sweat poured out and cooled, leaving me clammy. I didn't move. I stared at the neck of his robes, where his four layers of *jubon*, *kimono*, *koromo*, and *okesa* came together.

"Here," he said, pointing to his chin and thrusting it out to show me that doing so made his back slump in bad Zen posture. He looked up at me with wide, soft brown eyes, and a kind smile that exposed his crooked teeth. In a warm, encouraging voice, like a boy addressing his puppy, he pointed to his back and said, "Like this no good. Keep try!"

My posture is quite good; I've been told so by peers and teachers alike in the U.S. Did I cross the Pacific for basic posture instruction? Me? No, I've come to this temple to realize the Great Way, to advance beyond where my Western teachers—sincere but perhaps inadequately trained—have left off.

I pulled my chin in—what else could I do? Ashamed of my pride and overwhelmed with his love for me, I drew my body up from the crown of my head, took a breath down as far into my belly as I could, and exhaled. My shoulders dropped. As the deeper chambers of breath flowed out, my ears suddenly opened. I heard the rustle of robes in the hall behind me, the screech of a foreign bird. "*Hara! Hara!*" it cried.

"Continue!" Roshi-sama growled, suddenly fierce, slamming his hand bell in an explosion that dismissed me, evoking two strikes on the bell in the hallway and calling the next student to slip in through the left side of doorway and bow as I backed out through the right.

Leaving, I noticed a bloodstain on the tatami mat in front of Roshi-sama. For a moment I wondered where it came from.

My hara energized from the meeting, I intently returned to the meditation hall and rejoined the sixty practitioners—up from the usual core of twenty five or so—who sat out the sixth day of the monthly seven-day meditation retreat, or *sesshin*.

Not until I settled myself in the still, solemn hall, did I realize that my foot hurt and was smeared with fresh blood. I wiped it with the handkerchief I carry in my robe sleeve, trying to be silent and discreet, then crossed my legs in the lotus position—always a strain mid-sesshin, but somehow easier for a period or two after meeting with Roshi-sama—and sat upright in meditation. My foot throbbed, and the pain merged with the back pain and the neck pain and the hip pain and the knee pain that all rise and fall, like the breath and the mind, through the long, perfect, excruciating days of sesshin.

Now sesshin has ended and it's been two days of limping. After formal lunch, in the short break we have to rest and change out of our robes and into our monastic work clothes, I gesture for Shoryu-san, the kind senior monk with deformed hands and ears. I want him to join me behind the kitchen so I can discreetly show him my wound. He comes over, and immediately a crowd joins us. It is as mixed as Gendoji: laypeople, monks, Japanese, foreigners, men and women.

"*Ettoo*… I don't know…" Shoryu-san with the hands and the ears says gently in his accented English. "Maybe okay no problem…."

Others chime in. The Dutch woman Elaine says, "Just ice it."

Genzen, an American monk with several years at Gendoji, who will soon be my roommate, adds, "It needs heat; let's find a heating pad." He says that he's seen this kind of thing go untreated, and that it could be bad—he speaks my language—"Just go to the doctor," he says. "It's worth the price of the ticket home you'll have to buy if it infects."

Roshi-sama's attendant, the stern-to-violent disciplinarian Daiko-san, pushes through the gawkers and glances at my swollen foot. "What?

That's nothing!" he grumbles in Japanese. "Foreigners are such wimps," he adds under his breath, storming off in disgust.

Roshi-sama has retired to his room and is not present to offer the last word, so the chaotic discussion churns on. In the temple there are no movies, no sex to speak of, not much rich food. A possibly infected, swollen ankle wound is all there is some days to obviate the monotony of the spiritual endeavor, the stark silence, hour after hour of legs crossed in the sweaty meditation hall, day after day of picking tiny weeds out from moss.

Some people are advising me to go to the doctor; some are telling me to buck the hell up. Thirty blows either way, as the Zen saying goes.

Thirty blows either way is the Zen school's take on the Buddhist "Middle Way." When Shakyamuni Buddha taught it 2,500 years ago, the Middle Way was largely an instruction about lifestyle: he exhorted his monks to always find the Middle Way between ascetic self-discipline and idle indulgence. Not under-eating, not overeating. Below that superficial meaning was a philosophic principle of non-duality, elaborated voluminously by later generations of monks and scholars who taught that not only spiritual practice but Truth itself lies in the middle—the unification—of opposites. Open and aware of the oneness of all things, practitioners of the Middle Way are to avoid conceptual extremes like being versus nonbeing, this versus that, inside versus outside, and, the cherished and fundamental polarity at the root of all suffering, me versus everything else.

In the rigorous practicality of Chinese and Japanese Zen, spontaneous and creative expression of this ultimate, nondual reality took precedence over the detailed logic of Indian scholarship. Ultimate reality, though, as any glance at the nondual teachings will show, cannot be particularly expressed dualistically. It cannot be defined in terms of any opposites—and ordinary language is therefore of no use—because, as oneness itself, it has no opposites. It is the very reconciliation of opposites, which includes even their irreconcilability. In Zen's insistence on expressing the inexpressible, then, to speak a word of ultimate reality is heresy, but to devalue the phenomenal world by remaining silent equally errs.

"Thirty blows if you speak," the ninth-century Chinese Zen Master Deshan warns his assembled monks. "And thirty if you're silent!"

In most American Zen, the "wake-up" stick is rarely used, and even then only on students who request it, consigning teachings about "blows" to poetic encouragement. Japanese Zen does tend to cherish the kyosaku, but strikes from it, always delivered to the shoulder, are more jarring than painful. They actually release some tension, a sort of sudden, vigorous, unsolicited massage. But even though violent training is more metaphorical than actual, the "no-win situation" is highly regarded in all forms of Zen. It contains the "wisdom of no escape," as one Western Buddhist teacher has put it. In a bind thorough enough, reality itself overwhelms reality as we dream it, and our limited version of how things are and how things work, of who we are and how we work, tend collapse on themselves in spectacular or subtle implosions, opening the ground for a wider view. Zen students everywhere, then, are keenly open to the opportunity of the irresolvable bind. It is just at that impasse that we can find the great freedom—just there, something beyond opposites can unfold.

 

The monk with the hands and the ears helps me get to the doctor.

He is going to leave me here, I realize at the clinic doors as he starts to get back on his bike. To just leave me, though I can hardly buy a bus ticket in this incomprehensible country, much less understand a diagnosis.

"You're not going to leave me here?" I protest.

Reluctantly generous, Shoryu-san stays with me at the doctor's office. In the entryway, he shows me where to put my shoes and how to slip into the small plastic clinic slippers. I feel sort of bad for making him stay, but I can't imagine being there alone. To kill time in the lobby, he practices his English and I try out my Japanese.

He asks, "What is it like there, *Amerika?*"

I mumble something about "wide space," "open minds," something about "companies cut trees"—I want to tell him about home, but I don't know so many words. I don't think it makes any sense.

He looks up at the T.V. that hangs in a high corner of the lobby. An exuberant Japanese man talks while a chirpy, sexy woman nods, wiggles, and giggles at his words.

Shoryu-san and I are silent together for a moment. He looks over at me. He seems to have heard the wild rumors about the infant movement called "American Zen," because he asks, with disbelief and a tinge of awe: "Is it really true that in your American temple you can bathe whenever you want?"

I nod tentatively, ashamed.

When Shoryu-san lowers himself into the bath—only once every five days at Gendoji, in accordance with Zen tradition—he groans deep belly groans. I can't tell if it's pleasure or pain, for they seem inseparable in him. His ribs jut out of his chest; his bones are sharp against his thin skin.

One day in the coming winter I will see him standing on the scale in the bathhouse—"Not eating enough," he murmurs to himself. Freezing and famished, I am eating too much, not getting enough. Shoving rice down my throat, firsts and seconds as full as my formal rice bowl allows, swallowing without chewing to get calories in before the wooden blocks halt abruptly the meal. My desperate starchy eating adds kilos, centimeters, of fat to my pale body, to most of our bodies, but not Shoryu-san's. He takes the same slow, deliberate bites that he takes in the summer, and in the bathhouse he murmurs, "Not eating enough."

In the meditation hall, Shoryu-san sits still, but his frail body is hunched—just seeing it makes my own back hurt. His head twists sharply, and he leans severely forward and to the side. When he hears somebody walking behind him, he draws up his body, but even after he has straightened, he is bent. Many nights after the bedtime bells he slips back into the hall and takes his seat. Sometimes for this after-hours practice he sits up, but when he is too tired he just puts his head down in front of him on the mat, doubling his torso over crossed legs. Is it the hours of that posture that have misshapen his back and neck? Whenever I sit behind him, kneeling on my heels in the line for dokusan with Roshi-sama, I can't help watching the breath struggle through his bent body. Now and then he rolls his shoulders, or shudders as though trying somehow to wriggle free of himself.

In his decade or so at the temple, Shoryu-san has been home only once; even then it was just to get treatment for his chilblained hands and ears. His fingers could not move. He could not hit the bells, or carry the kyosaku stick, use a broom. His ears burned. He had no choice but to go home to recover, inasmuch as he could recover.

Having been home, he can move his fingers a little, but his hands, in the *gassho*, palms together, of reverence, are like warped, knotted wood. His ears sting.

As we talk in the clinic lobby, in hard chairs, toes sweaty against the slick plastic slippers, I realize that my foot is already better. It still aches, but it isn't so bad. It's nothing really. The disciplinarian Daiko-san is right—even with my scant Japanese I understood his scoff as everyone stood crowded around my precious foot. We foreigners really are wimps. I am sure that Shoryu-san, the kind monk with the hands and ears, though he would never say so, also thinks it weak of me, self-indulgent to have come to the doctor. I am sure of it.

"Would Dogen have seen the doctor for a hurt foot?" I ask tentatively, invoking the austere and prolific founder of our Soto Zen school.

"Dogen-*Zenji*," Shoryu-san corrects, slightly jarred by my neglect of the Zen master's honorific suffix, as though I had implied that the great medieval saint was my pal, or my dog. "I don't know so much about Dogen-Zenji—Roshi-sama says not to study," he answers.

I try again, prying for him to just come out and say how pathetic it is that I've come to the doctor. "Would the Buddha have come?"

Shoryu-san pauses. "You should ask him."

Does he mean Roshi-sama, the "old Buddha" who is our abbot? Does he somehow mean the historical Shakyamuni Buddha? Does he mean the Buddha that is only ever here and now, that I am Buddha, he is Buddha, plastic slippers, bikes, and swollen feet and heat and wind are Buddha, and that asking, too, is Buddha?

I am no newcomer to Zen one-liners, and am less impressed than annoyed by Shoryu-san's answer. If he isn't going to criticize me, at least he could give me some affirmation, some confirmation, a dose of the support that is a cornerstone of the American Zen of my religious formation. I want to know what he thinks, what *his* practice is, what *he* would do, how Shoryu-san himself, with his cracked hands and ears, understands taking care of the body in the midst of our bone-crushing, no-holds-barred pursuit of enlightenment.

I say nothing, and finally I am called in to see the doctor. He sits in a big leather chair, in a dark Western suit. Half a dozen nurses in little pink skirts shuffle around at his orders. They put me in different places, bandage me. The doctor leans way back in his chair. It doesn't make any sense.

"It's nothing really," they say. I'm shown the door, and the window where I am to pay. "Take these pills," they say. I fumble for the right bills, the right coins.

As fall drifts toward winter and I am assigned to the temple kitchen duty, I learn that the bent-over Shoryu-san comes into the kitchen at all hours. We kitchen monks aren't bothered when he comes, though we are busy with food and might resent the intrusion of a lesser monk. If something is on the stove, he sidles up to it and peels off his cotton gloves as though stripping gauze from a wound. If nothing is cooking, he screws up his face in apology, lights the range, and squirms as the fire brings life back into his swollen hands.

"What *happened* to you?" I ask once or twice, trying to understand his injury. But it isn't anything, exactly, that has happened. It's just the cold, the constant and unmitigated cold of temple winters.

"In the summer it's not such a problem," he says.

He clenches his teeth as he tries to bend a stove-warmed finger, and I remember meeting him in the summer: his misshapen hands, his strange ears.

# 2   No Zen in the West

"It's *bullshit*," I tell my American teacher. We sit face-to-face on the floor on black cushions, bodies still, our legs folded neatly and our backs strongly upright. Beneath a small wooden Buddha in the windowsill, a short stick of incense releases strands of smoke in chaotic, dissipating patterns. The scent, like the silence, suffuses the air in the weathered wooden cabin that teeters over a creek in our California mountain temple.

I hold the word on my tongue, *bullshit*, so he'll know that I'm serious about this. I'm not just complaining. He needs to meet me, to understand that I'm tired of this American Buddhist "Upper Middle Way." I'm tired of the sexual dramas, the talk of "income streams" and "personnel costs." I don't want any more of the peanut butter that's refilled in the snack area as quickly as it's used. I don't want a snack area, period. The great monks of old didn't have a "snack area," much less one stocked with blueberry-tofu-cashew smoothies and leftover chocolate cake.

The accounting office sends out memos. *Accounting office? Memos?* Each year they raise the overnight guest fees, even the meditation retreat fees. They inquire after under-spending temple cooks—is their frugality thinning the guests? A payroll company delivers stipend checks; pay rates advance with seniority. What does any of this have to do with the Buddha Way? What are we up to?

"It's bullshit, Lee," I tell him. When I'm feeling particularly pious, I call my teacher, "Teacher," and he tolerates that with a smirk. If I tried to call him "Roshi," he'd just laugh, or worse. So, today, like most days, I just call him "Lee."

"I think you mean *dried up shit stick*," he answers light-heartedly. "But yes, it is bullshit as well, and deer shit. Did you notice that the almond in the garden has just started to blossom? It's that too."

I nod, and I smile. A thousand years ago in China, a monk, maybe a young monk like me, asked Zen Master Yunmen, "What is Buddha?" Yunmen answered, "Dried up shit stick." Today it's the same conversation: I tell my humble teacher about "bullshit" and he answers back, "Buddha." Yunmen, and no less Lee, remind their students that Buddha is everywhere, everything—even, or especially, right here in the "bullshit."

Lee continues after a pause, his voice quieter, unmistakably pained. "A disciple of Buddha does not disparage the triple treasure. Please be careful. Don't make yourself better than the rest of us. I think you know that's the furthest thing from our practice."

I do know that; I have heard it many times anyway. But I'm frustrated, and I'm tired, and it's dawning on me, like a slow, unstoppable train, that if I'm really serious about this Buddhism thing, I may well need to abandon this California imitation of it. I don't mean to disparage the Sangha, my peers and my teachers, but I have vowed to end all suffering, my own and others'. And I've glimpsed the possibility of that kind of salvation, but the lifestyle here is not pushing me to take the plunge, to realize the one final truth that will shatter all delusions and liberate all beings.

It is not that I'm averse to problems; I understand that they are the stones that lay the path. I am tired, though, of these corporate problems, *"Are we making enough?"* and these hippie commune problems, *"Who's fucking who?"* I want to live more humble problems: cold wind through threadbare robes, the faint, holy fragility of a diet of watery rice. I want monks' problems. The problems implied in the ancient admonitions like Dogen's *Zuimonki*, and the original Buddhist monastic code, the *Vinaya*.

Dogen in the Zuimonki says over and over that the pursuit of the Way must be our only concern. He demands that we renounce all of our attachments, all of our belongings, all of our loved ones, and fling our bodies and minds into the Way. Like a man in desperate and total pursuit of a woman, he says, like a thief completely engaged in a heist, we must give our full effort, allow no diversion. So what is this overexcited "skit night" that interrupts our three month retreat? Why instead of meditation tonight are we breaking into small groups to discuss our feelings? Why do my elders all tell me that I should not turn away from this lust that I have, this longing I have, this girl who haunts me? Why do they tell me that we need to work all day to make beds to bring guests to bring money? Why am I eating this asparagus timbale?

Wasn't the simple, austere life good enough for Zen ancestors like Dogen and Nanquan? Wasn't it enough for Shakyamuni himself, who left home, left everything, and went into the forest to follow the primordial Buddhas? Should he have sorted out his "issues" first? Was he "running away" from his life? Did the Indian monk Bodhidharma need communication exercises to tell the Chinese emperor, "Vast emptiness, nothing holy," or to tell him with supreme clarity and confidence, "Who stands before you, I don't know?" Did Xuefeng need group processing workshops to lead a harmonious assembly of 1,500 monks?

Even Dogen admits that to shatter our bones is beside the point. Our Way is the Middle Way, and we don't need to starve or hurt ourselves. But on what graph do we chart this Middle Way? Dogen would perhaps at one extreme draw the ancient Indian mountain ascetics, naked, long-haired, eating grasses if they ate at all; and, at the other extreme, he might put the pampered nobility of his own day. Given those poles, his model of the Middle was Shakyamuni, the renunciate monk who ate one meal a day and lived simply in the woods.

Shaykamuni, as recorded in the Vinaya, is clear how monks should live out the Middle Way: don't light a fire just because you're cold, don't hand a woman anything, or ever be alone with a woman. Don't ride on a carriage, don't handle so much as a penny, and if you must lie down, sleep on your right side, in your robes, mindful. This was by no means Shaykamuni Buddha's view of asceticism—this was precisely his teaching of the Middle Way.

But we American Buddhists, calling ourselves disciples of Buddha, find Shakyamuni's own Middle Way too extreme. To find our Middle Way we seem to set Shakyamuni himself at one extreme, and the likes of Donald Trump at the other, so naturally we find our middle in soft beds and lazy practice schedules, in romances and *The Times*. But how can we call this following Shakyamuni? How did we manage to make the original Middle Way into an extreme to be avoided?

The texts like Zuimonki and the Vinaya scriptures thus recede into spiritualized metaphor—they aren't about how we should actually live, but just about an inner attitude we should have. In their place, books like "Zen and Business" and "Zen Sex" spring up and dot the bookstores, excerpted in glossy, pop-Buddhist magazines. I hate those magazines, though it's true I have liked some of the articles. There was that one about Zen and sex that I nervously skimmed, leaning against the shelves in a big city bookstore, but that's just my own weakness.... Hate, too, is improper, but I quite nearly hate the celebrity Buddhists who, I'm told, dash their *People* interviews with Buddhist terms. My negativity is my weakness, I know. I should not disparage the Sangha. I apply myself to my studies and practice. I meet with my teacher again and again, hoping he can free me from my bias.

"What about those old books: the Vinaya, the Zuimonki," I ask Lee. "What about the old way of life?"

Lee's eyes light up. "I love the Zuimonki!" he says.

I hate that he loves the Zuimonki. Does he have the right to love the Zuimonki? I hate the Zuimonki because it reminds me how I'm not living, though I try, though I would. My teacher is married, has a car, and loves the Zuimonki. This is maddening.

"In the Zuimonki, Dogen is talking to monks, reminding them to be sincere," Lee says. "And we should be sincere."

I love my teacher.

"Our problems are problems of wealth," he tells me. "So what? There are always problems. Our practice is good."

The hum of the creek rushes into my ears, deepening the silence in the cabin. The incense stick has burned down; the Buddha sits, still unmoving, on the windowsill.

I believe that our practice is good. I love my teacher; he is wise and sincere. But I am at heart a monk—why is that so hard for people to see—and I hate the stipend checks, the aftertaste of peanut butter, my girlfriend/ex-girlfriend's soft, warm cheeks.


For *takuhatsu* alms rounds in Japan, we wear enormous straw hats, *ajirogasa*. The hats keep out rain and sun; they mute the bright lights of town, the traffic and comic book shops, luminous young women on bikes. Although one can wear the *gasa* degrees back on the head, and thus see the world degrees better, the design is meant to keep monks' focus downward, like a city horse's blinders.

The hat discourages eye-contact; obscuration is a virtue of the gasa's wide rim. This can be taken too far—I, for one, try at first to hide my face behind it. I want to hide my monstrous nose and round eyes. Deep inside my hat, with bell and bowl extended toward the door at which I stand, I try to chant so crisply that it will occur to no one that I am not Japanese. Of course, this is a non-standard use of the ajirogasa: proper use rests in a middle way between exposure and concealment, sight and blindness. It should be worn straight, as Daiko-san reminds me with a shove.

We hold our bells and lacquer bowls, hoist up our robes, and set out. The robes should be our formal meditation robes, some monks hold. Others wear shortened robes used just for takuhatsu; formal robes, these monks insist, get bleached by hours of sun, and torn at the feet of shrines where lunching monks slip underneath their hats and sometimes raincoats, napping. Though I will meet dissenters, most monks agree that modesty and underbrush demand that wrists and shins be wrapped by white, sock-like *tekko* and *kyahan*. Kimono underneath the outer-robe is hoisted up: kimono-freed legs move with much more ease, cover more begging ground. Jubon shirt beneath kimono. On winter days, long underwear will be acceptable, but to be worn at the risk of overheating. Noteworthy is the monk who can divest himself of long johns between houses while disrupting neither his layers of robes nor the communal gait.

Cloth bags hang around our necks and bounce on our bellies as we walk. The temple's name is printed on them in three characters: Gen-do-ji, "Actualize Way Temple." Inside fits any uncooked rice received on takuhatsu, and perhaps, if it will be a full day, a temple-prepared lunch box for the midday break. We also carry water, or green tea, or cookies bought at the department store, hoarded sweets to secretly invigorate midmorning.

We wear rope sandals, *waraji*. We make them when there's time, on snowy winter days or lazy *shikunichi*, weekly bath and rest day, afternoons, weaving hardware store rope into the rough shape of a foot. The coarse rope pulls between the thumb toe and the others, like flip-flops, and wraps up the ankles, tying tight behind the calves.

"There will be a little blood the first times," the young monk Ejo-san warns me on the eve of my first takuhatsu, as I walk circles in the courtyard in my new temple-issue waraji, exploring that soft vertex, thumb and first toe.

After breakfast we tie on our gear and chant the *Heart of Great Perfect Wisdom Sutra*, the *Makahannya Haramita Shingyo*, in the *genkan* entryway. Roshi-sama in his old age doesn't come on takuhatsu, but he comes out to chant with us while the straggling monks, myself invariably included, scurry to tie on waraji and fill up water bottles. After we recite the sutra, he looks us up and down, fixing our collars and straightening our sleeves.

"*Yooshh*," "Good," he hums, beaming like a proud father. He bows and hollers out some stern admonition that my failure to understand cannot diminish.

"Just become one with takuhatsu," I decide that he said—it is true that he might say such a thing—and I bring all of my attention to my breath and body as we file out through the temple gate.

When it has been some time since we last did takuhatsu in the area, we simply walk to an outlying village or neighborhood of Maibara. If the schedule has us begging farther away, we process to the train station, remove our giant hats, and fill a train car with our robes and silent faces.

In whatever town we arrive, we walk single file in the streets, our bells ringing and our throats and haras vibrating the takuhatsu mantra: "*Ho*." "Ho" fills the streets: "truth," "Dharma." A symphony of "ho"s and clanging bells. Some "ho"s are hara-driven. Some are throaty, voiced "ho"s, or growled, shouted "ho"s—we try them all, in the course of a day. All are equally Dharma.

It is not that monks are good, just that we are equally Dharma. This is the teaching of Dogen-Zenji. He states in his Zuimonki that the laity should not donate based on the virtues or merits of a monk. Monks, too, of course, should think this way, and not discriminate or judge. But still we gauge ourselves, each other, inevitably wondering who chants the best.

"Today, by the lunch break, I broke *ichimanen*, nearly one-hundred dollars! *Ichiman han* total. What a day!" says Genzen, another American monk. The fastest and strongest, the most insanely devoted among us, Genzen out-collected us all today, though perhaps he lost some merit by counting. Every morning he is the first to wake up, ringing the bell that wakes the temple, though some nights he reads trashy novels in bed with a flashlight, and other days "actualizing the Way" feels so heavy that he can't get out of bed at all. He sits more than any of us, seeming to be in the *zendo*, meditation hall, during every moment of his free time, though occasionally instead he sneaks out on a bike he keeps stashed at the neighboring Shinto shrine, and darts around town charming women and drinking vending machine beer.

It's not that monks are good, but just that we walk single file, belting out our "ho"s as suit the moment, in accord with our sincerity, exhaustion, or vigor. We "ho" and walk and find ourselves at a doorway, ringing our hand-bell furiously or softly, filling our mouth and hara with the chant of blessing. "*Kanzeon namu butsu yo butsu…,*" we roar, standing alone at a house, ringing, invoking *Kanzeon*, who is *Quan Yin, Kannon, Avalokiteshvara*, the Buddhist embodiment of perfected compassion.

We believe in this Kanzeon Bosatsu we invoke. Our chanting is not a psychological trick, it is calling Kanzeon. Every morning we chant a long scripture in praise of her, proclaiming that when shackled, when pursued by demons, thieves, or killers, just to say her name is to be protected, freed. And here we believe it. In the same way, here in Japan when we chant for the dead, we chant to aid the dead; our ceremonies are not just to console the living, as the pop-psychological American Buddhists suggest. This isn't to say that Kanzeon is outside me exactly, or even inside me, but wherever she is, she is real. Whether she comes forth from within or swings down for above, she is called, she arrives, and she frees. This faith here is strong. Chanting at a doorway, hammering on my bell and roaring out her name, I don't know what she is, but just as the layperson at whose door I'm chanting, I know she is far more than metaphor.

The bell fills itself, fills everything, and the ringing merges with the chanting, with the standing, with the doorway, the whole of the moment merging as one blessing, a simultaneous receiving and offering. This is not something I eventually uncover, but is from the first the reality of takuhatsu. It is just evident that this interpenetration of all things is our walking, our "ho"ing and ringing, our invocation and blessing. How could it be otherwise?

Mostly we receive coins from our begging and blessing, but no offering is refused. The young monk Ankai-san receives a cabbage one morning. Cabbage only seems light to those who haven't carried one around for a day. I receive a slimy bag of home-pickled *umeboshi* plums, and the Gendoji bag I wear around my neck is thereafter never quite the same. Persimmons.

One rainy day, a woman runs out of her house to offer me a steaming cup of tea with a pickle at the bottom. It seems that I've been inadvertently chanting at a temple door; the temple wife, temple mother, rushes out to greet me with the perfect treat. She understands. Perhaps her son is at a training temple somewhere, out on alms rounds—I don't know—begging in the rain. Perhaps she thinks of him. But still I should not be begging at a temple door. It's that it did not look like a temple at first, and I thought it was an ordinary house. Such is the confusing state of modern, mainstream Japanese Zen—the monasticism getting more vague by the day since the 1800s. After the floodgates to the West opened, and married clergy were established, Japanese Buddhism got quite a bit more complex. Monks haven't quite shaken the weight of the celibate tradition, but there is no going back to it either. In the resulting blur, I can't tell if it's the houses looking like temples or the temples looking like houses. Still, there's no excuse for begging from fellow monks.

Banks, yes. Stores, yes. Residences, yes; farmhouses as well. Churches, no. Temples, no. Bookstores, museums, *pachinko* parlors, porn shops, *patisserie*, yes. Gas stations, yes. Schools, *"chotto"*—"maybe not." Apartments, no. Mechanics, yes. Convenience stores, yes. Slums, somehow not so much. I don't know why, but we just don't stop so much at poor spots. Perhaps we fear we'll spend a day just blessing poverty, and walk home empty-handed. On the other hand, at one of the most beautifully crafted, luxurious homes I will ever approach with bell and bowl, I receive from the matriarch, through her child, about ten cents. Ten cents from a mansion! Monks do not complain. It is touching really, even that token generosity. But *ten yen*? What's the point? I do not claim to be a good monk. The Buddha said that monks should favor neither rich nor poor, but somehow that teaching has slipped through the wide-mesh net of Japanese Buddhism. Practically speaking—at the bottom line—both extremes are unreliable. It is in the humble and the tidy parts of town, the farming villages, the rustic, temple-heavy neighborhoods, where as we bless we are most blessed in coins, and rice, and cabbage.

Whatever the offerings we receive, at lunch most of all we realize our gratitude. Fanned out in a park or Shinto shrine, we each quietly take our *obento* lunch box out from our Gendoji bag, say a silent blessing, and eat the soft brown rice and pickles that we packed early in the morning. As we eat, we realize that which we've received: quite literally we eat the offerings from prior takuhatsus. We see that though we have nothing, we are totally provided for. Lunch realizes that we are held, that needing nothing, having nothing, lunch arrives. We rest and eat: this life provides this life.

After lunch, we walk again, and the walking purifies still more. It is not that I don't get tired, in waves, from the marching and shouting. But I sometimes come to glimpse the Way that's truly empty-handed, like on the day when walking near the ocean along a big street and across from glistening pachinko parlor, I feel suddenly an empty-handed bliss—*I can just die with each step, I am taken care of, I am held, I truly don't need anything.* The English layman Harold speeds up to talk to me, breaking the single file and the silence, and the feeling fades but I do not pull away from chatting because chatting is included, the feeling of not-needing is so excruciatingly inclusive that even it isn't something that I need to hold onto.

The Buddha too practiced takuhatsu, and he walked and taught with the same open hands. Dogen pronounced on returning to Japan from China that he came "empty-handed." Everything let go, nothing carried forth; an empty vessel receiving and offering the moment, the Dharma. Reality invited and relinquished; the whole world falling into and passing out of empty hands. Nothing sticks in takuhatsu. Not even thoughts of Sakura-san, the gorgeous Gendoji laywoman who has already begun to complicate my stay.

On a sunny August takuhatsu, in a quiet part of a remote town, walking with my mind empty even of her, I notice a dignified, well-dressed, and attractive woman, not more than thirty, walking down the street holding a parasol. Struggling to keep my eyes lowered, shaded by the giant rim of the ajirogasa, I round a corner and approach the next house, following a narrow stone pathway through a small, well-trimmed garden to a western-style doorway. I straighten my body up at the door, ring my little hand-bell, and start in on my blessing, "*Kanzeon namu butsu....*" As I begin, the same woman suddenly appears behind me, a gust of her perfume prickling my rice and pickle-accustomed nostrils, suddenly slurring the words of my chant.

She ducks and mumbles in apology and slides past me into the house while my eyes, despite themselves, follow the curves that push tight against her pressed suit skirt. She disappears to find some coins and then emerges again, wide-eyed and smiling, looking coyly up at me.

A foreign monk can't help but to draw attention, but nonetheless it is taught that on takuhatsu one should not make eye contact, not linger at a door, indulge in "Thank you's" and "Excuse me's" and "*Sou desu ne, Amerika kara desu ne*, yes, yes Zen life is difficult but do you know it's wonderful—I just received the universe in your one hundred yen coin." There are many such things that should not be done.

Our eyes brush, fire. She is beautiful, almost as beautiful Sakura-san, more so if I factor in her perfume, her parasol that leans against the open doorway, her painted, worldly lips. She says—I am not sure—she says, "Come in, have some tea, maybe we should make love before you head back into the streets... It's early, spend the night. We'll say that you got lost, slept in an alley; we'll put dirt on your robes and send you back in the morning...."

The money clinks into my bowl.

She is very close, or I am too close, or the day, the sun...

I try to step back but the stone pathway doesn't hold me; I stumble backwards, mumbling the gratitude verse, "*Zai ho nise...,*" falling, wanting just to say, "Yes, let's—let the others worry, we're in love, and love—love conquers all."

She is beautiful, but I can only pick myself up, brush off my robes, and walk away. My bell rings more softly now, my "ho" choked and muffled, my mind aflame with the life I've left behind.

A would-be American monastic, I find myself snacking again. In another relationship. Paying a credit card bill. I blame myself; I blame others. It's not Buddhist to blame, I know, but there must be accountability. People are not helping me to realize the Way. I blame my teachers, my country, my culture.

I at least will be accountable; I will take responsibility. I vow to stay away from peanut butter. I break it off with my girlfriend yet again. My tears spot the worn pages of my copy of Dogen's *Zuimonki*. I know that I have a chance at the Way, and this is the only true thing, the only important thing, but it's like swimming upstream. People even talk at some meals, laughing and chewing and remembering movies. What does this have to with Buddhism?

On a day off, I borrow a car, drive up and down the steep mountain that buffers the temple, drop my laundry off at a laundromat, and go to a movie. Guys shoot each other, get laid. I click prayers on my *mala* beads through the whole second half, but I can't bring myself to walk out.

My teacher Lee says, "To always want to sit *zazen* is just another dualistic idea. You need to find the continuity of practice through the mundane." I believe him.

One night of sesshin, sitting late after bedtime on a deck outside my small hillside cabin, I am overwhelmed again by life. Swarms of stars, tall pines. I exhale. This very moment, I die, I whisper. This very moment is exactly the moment of everything that has and will ever be. *There is rest here*, I whisper soundlessly.

After sesshin I go to my parents' house and throw away all of my old letters. They lock me into the past. I give away all of my books, Buddhist and otherwise, and my Bob Dylan collection. *Lay down your weary tune....*

"It's okay," Lee says, "to get rid of everything. But also in our school if we have something, that is good, because we have something then to give away at the right time."

I love my teacher very much, but I don't understand him. I love my teacher's wife, and I love to ride with my teacher in his car, but I hate that he is married, and I hate that he has a car. Buddhists shouldn't judge. But what's a monk doing with a wife and a car?

"I want to be a monk," I tell Lee again. "Then live that way," he says once. "You already are a monk in your heart," he says the second time. "Can you let go of even that?" he says another.

I learn the formal ceremonies, the through-line of Soto Zen practice, and I see that what I thought was highly formal is in fact, from backstage, rather loose. It shouldn't be that way. The ancestors are all clear on this point: there is a way to meet and accomplish each detail, each gesture, each offering. The key to our school is *menmitsu no kafu*, total care and consideration for each thing, however minute. So how is that even the head of the zendo seems not to notice, or to care, when students pick up bells like rag dolls, hold sutra books like yesterday's paper? I'm starting to wonder whether the authentic transmission of Dharma to the West is really complete. When I hold my elbows straight out, parallel to the ground, straighter even than the ceremony instructor demonstrates, and hit the *inkin* bell just so from the back, I know a kind of magic.

It's not that I don't know that the teaching is fundamentally presence, release, and awareness alone. Once, in fact, I ripped down my altar and threw my Dogen on the floor.

"Trash!" I shrieked, "trash!" and collapsed on my bed. My sometimes girlfriend came by after evening chanting.

"Where were you?" she asked.

"It's not about Buddhism at all," I said.

"I know," she said, climbing on the bed and straddling me.

I know that the ceremonial forms are provisional, that Buddha is everywhere and in all things, and that temple life just points to what farmers, clerks, and mechanics all see just as clearly. But still I am absorbed in the magic of elbows extended, the just-so way to strike a bell and how it draws the body, mind, and vow into one indivisible instant.

"It's just that it's a gate," I say to Lee. "It's not awakening, but it is a gate into awakening. I want to enter there. I want to be ordained, and I want to practice the way the ancients practiced. I want go to Japan."

It is my fourth year of living in the temple, and still a year or two before I finally get to Japan. I sit facing my teacher whom I love, though I hate how he doesn't shave his head quite often enough, as often as the scriptures suggest, as often as I know that I will once I am ordained. We sit in the wooden cabin that hangs at the edge of a drop-off into the creek. It is fall. It is quiet. The creek hums.

"Yes, I will ordain you," he finally says. "And you should go to Japan, since you want to. Maybe for a year, but maybe for five years. Don't know—just go. Meet teachers and live out their teachings. Come back and tell us about it."

A shikunichi bath day a few weeks into my stay at Gendoji and two days before the August sesshin meditation intensive, I meet Keishi. I am still sweaty and sore from yesterday's alms rounds, still replaying in my mind the sweet, seductive smile of the woman with the parasol for whom and based on nothing I nearly abandoned the Way. Standing in my dorm room that doubles as the dining room, in front of the section of the communal closet that holds my bedding and belongings, I picture her looking up and smiling, looking up and smiling, as I anxiously fumble with my toiletries and await my turn in the hierarchy of baths.

The sliding door of the large room opens, and a shallow-faced, austere Western monk, two or three decades my senior, steps in, flushed from the bath and wearing the full meditation robes that entering and exiting the bathhouse require. Though we haven't met formally, I recognize him from last month's sesshin, my first at Gendoji; this sesshin again he is among the crowd of foreigners and Japanese who descend on the temple only to vanish once the retreat ends. Something about Keishi—perhaps the way he reaches to unfasten his robe belt, slowly, deliberately, with intense but relaxed concentration—makes me assume that he has lived dozens of years in Japan. I won't until much later learn that it has only been a few years since he left his family and country to come to Japan to finally resolve the Great Matter of Zen.

"Where are you from?" he asks, his intonations distinctly Midwestern.

I abandon my distracted luggage arranging. I wonder if his presence means that it is now my turn for the bath, the bath I perhaps should have taken during yesterday's takuhatsu instead, lathering and being lathered by the smooth fingers of the parasol woman in her cool, tidy home, giggling and submerging ourselves.... I turn to face the monk.

He looks closely at me, while his fingers gracefully disentangle the loops in the belt that he removes as he starts to get out of his outer koromo robe and relax in the cooler single layer of kimono.

"The States," I answer.

"Yeah?" he says, "You have a teacher out there?" He smirks slightly—perhaps I'm only imagining it—and I swallow hard and turn back toward the closet, folding my towel yet again and draping it over my toiletries bag.

"I doubt you know him; he's not so well known... Lee deBarros," I say.

Keishi breaks into a grin: "Sure I know him!" He looks amused and bewildered. "He's your teacher?! Jesus! Sit down, kid, sit down," he says emphatically, gesturing for me to sit on the tatami floor, and sitting down himself in seiza.

We look out of the sliding glass doors onto a small back garden that can't really be seen from anywhere else in the temple. It is littered with branches and weeds. "Doesn't anyone do weeding back there during *samu* period?" Keishi asks, with the judgment of an insider and the impunity of a guest. I assume it's a rhetorical question.

"You know Lee?" I muster softly. "So you must know my American temple..."

"Know it? Hell, I'm from there, from the old days!" He laughs and shakes his head. "But Lee deBarros is a teacher now? I mean with all due respect, he's a good guy, I'm sure he's a good priest, but come on! I've no doubt he helps people out, but really... *he's* got the certification of Dharma Transmission?!"

Outside the sliding glass doors, a little brown bird hops from a rock to the ground. We watch it together for a moment before Keishi goes on.

"I don't care about that, Transmission doesn't mean anything out there. It's ludicrous, though, those people start teaching before they've *realized* anything! They're good people—I'm not saying they aren't good people—but they're just leading others astray. It isn't Zen. I'll tell you something, there isn't any real Zen in America. No real teachers. It's a sad situation. You're lucky you made it to Japan, kid. Now maybe you can really start to practice."

He pauses and tenses his body, as if considering taking control of the righteous flood that washes over him, but just as soon he relaxes and continues.

"Everything out there is just about seniority, like any corporation. Even 'abbot' is just another position—nothing to do with enlightenment. Jesus! I tell you what, I'm senior to all of them, but you won't see me teaching. Not pretending to teach like those phonies.

"They're up to their ears in stuff! Their positions are just like more stuff! Their wives are more stuff... their houses and cars. Their *kids*. Practice is renunciation—how do they expect to get it, much less teach it, with all that stuff in the way? They mean well, but come on."

Despite myself, I find myself nodding. I think again of my home temple: the bread, fruit, and peanut butter, the pampering of the paying guests, the sub-floor heating system that each year infects more cabins. Isn't he saying exactly what I think—aren't I also sick of all of the *stuff* that American Zen people can't realize is obstructing them? Haven't I too tired of the constant romances and emotional intrigues, the family pressures that pull the senior teachers away from the students who rely on them... the sex, in short, that American Zen people can't see is just more grasping attachment?

I have my inadvertently imagined sexual adventures—the parasol woman lingers in my mind—but I don't claim that they are appropriate. They are merely further evidence of my delusion. Romance is contrary to Buddhism. The relationships and marriages, even among ordained people, that are taken as natural in my American temple increasingly seem revolting to me, perversely transgressive. On a recent takuhatsu, as we crossed the Fushihara highway near the temple, the two-lane road that shoots into the gaping, rumbling tunnel through the mountain, my stomach turned to see a monk and a woman on the sidewalk together. He was a beautiful, upright, and dignified monk; his head was polished and his dark gray robes flowed around him. Beside him, the woman's sophistication and figure cut a streak of brightness through the gray Maibara day, the rush of Fushihara traffic. Perfectly black hair streamed down the back of her long, tight, shoulderless dress. The two walked shoulder to shoulder, brushing.

It was not his poise or her beauty, nor his beauty nor her poise that cut into me, but something in the pairing. Their beauties clashed, as though the principle on which each staked their beauty was in the other violated. If ever I should walk alongside such a woman, I resolved, let me not disgrace her beauty with my robes. And should I base my beauty on my robes, let me never walk alongside such a woman.

"I mean, how can they even call themselves monks?" Keishi says to my nods. "Monks don't have sex, don't have stuff! So they call themselves 'priests,' what's that? Buddhism doesn't have 'priests'! It's meaningless. Buddhist ordination has always only been about monasticism. Just because they live communally doesn't make them monastics! They're just a bunch of leftover hippies."

"Yeah, I know what you mean," I venture, careful and distant, not disagreeing exactly, but feeling like I should offer some defense of my lineage, and by extension my own "monk" or "priest" ordination. "But I don't know if we can totally dismiss them. I mean can't their ordinations be a legitimate way to express commitment to the ritual forms, to affirm that Buddhism is the central aspect of their life, is their livelihood?"

"No!" Keishi looks at me incredulously. "If you want Buddhism to be the center of your life, just make it the center of your life! Ordination isn't about creating a new class of people who claim to have 'Dharma at the center of their lives' while they pursue their academic careers, raise kids, run companies... Buddhism isn't about that!"

"Yeah... but," I struggle, amazed that I am so little inspired to stand up for the tradition I've come from, my American teachers, my American Sangha. "Couldn't ordination be a way not so much to identify a particular strict lifestyle, but just to identify people who are really dedicated to the Dharma, who want to help share and spread it?"

"No! Jesus, kid, do you hear what I'm saying?! If someone is really dedicated to the Dharma, *it will show*, they don't need to pose as monks. Take Aitken Roshi—he never bothered with a phony ordination, but people came to him anyway, because they felt his dedication. I'm not saying he's enlightened, but he had some deep realization, and people noticed. That's how it works—there's no point creating some special class. A person's realization just stands on its own. And if it doesn't, there's nothing to 'share' or 'spread' anyway, except a whole lot of hot air.

"The ordained teachers out there are all bogus. Ordination means monasticism, but that's not how they're living. To go around wearing monks' clothes, call yourself a 'monk,' and live in a house just like anyone else—it's ludicrous! And it's damaging, it's confusing to people."

"I know what you're saying," I say, looking out the sliding glass doors into the garden, and looking over at Keishi, the unequivocal monk. Again I half-heartedly muster a defense: "But we did get the tradition from Japan—after all, it is more or less the same here. Maybe pure monasticism is fading naturally, and this new way is an appropriate development of the Buddhist tradition..."

"It's not a development," Keishi interrupts. "It started with a Japanese government persecution of Buddhism. A hundred and fifty years back they wanted to weaken the monastic order, so they made a law that made the monks marry. Everybody went for it, and it destroyed Japanese Buddhism. Politicians killed it. And now the American Zen 'priests' are telling you it was a spiritual development?"

We sit together on the tatami, looking at each other and out the doors into the unkempt garden. The little brown bird pecks and hops, apparently uninterested in flight. I am disoriented—I've never heard such a confident and sharp attack of the modern Zen way of life—but I am at the same time inspired. I think of *mappo*, the old idea of the decline of the Dharma, the last age of Buddhism, in which there is no longer practice or enlightenment, but only superficial observances. The weight of it presses into my shoulders, my jaw. We are indeed in the last age, I realize.

But there is also a new hope: the tatami-floored room in the humble temple is like a last mountain peak still dry in a world-flooding deluge. Amidst the astounding decadence of both American and mainstream Japanese Zen, I've finally found a place that knows what Buddhism really means. I resolve, yet again, to stay pure.

Keishi looks at me again in the eye, and we hold the stare for a moment, as though something immense, cosmically true, has passed between us.

"Retirement!" he scoffs, continuing suddenly. "None of them care about practice. They're making *retirement* plans, trying to ensure their comfort. That isn't practice! When they're on their death beds they'll regret it. They'll regret that they didn't practice and wake up when they could. Their retirement plans aren't going to save them."

Suddenly his voice changes, and his eyes seem ever so slightly to moisten. He grabs with both hands the priest belt he has been holding while we talk, and he winds it carefully in a coil on the floor. He takes off his *rakusu* surplice, folds it, and lays it down on the coiled up belt. His movements are precise and beautiful. Here, finally, is a real Western monk.

"Listen," he says, "I've got nothing. I'll probably die on the street in a cardboard box. I've got no inheritance, no family, no insurance. But I'm a monk. I'm getting old, I have to push now, practice hard while I can. Life is short, I'm telling you, kid, in the snap of a finger you'll be my age. But monks can't go around making retirement plans. We've renounced things, we don't need those comforts! Listen, I don't usually tell people this, but take it from me, there is no real Zen in America. There are no monks, no teachers, no enlightenment… It's dying here too, I'll be honest with you, but there are still a couple of enlightened masters left. Roshi-sama is one," he says, gesturing with his chin toward the dokusan room behind the ceremony hall.

I nod in agreement, and Keishi pauses again, looking me up and down, "Why are you here anyway, kid?"

What can I say? One anticipates such questions, sure, imagines being asked them at the temple gate, proper answer allowing entry, shallow answer inciting a humiliating "Go home!" One thinks, perhaps, that one will reply, "Not even the 10,000 sages could say," or, "Who says I have come?" or, "What do *you* call it when ripe fruit falls?" One turns such questions over, perhaps, in one's head. But none of the answers seems quite right when the question has a voice, a body.

"Umm..."

He continues, "I mean if you want to just live a good life, go back to American Zen. Move up the Zen corporate ladder, make your little Zen career like the rest of those guys out there."

I look again out the sliding glass doors. We are both kneeling in seiza; my knees are starting to tingle but I dare not to move. The little brown bird hops around the scraggly bushes and the unweeded moss.

"I was frustrated with the life there," I say finally. "I saw it starting to happen, the thing that you're talking about."

Here, finally, is a monk who understands the pain of being at a comfortable, pop-psychy American Zen place, while really wanting to realize the Way. I can talk to him, and say the things that seem too hard, or too unkind, to say at home.

"I saw myself moving up that ladder and I got terrified," I say, hesitant. "I saw my little Zen career laid out right in front of me, and it seemed so vacant, so small. I mean they're not really monks there, you know? It's frustrating, for people who really want… I mean it gets so psychological sometimes—I don't know, 'check-in's—I mean what are we really doing there, I get to wondering."

Keishi snorts, "'Check-in's! What do you expect, women run the place!"

His comment jolts me a little, but I am enthralled with him, entranced. He is mouthing my criticisms, my own fears and frustrations with life in American Zen. His sincerity and his pain are so obvious, so crisp, and so inseparable. I appreciate him; he can understand what I really want, why I've really come.

"Listen," I say, and I try to look him straight in the eyes, the way he's looked at me. "Listen, I want to do this. I'm here because I really want to do this, not just to settle for an awakening that other people think

I must have by virtue of some seniority. I've vowed to do this and I've got no choice but to really do it, to do it totally and completely."

Keishi nods. Somebody slides the door open and comes into the communal room, but neither of us look up; we hardly notice.

"If you really want to be able to help beings you have to wake up," he says. "You have to really wake up. That's what it means, the vow to 'save all beings.' Those American Zen 'teachers' think they're saving beings but they're just stopping some children from crying. They aren't themselves awake, so how could they really save anyone? Roshi-sama helps people, really. You've met him; it's obvious. If you want to help people, you have to become like him, you have to wake up. It isn't easy—did you know Roshi-sama didn't lie down or look up for three years in his training? You have to train hard. And even if you do the real training, it doesn't happen much. Genuine awakening is very rare."

Keishi pauses. "It hasn't happened to me yet. I was just talking to Roshi-sama, I told him, 'I haven't gotten it yet,' and he said, 'Just continue!'" He chuckles. "He said it took his teacher the great Rodaishi thirty years to have *satori* awakening. He told me just not to look off."

He is smiling now, but his voice is sad. "I don't know if I will ever really see," he says quietly. "It hasn't happened yet, and it may never happen to me, but I'm going to give it my best shot, and while I do, before my Dharma eye has truly opened, I'm not going to go around pretending to teach like those guys out there." He gestures vaguely toward the ocean.

"Zen is about nothing other than waking up," he continues. "You know, it might last in America, the way it is now with no real teachers, no one really bothering to understand the essence. It might last that way as a religion, but real Zen won't last there. It'll die with these last couple of enlightened Japanese masters. Not many people are able to wake up, but we have to really strive for it to even have a chance. Zen is about becoming enlightened. Hell, the whole monastic set-up is to support one or two people to really get enlightened, that's all. The rest of us are beside the point."

He is crossing lines that I've only crossed privately, but he's saying nothing exactly that I disagree with. A little uneasy, though, I try one last time to offer some words from my lineage.

"But can't people share something of value about Zen before getting completely enlight..." I begin.

"Baahhh!" he cuts me off with a snort. "No one out there is even trying to get enlightened! Take it from me, if you really want to practice and wake up your only option is to be in Japan while these couple of enlightened teachers are still around. They won't live forever, so now is the time. Ok? So what are you gonna do? Are you going to tell me you're going back to the States?"

Keishi looks squarely at me for a second, and then laughs. I start laughing too.

"Yeah," I scoff, flushed with sarcasm, *"the States."*

# 3   Home Leaving

A train from Kyoto deposits me at a village station where I board an air-conditioned bus that winds school kids and middle-aged women through densely forested mountains and rivers. After about an hour, the bus pulls into a terminal in a medium-sized town on the coast. With my limited Japanese character literacy I can tell from the signs only that I am somewhere "relating to a city." I stand up on the slowing bus and ask a young man across the aisle from me, in my fresh, best Japanese, "*Maibara Eki desu ka?*"

I don't know what people think of me. I have gotten strange glances since arriving in my monk's clothes in Kyoto day before yesterday, some looks reverent, some amused, and some, from the corner of my eye, with a disdain that reminds me of the Japanese language tutor I had who when we first met asked me what I did for a living. We were in a room on the eighth floor of a downtown San Francisco office building, windows overlooking an alley, other buildings' windows, and a thin swath of sky—

"I'm a Zen priest," I said. "I live in a Zen temple. I don't really think of it as work, but the temple does support me, so I guess I do Zen for a living."

My new teacher bobbed his head, staring at me as though I had just stolen his stapler.

"Do you hate the world?" he exploded, and I glimpsed suddenly that Zen in Japan might not be as clear-cut as I'd hoped.

I tried to explain how instead it was that my *love* of the world overflowed out of me, becoming—the way blood turns red on touching the air—my aspiration to practice Zen, but he just went on with the lesson…

"*Maibara Eki desu ka?*" I ask, hoping that the young man on the bus won't give me that same look, or laugh out loud at my shiny, American-made, Japanese-style *samue* monk's clothes.

"*Eeeehhh…*" he says. *Eeehhh?* Is that closer to *hai*—the word I've learned for "yes"—or to *iie*, what I've learned for "no"? *Did I learn* "eh"? I vaguely remember the sound; I did study it. I remember it definitely as the casual version of some word.

"*Arigato gozaimasu,*" I say, thanking him, and get up from my seat, relying on my instinct and optimism in the absence of information. Before stepping down from the bus, though, I hesitate again and turn to the driver: "*Maibara Eki desu ka?*"

"*Eeeehhh…*" he says.

I'm washed over by an incredible desire to grab him by the pressed uniform and shake him, shake everyone on the whole goddamn bus, jump up and down the aisles flinging copies of my A+ Japanese final at all of them, screaming, "See! See! I *do* speak Japanese"…

"*Arigato,*" I say, and I take the plunge onto the concrete, out of the air-conditioned bus and into the hot and humid probably-Maibara air. I pull out some instructions and a rough map that my American friend Shoko, who spent time at Gendoji himself, had sketched for me on the back of his temple's utility bill envelope—I look around and orient myself. The station in front of me has high glass walls, glass doors. Inside, businessmen and schoolchildren bustle, and beyond the ticket booth I see a train pull out. At the edge of the station, a long staircase climbs to a walkway that crosses over the train tracks. I hoist up my bags and walk towards it.

I come down the other side and I cross a two-lane highway. I wander through a quiet neighborhood of farmhouses and rice paddies and end up on a street that dead ends in a steep, tree-covered hill that connects to others in a series of hills that reveal themselves, from the crest at least, as a genuine mountain range. At the base of the hill is a temple complex. A gravel parking lot lies at the end of the street, and near it a tall stone pillar carved with *kanji* Japanese characters stands imposingly at the bottom of wide concrete steps that lead up the slope to a wooden gate.

I compare the kanji to Shoko's instructions, but already I recognize them from my studies. "Gen-do-ji" Whole Way Temple. I have arrived. American Zen is behind me: from here on, the Whole Way, the true Way, unfolds.

Though Gendoji's site has housed a temple for at least five hundred years, it is by no means of ancient proportions: it is a small and unimpressive patchwork of traditional architecture and cheap but functional afterthoughts. Beyond the traditional Zen temple gate, *sanmon*, which is large to my American eyes (larger at least than the steel cattle gate that marks the boundary of my home temple), but tiny in comparison to the stories-high ancient gates of the Kyoto temples, the concrete steps turn into a path that leads straight through the compact temple complex to the *hondo*, ceremonial hall, which is the only Gendoji building with the traditional sharp-pitched, curved tile roof and enormous sliding doors. More steps lead up from the end of the path to the hondo doors.

The hondo hall and sanmon gate enclose the north and south sides of a courtyard cut by concrete paths and landscaped in gravel, rock, puddle-sized ponds, moss, and artfully pruned trees. Statues and engraved pillars stand here and there, and a roofed platform elevated about four feet off the ground is tucked in near the gate and holds a large, suspended *bonsho* bell. Next to the hondo, along the same line, is the kitchen and dining room, and above on a second floor is Roshi-sama's bedroom and living space. Enclosing the sides of the courtyard are the flimsy and box-like zendo and living spaces to the east, bordering the run-down and generally abandoned neighboring Shinto shrine, and to the west, the *Kannondo*, where the handful of lay resident practitioners complete morning service each day. Above the Kannondo, a rickety loft serves as additional living space. Behind the Kannondo, the property expands out into a cemetery that the temple maintains—and that in turn largely funds the temple—and beyond it narrow garden plots run alongside the base of the mountain, opposite several rice paddies and vegetable gardens associated with the farmhouses that share the edge of Maibara with Gendoji.

At the parking lot in the shadow of the mountain and temple, I put down my bags. My heart is pounding and my shiny new American polyester-wool blend samue are covered with sweat. I imagine ripping off my samue top and feeling the slight breeze through my tee-shirt, but I don't dare. It is too early to cut corners on decorum. This isn't the U.S., after all.

I rummage in my bag for my formal bib-like priest's rakusu, touch the small, symbolic robe to my forehead, and drape it over my neck.

Climbing the wide stairs and passing nervously through the gate and into the courtyard, I make my way across the grounds to the entryway at the end of the hondo, where the big hall meets the dining room and kitchen. As I walk through the temple courtyard among a scattering of people, slouching under my heavy red backpack and handbags, no one seems to notice me. The temple is quiet and oddly still, even though I can see people walking around in the cemetery beyond the buildings, a man scrubbing a row of stone statues, and a few women hunched over the ground in a mysterious activity that I will learn (in great detail) to be weeding, extracting tiny grasses from mossy rocks without disturbing the delicate moss. I don't feel unwelcomed by the silence and the coldness of the people—I am instead inspired by their diligence and concentrated meditation on their work. In the U.S. Zen students might have looked up, or called out, broken their concentration for some trivial formality of greeting. But not here: I am among real meditators now.

I set my bags down outside the entryway, where a small wooden block *han*, the instrument that in my American temple is used to call practitioners to zazen, hangs on the outer wall. Above the han is a sign in Japanese; I make out the character for "three"—three horizontal lines—but beyond that the writing is lost on me. The vulnerability of being newly illiterate sends a spasm of panic through me, but I collect myself and, as Shoko explained, I tentatively lift the han mallet and strike three hits, loud and slow, to announce my presence. Nothing happens.

Monks and laypeople scurry around, working and ignoring me still. A few minutes pass, but I am prepared: it is just as Shoko described. After another half an hour of so—resolutely standing with my bags on the ground beside me—a pair of wooden blocks crash together in an accelerating crescendo and people start to converge in the kitchen courtyard area where some low tables hold pots of tea and trays of tea sweets. Some practitioner talk softly, others sit on the hondo steps or walk across the compound to the cemetery and perch on a memorial stone to take their break. A number of people seem oblivious to the tea break, and just continue their delicate weeding. No one pays me the slightest attention. One monk sits with his teacup and treat on the stoop right next to where I stand, without even looking up at me once.

Two or three hours pass while I stand formally in front of the doors, upright, with my hands clasped at my chest in the *shasshu* position. My shoulders cry out, but I do not dare to drop my hands. My calves ache. Sweat drips down my face and legs.

Finally I hear a loud "*Hai?*" from inside, and a tall, thin Japanese monk, his bare chest visible far down the neck of his tattered, loose samue monk's clothes, steps out to greet me as though I had just arrived.

"*He-rro*," he says brightly, approximating English. "Yushin," he says, pointing to his nose, and directs me up the steps to the hondo.

He lights a stick of incense and gestures for me to offer it at the main altar: "*Sampai*," Yushin-san says, inviting me to do three full bows.

I scoot up to the altar as I've done many times in the States, and watched countless more, take the incense stick with trembling hands from his fingers and touch it to my forehead in blessing. As I raise the stick, I take a closer look at the altar. It is crowded with implements, statues, envelopes, and plaques, and it is multi-leveled, continuing back and further up into dimmer recesses shaded by the hanging curtains. The main altar statue is at such a dim and high level of the altar that I can scarcely make it out, though I assume that it is Shakyamuni Buddha. Such a complex and almost esoteric altar seems odd to me, given that in the Sates all the main altars I've seen have been uncluttered, with bold, unmistakable statues clearly exposed atop them: all revealed, no mystery. I set the incense stick solidly to stand in the deep, ash-filled incense urn.

The thin, smiling monk Yushin-san, I will learn, is the mild-mannered head cook, *tenzo*, who can fry some mean *tempura* and is the only monk trusted to make the *dashi* noodle broth, but whose frequent "dentist appointments" in town sometimes strain his kitchen assistants' morale. He somehow coasts through the rigor of Gendoji, comfortable in his kitchen rhythm, his seniority, and his humble living space in a less-traveled branch of the hallway behind the kitchen, but he always wonders, I will hear, whether it is the right time to leave the temple where he has lived almost fifteen years and served as head cook for eight. His plans never materialize, though, and years just keep ticking away. When I begin carrying the kyosaku stick in the meditation hall I will notice that whenever he is there, he sleeps. Of course I won't ever hit him, no one does—and anyway one mustn't correct a senior—but the relaxation with which he seems to sleep is startling to me. I'll sleep my share, no doubt, but never comfortably or happily, always only angst-ridden, failure-speckled snatches of sleep broken by fits of resolve. He has a place at Gendoji, a groove or a rut, and his low-intensity but big-hearted presence is an asset that even his most annoyed assistants don't contest. My opinion of him will alternate, sometimes quickly, between disrespect for his laziness—can't he see that he is stuck in the way he found to work the system to make temple life comfortable without really engaging in it?—and a sneaking, terrifying suspicion that he may in fact be the only disciple in the temple who really has any clue about the meaning of Zen.

Yushin-san takes me to the large room next to the hondo and across from the small office and kitchen, and shows me a section of closet behind a sliding door that covers a long wall of the room. A *futon* and bedding are folded neatly at the bottom of the closet, and he points to the space for my luggage.

"*Banka* fo-ru sa-ti *desu*," Yushin says, leaving me to arrange my things in the closet of the dormitory that doubles as the dining room. *Banka* is a chanting service, I recall, but not until I have organized my corner of the closet do I realize that "fo-ru sa-ti" was an attempt at English—four thirty.

I step out of the room into the hallway, somewhat urgently looking for a bathroom after my extended vigil outside the hondo doors. The sliding door of the office, where a different Japanese monk spends each day, like Yushin-san today, greeting guests and answering the phone, is open. Yushin-san is nowhere in sight, but a woman sits on the tatami floor of the office, her back to me, arranging tea cups on a tray.

As politely as I can, with rehearsed fluidity, I inquire as to the possible locale of a room in which to wash my hands.

The woman turns to face me, smiling, her eyes soft and warm. She is gorgeous, in her late twenties. I did not expect that; I knew that there would be some women, somehow I didn't imagine that *such* a woman would be allowed. No problem. I'm just trying to get to the bathroom. I look down at the ground, massaging my hands.

"*Migi*," she says, pointing down the hallway.

I nod—taking just one more quick glance at her silky face, her shimmering black hair that cascades over a gentle, curving womanness that not even her baggy temple work clothes can temper... and I thank her. *Migi*, I repeat to myself, unperturbed. Just down the hall and turn *migi*.

I have not come so far to be distracted by even such beauty as this woman's, and I will not be, I am certain, and I simply smile and nod. I will be courteous, but nothing more. I will simply return her courtesy. I drop all thoughts of her and walk the few steps down the hallway and turn left, *migi*, as she said. But there is no left. No door, no opening, no turn in the hallway, just a blank white wall with a wooden bar mounted on it, for monks to use to hang up outer robes before entering the toilet. There is a door in front of me, though: I try it and peer in, but it is a small bathing room, no toilet, just a deep Japanese *ofuro* bathtub, a sink, a mirror, and a showerhead. I close it.

I look back up the hallway and I see that the "*migi*" woman is leaning her slender body out from the doorway of the small office and into the hallway, watching me. Her faded, baggy black monk's clothes hang naturally from her, as though accustomed to her shape—I cringe at the thought of how ridiculous the polyester sheen and crisp straight cut of my American set must look to her, and I pull the two sides of my slipping collar more tightly around my neck as I look up the hall at her looking at me. Her long, straight black hair falls off her shoulder, towards the ground against the angle of her leaning body, and her thin, smooth hand lifts from her side and waves out towards the right.

"*Migi!*" she says again, giggling and gesturing to the right.

I smile, nod awkwardly, look up at her, re-close the stubborn X where the collar of my shiny American samue fails to come together, and I open the door to my right. Of course, *migi* is right. *Hidari*, left. *Migi*, right.

"*Migi, migi, migi,*" I say to myself, "right, right, right." But as I say it, opening the door to the small bathroom off the hallway near the kitchen and the small office and my dorm that is also the dining room, I only hear her voice saying it. "*Migi,*" she whispers, giggling, nasal, the *g* more like an *n*, but not as harsh as my own *n*, not as though I could think "*mini*" and in that way capture it. Perhaps "*migni*?", but melodic somehow, as her smooth hair plummeted from her leaning head, her flawless hand rising from her faded black cotton covered hip.

Or even "*mignyi*", I think, trying the syllables myself, chewing on them like clay, like glutinous rice, unable to say them properly, or to say them at all without picturing her gentle, kind, smooth face and flawless hand, this woman's—unzipping my pants, and crouching over the open Japanese-style toilet, remembering the instructions on the sign I read in the hostel, and the paragraph in the guide book, and facing the correct way, such that the concave porcelain protrusion would capture and re-direct my wayward urine.

"*Mignyi,*" I whisper awkwardly, inaccurately, and I piss my first Gendoji piss.

I say goodbye to *Amerika* in a large suburban house, which no one is allowed to call a house, as it has been reclaimed as a "hermitage" by some friends of mine, monastics who like me long for the Ancient Way, hovering and agitating from the margins of the American Zen institution. At the hermitage they live the Ancient codes, sit long days in meditation and study, beg for food outside the nearby grocery store, don't stretch their feet towards altars. They are liminal luminaries waiting, laying the ground, for the perhaps impending monastic revolution that will bring the American Zen lifestyle into accord with the Ancient Way. In the hermitage ceremonial hall—a disguised living room with wide windows, a vaulted ceiling, sitting cushions, and a grand three-tiered altar with a seated bronze Shakyamuni Buddha—I touch the bottom of a smoking incense stick to my forehead for a moment and plunge it into the incensor.

I was up late the night before, listening carefully to one of the hermitage's founders, Shoko, who spent time in Japan at Gendoji and can go on for hours sharing survival tips and stories about the practice there. The nun Jusan, the other hermitage founder, had offered to drop me off at the airport shuttle stop at the base of the hill. Before morning zazen, four a.m. and still dark, I awoke and packed my last things into my enormous red backpack. I draped my rakusu informal robe over my samue monk's clothes and climbed down the stairs to the high-ceilinged service hall. Leaving my bags by the stairs, I lit a stick of incense.

Offering it at the main altar, I do three full bows on the wooden floor. My hands tremble as they touch the ground; my heart pounds.

Suddenly I doubt everything.

The three hermitage monastics line up in the service hall, witnessing my bows as a silent goodbye. Something sweeps over me: the sweetness of the hermitage, and my nearby home temple, the warmth of the wide American Sangha, the strength of the practice, the depth of it. My debt of gratitude to my temple, to American Zen. How can I walk away?

*Why leave behind the seat that exists in your own home, and wander in vain through the dusty realms of other lands?* Dogen-Zenji teaches in his *Fukanzazengi* meditation instruction. *If you make one misstep you stray away from the Way directly before you.*

I see my teacher's face, his flexible, steady zazen. His relentless, joyful kindness. His relaxation and curiosity. I remember how, in his way, my teacher has never failed to meet me, whether or not I have been able to see the meeting or understand a word of it. I am overcome with gratitude for my teacher's devotion to practice, which is his devotion to me.

*Is ordination with a teacher meaningless?* I ask myself. *How can I leave behind the teacher that is in my own home? Why scramble to understand somebody who won't speak my language or understand my context? Do I think that the Japanese Way can possibly be relevant to me? Isn't the Way to proceed always clear—simple, present attention, and wide mind—why seek further teachings when I can barely practice those I've already received? Don't I have enough to work with? Don't I have all the support I could dream of having—Sangha treasure, Dharma treasure, Buddha treasure? 'Why wander in vain?!'*

"Enjoy your life," my teacher told me, smiling, looking at me kindly after dropping me off at the hermitage the day before my departure to Japan. "Enjoy your life," he repeated, before closing his car door and driving off down the hill.

It is time to go. The door is open, and the concrete garage is dimly lit by the light over the open garage door. A damp, cold breeze licks through the open door and into the hermitage, swirling to rest in the service hall where we stand. My old Dharma friend, the nun Jusan, gestures to me: It is time to go.

She has already loaded my bags into the trunk. I stand on the threshold and bow—what else can I do? Can I back out? Everything is already in place, but.... The hermitage monks bow back deeply to me. Jusan starts the engine.

I stand on the threshold. The candles on the main altar flicker in the intermittent breeze; a breath of exhaust blows in from the garage. *Do I have to go?* I wonder. *What am I thinking? Won't Japan just be overkill, burn out, just agony, relentless rigor? The Way, my Way, is right here, in this quiet hermitage, quietly, sincerely proceeding....*

"Why am I doing this?" I squeak, trembling. "What am I doing?"

The hermitage is silent. The car engine hums behind me, the incense smoke streams up off the altar a few inches, then catches a different air current and swirls, spiraling and ballooning, vanishing into the room.

Shoko steps forward slightly. He raises his hands out of the shasshu formal position and into a gesture of offering, or somehow of questioning, almost—but not quite—as though he too has the same doubts.

"The One Great Matter," Shoko says slowly.

I step into the garage, get in the car, and within eighteen hours I find myself alone in Japan, a twenty-six year old monk with no ticket home.


The day after I arrive at Gendoji, the disciplinarian Daiko-san, a stern, senior Japanese monk, drives me in an old, tiny Japanese van out through the neighborhood streets to the highway, then speeding into the dark tunnel—I brace myself as we enter, and he shakes his head— through the mountain and along the highway for a few miles before turning down a winding dirt road to a moss-covered Shinto shrine. I remember Daiko-san's voice from when I first called Gendoji, asking permission to come from the basement phone of my home temple. In a strange blend of English and Japanese—sometimes a sort of English with Japanese grammar and sometimes Japanese with English grammar and phrases—he asked me to hold while he went to ask Roshi-sama. Soon, he returned to the phone and told me that Roshi-sama thought it would be fine if I came.

"Question *aru ka*?" he asked on the phone. I didn't have any questions, except maybe "Did you really just go ask the teacher if I could come—no application form, no interview? And did he really just say yes? Based on what? Nothing? Some psychic affinity? A good mood?" I had no questions that I knew how to ask, so I just told him my intended arrival date and hung up the phone.

"Squat if you pee—monks don't stand," Daiko-san tells me after we climb the mossy steps of the Shinto shrine and together chant the *Heart Sutra*. "This will be useful to you someday," he adds. I can't quite imagine how it will ever be useful, but as he gets back into the van with every sign of abandoning me at the Shinto shrine, I am less concerned with any future use as much as with finding my way back to the temple.

Before pulling away, Daiko-san tells me that—well…—if I *want* to, I can walk on the right side of the narrow road. That seems logical to me: *walk against traffic*, I recall, which, in the case of left-side driving Japan is the right side. However, I should know, he continues, that the tradition is to walk on the left. Granted that tradition is now complicated by cars… Daiko-san admits, having apparently given the matter deep thought, and concluding that either way is acceptable. Grimacing as though exhibiting an almost unbearably radical flexibility with the tradition, he leaves the decision to me, slams the door of the van, and squeals away in a great cloud of dust.

I start off, on the right side of the road, feeling like a medieval football player beneath the layers of monastic pilgrimage gear and the various objects hanging from it. I wear the standard takuhatsu outfit of straw sandals, hitched up koromo and kimono, white leggings, and straw hat. Tied to my back is a lacquer box, containing my okesa robe, a Dharma protecting "Dragon Scroll," and my American *kechimyaku* lineage papers, wrapped in the clothes from my *oryoki* eating bowl, the bowls of which are in a long cloth tube that affixes to the outside of the box. Additionally, a bamboo basket, containing toiletries, is wrapped elaborately in cloth and tied to the outfit in an esoteric knot that the kind young monk Ejo-san, after working for half and hour in consultation with a ratty manual, tied for me last night. I wear my rakusu, which usually hangs over the chest, over my left shoulder, and I walk with a round, black *zafu* sitting cushion tucked under my arm, as though ready at any moment to sit zazen. Unprepared for the details of this particular formality, my get-up is mostly borrowed, pieced together late last night from different monks' supplies: Ejo-san's "Dragon Scroll," Ankai-san's lacquer okesa box.

The walk is uneventful, excepting the precarious stretch through the damp, dark highway tunnel, the dim shapes of cars whipping by me as I clutch my zafu and try to balance on the thin walkway that runs along one edge of the tunnel, and I am surprised when I arrive back at the temple. I have been struggling to manifest the ritual—excruciatingly conscious of how beautiful it is but still somehow unable to bring forth the primal monk in me that should come forth to occupy it, the ancient heart to fill the ancient robes. I have been present, careful, attending to mind, but still nothing magical has happened, nothing profoundly old. *Just as the ancients have done*, I urge myself with each step. I even try walking on the left side for a quarter mile or so—nothing....

I hit the wooden han signal to announce my arrival, and I am non-greeted again by monks scurrying around, playing oblivious. I stand outside the entrance for another two hours. *What an honor!* I think, welcomed by the cold formality again, as though the walls and gates of the temple were widening to receive me—*just stand here*, they say, *now there is nothing you need to do*. Strange and familiar freedom.

Finally Daiko-san "notices" me and waves me in. He leads me in another incense offering at the main hondo altar, and then together we walk to the shared dorm room/dining room where I spent last night. He opens the closet where my bags and bedding are, and pulls down my big red backpack and duffel bag. He puts them on the ground and gestures for me to open them.

"What?" I say.

"*Akete!*" he elaborates. *Open.*

I unsnap my backpack and unzip my duffel bag, and Daiko-san sits next to them on the tatami mat and starts rummaging through my things. He finds the bar of chocolate that Jusan had snuck into my bags before we left the hermitage, and the zip lock bag of black tea that I brought with me just in case.

"*Dame!*" he shouts, throwing my contraband on the floor. "*No good!* You are a monk!"

# 4
# Deluded About Enlightenment

*Those who are greatly enlightened about delusion are Buddhas; those who are greatly deluded about enlightenment are sentient beings. Further there are those who are enlightened beyond enlightenment, and who are in delusion throughout delusion.*

—Dogen Zenji, *Genjokoan*

Daiko-san shoves Ankai-san, apparently communicating that it is Ankai-san's turn to hit the big taiko drum for the formal gyocha tea and Dharma address that is held mid-morning each shikunichi bath and rest day. Ankai-san understands the demand implied by the silent shove by means of a Japanese nonverbal skill set that eludes me. He replies with a forceful "*Hai!*" and takes his place, with too stiff a dignity, at the base of the rickety ladder that leads to the taiko drum resting in a high alcove of the ceremonial hall.

Ankai-san is the youngest of the Japanese monks and reputedly a martial arts adept, although he is forbidden from practicing his art on temple grounds. He is kind and thoughtful, but ambition pours from him like streams of color, painting everything he does. Sometimes, when he is bored during his turn in the office, waiting for parishioners to wander by and assuming that no one can see, he picks up a *kotsu* stick or a whisk, the ritual phalli that senior priests hold while officiating services, and practices his Zen Master posture. He bends his legs, his elbows up at attention, his chin high, the kotsu upright in his hand with its long tassel draped just so, and grunts an imitation of Roshi-sama's satisfied, centered "*Yoosh*", which blends into a cough and a quick look at a pile of papers when I walk by the office window on my way to the kitchen.

We monks rotate through the gyocha positions, one week whisking or carrying tea to the assembly, one week serving it to Roshi-sama, one week playing the taiko drum that accompanies the procession and opens the ceremony. I'm glad that this week it isn't my turn for anything. In the course of two months in the temple, I have only had to carry tea once or twice, and though I enjoy it, today I would like as little responsibility as possible. The last couple of gyochas have been markedly unpleasant, with Roshi-sama dragging on far beyond my language comprehension, my seiza-raw knees screaming out each instant of their slow descent into fiery hells, and my mind tightening and tightening around the fact that the one ostensibly free day of the week will again be swallowed up not just by gyocha, but by morning meditation and chanting, three formal meals, evening chanting, three hours of evening zazen, and my cruel usual shikunichi assignment of afternoon kitchen cleaning. What time does that leave for the "rest" I've spent most of the week looking forward to?

The "day off" at my American temple, starting before five in the morning but broken by just two or three hours of formal events, never seemed so spacious when I was in it, but lately it seems to have been a vast expanse of free time. At the very least in the States on day off I never had to wash the kitchen floor, or spend two hours finely chopping boiled *daikon* greens (after which they are still only remotely digestible, I grumble inevitably when aboard this particular thought train). Even if by some chance I had needed to work on an American day off, I would have demanded and surely received generous recompense in "comp time," a concept for which I'm certain there could not possibly be a Japanese translation.

Precisely at 10:15 am Roshi-sama starts down the stairs from his room, with Daiko-san attending close behind him, swishing through the hallway towards the hondo in the ornate vestments I think of as his "Sunday robes." Taking the cue, Ankai-san scurries up the ladder and starts pounding the drum, slowly at first, then gradually building speed.

He hits hard and loud, with martial ferocity, but the sound is flat, lacks the fullness that sometimes reverberates through the taiko.

"*Dame!*", *no good!*, Roshi-sama shouts furiously as he nears the drum, breaking into a run out of the solemn procession of two and waving his arms at Ankai-san, who stops and climbs meekly down from the ladder. Ripping the drumsticks from Ankai-san's hands, Roshi-sama scrambles up the wobbly ladder himself, his floor-length robes tangling around his legs and his elderly body heaving for breath. The assembly seated below watches anxiously, and Daiko-san rocks nervously at the bottom of the ladder, poised to catch his frail teacher as he falls.

High up in the drum alcove, Roshi-sama strikes the drum once. It sounds flat, at least as dull as Ankai-san's. From my place on the tatami floor, I look up at Roshi-sama and feel a little embarrassed for him. I hope he wasn't trying to make a point about the drum. He's an old man, I remind myself, and just because he's enlightened doesn't mean he has the strength to hit a drum.

Unfazed, Roshi-sama hits the drum a second time. The clear sound shakes the sliding wooden doors, reverberating through the weave of the cool tatami. *Good hit, old man*, I think.

He strikes a third time. An explosive, expansive boom fills the temple, not so much shaking things as settling, silencing them. The sound blankets my mind with its clarity and weight, snapping me into a new, immense consciousness. My whole field of awareness smoothes out, crystallizes, and fills to overflowing with the vastness of my being.

Roshi-sama, now himself a stillness that flows through the stillness of a hall that is no longer any other than my body, descends from the alcove. He crosses his legs under his robes at his seat, rests a moment—complete unmoving—in his place, and then addresses the assembled monks and laypeople.

"I hit the drum three times just now. The first time I hit it like Ankai-san had. Ankai-san, your hits were no good! Your arm was extended, your body was bent, you were off balance. The way you were standing, it was impossible to hit the drum well.

"The second time, I hit it correctly. There are ways to do things. When you do things in certain ways, it is easier to become one with them. When your body is close to the drum, you can hit it with ease. When an action comes from your hara—when you hold the drumstick with your hara—the result is always excellent. We must learn this in our practice, to fully use the hara in everything we do. That is the way I hit the drum the second time: I hit it correctly, the way it should be done.

"The third time—did you hear the third hit?—the third time I just became one with the drum. The drum, the old teacher, no separation."

I am in awe of him, absorbed in his sweet spell.

"When I met my great teacher I just gave myself completely to him," Roshi-sama begins again, after the tea and sweets are offered and silently consumed, and the tea bowls retrieved. The words are familiar to me already, one of the few simple points that make up Roshi-sama's teaching, that he repeats over and over at every opportunity. "I just followed my teacher completely."

Sitting in seiza in the concentrated, upright row of monks in the hondo, the feeling I have is also already familiar: I want more than anything to be as he is, to do as he did. If he says that the path is surrender to the teacher, sign me up—I will give myself over to this great teacher and to his great awakening. How could I not? His enlightenment clearly and abundantly manifests through his presence, his kindness, and the way his body radiates a sort of brightness. The many Western teachers I've met all pale in comparison.

And yet I harbor a quiet, lingering doubt: Roshi-sama's foreignness is devastating. The training that he himself endured under his teacher, by "just following his teacher completely," is so distant and mythic that I can't quite believe it is available to me, no matter how devoted to him I feel. He seems more an artifact than a person like me; he is a remnant of an ancient world, of a fiercely focused culture of lifelong apprenticeship and single-minded study. A product of "the sort of people that would spend their whole life making *one* doll," as a friend likes to express the intensity of Old Japan. I can surrender to him as completely as my American being will allow, but I am not sure whether it will be enough, whether my surrender can possibly lead me, a foreigner with foreign views and foreign needs, where it led him. But how could I fail to try?

Roshi-sama was born to give himself over, and gave himself to his nation even before he met his teacher. He leapt into the World War with the same fervor with which he would later plunge into the Way. It was his great service, sacrifice, and honor. He lied about his age and entered the ranks of the *kamikaze* at sixteen. He now regrets war—"Right hand against left hand," he says sadly, raising and joining the two hands of his one body—but to this day he loves airplanes. One jovial shikunichi day he runs through the temple courtyard laughing and making a puttering engine sound with his mouth, arms extended like wings, flying over the rock and moss garden.

"Planes are a little different now," his Australian disciple Simon quips. "They have landing gear."

Roshi-sama looks puzzled and looks to Shoryu-san, the Japanese monk with the swollen hands and ears, who clarifies the translation. Roshi-sama laughs heartily, extends his wings, and flies away towards the bathhouse.

Before he could fly the noble flight, the war ended. His heart was broken: how now could he give his life? What meaning, what honor was left for him? In despair, he sought out his great master, "Rodaishi," a pre-eminent Zen teacher of the generation, of the century. His master showed him another path to meaning, another meaning of service, and the young Roshi-sama stayed with him for ten years, until he came finally to thoroughly embody the old Rodaishi's way.

"What is the meaning," Roshi-sama asks me in dokusan, nearly six decades later, sitting stern and smiling slightly beneath the larger than life portrait of his master that hangs above him in the narrow interview room. "What is the meaning of Dogen-Zenji's vow in the *Eihei Koso Hotsuganmon*, the vow to 'renounce worldly affairs and maintain the Buddhadharma'?"

"Not acting from self," I say, after a pause. I'm always inspired, ignited, when facing Roshi-sama, and the voice comes up from deep within me, bringing with it again the possibility of real awakening, indeed the vow to attain it. I feel again, right now, that my self is just the surface of an ocean that acts, an ocean that moves lips before Roshi-sama, that sees Rodaishi's portrait above him, that hears the sudden caw of a nearby bird. "*Renouncing worldly affairs and maintaining the Buddhadharma* is just to allow all action to rise up from the source far deeper than self," I continue. "As Dogen-Zenji puts it: not carrying oneself forward to things, but the myriad things realizing themselves."

"No!" Roshi-sama shouts, a surge of righteous wrath rushing though him. "Very bad you do not understand this!"

He settles himself and looks me up and down with wide eyes. I can feel how boundlessly deeply he wants me to understand, but I can't see what it is he wants me to see.

"When I met my teacher," he says, "I gave myself to him. Doing only what the teacher says is to *renounce worldly affairs*. This is very important! To completely follow the teacher is the only way!"

It is? Hasn't my expression of "no-self," of the true depth behind the dream of the acting self, gone far beyond a mundane, procedural teaching like "follow the teacher"? Haven't my words illuminated a deep inner meaning of Dogen's vow *to renounce worldly affairs*? Isn't leaping beyond self and other the true way of renunciation; don't we revere those who can see for themselves, who "attain the teacherless state"?

"Follow the teacher is the only way!" he shouts again, before ringing his hand bell furiously to banish me from the room.

"Kind of guru situation," Lee notes. I have at last arrived in Japan, and I sneak out of the temple to call him, brimming with enthusiasm for Gendoji's Ancient Way and the enlightenment of this tremendous old master. I don't say in as many words that Roshi-sama's enlightenment makes Lee's understanding seem trifling, negligible, but I can hardly contain myself, and no doubt it comes across in the long string of adjectives I use to describe the Japanese teacher.

"Good…" he continues. "Do the practice that's offered."

He pauses, and the silence crackles with our distance. He has always maintained that my study with him includes, and is enriched by, my study with others; just as he insists that my study of Zen includes, and is enriched by, whatever "non-Zen" study or "non-Zen" circumstance may arise and attract me. "Everything is included," he likes to say, "nothing is outside of Zen." Since for him there is no particular way to do Zen, not even any particular thing that Zen is at all, the key point of our study together is just this including, this fully engaging with our life as it arises.

I am not entirely surprised, then, when he says, "The Roshi there is your teacher now. Follow your teacher."

He is simply nudging me towards my life, inviting me to fully engage with my conditions, but still my heart sinks at his words. They carry a kind of finality; they sound like "goodbye." My original teacher is encouraging me to leave him behind as I set out on a path that perhaps even he sees can take me farther, deeper, than the practice we once shared in the strange, rootless wilderness of American Zen.

*Perhaps I will cut off my finger*, I think. I've heard that great Zen adepts do such things on occasion, a gesture of gratitude and devotion upon leaving one teacher for another. And it feels like that to me now, a cutting, a leaving behind of someone who has become part of me. *What sort of knife will I use?* I wonder. *And which finger?*

"Have you seen his hand?" people will surely whisper, in hushed awe at my resolve and my passion.

*Yes, yes—I might well cut a finger off sometime soon…*

It would be a fitting expression of how I love Lee, how I have in my own way given over to him. It may at times be hard to say what I've given myself over to exactly, as he never quite tells me what to do. But I've given myself over to our conversations at least, conversations in which teachings arise.

"We bring up the teaching together," he told me once. "It's not that I'm bringing it up and giving it to you."

I nodded, a little disappointed. Better he do the teaching to me, given the tangle of my mind! But I also had a glimpse, tiny and profound, of a truth and a path that he was in this wide open way transmitting.

That truth notwithstanding, I sometimes try quite hard to get him to tell me to do something, but he simply refuses, and tries instead to draw out my own wisdom. It would make things so much easier to just have clear instruction, to just know what to do, but though Lee guides me in principle, he withholds detailed demands. "You need to include people," he might say, or "Don't draw other people into negativity," or "Are you breathing?" He might even suggest something like, "You should study Bodhisattva Precepts," or, as he does over the phone line that crackles to span two shores, "Follow your new teacher." But he will never quite say, "Go there," "Come back here," 'Bring me tea," "Break up with her," or, "Practice this meditation."

And it's furthermore always been clear that even if Lee does suggest something, it doesn't mean that I should necessarily do it. Maybe I will, but maybe I won't, and it is perhaps that very principle that opens up our conversations, that allows them their power and intimacy. Sometimes I do what he hasn't suggested, or I suggest to him what I think I should do, or tell him what he should do, or what he should tell me to do. In whatever case, a conversation ensues. Sometimes a cosmic conversation, sometimes a mundane one, but in any case a shared feeling for the Way arises through it. In those moments it is clear that the Dharma is not turned by the wisdom of the teacher or the aspiration of the student, but only by the sincere meeting of the two.

In the phone booth at the train station in my new and still strange Japanese town, heavy with the reverberation of the words, "Follow your teacher," I nod. Lee is handing me over, passing me on to my Japanese teacher, knowing that there is something for me here with Roshi-sama, something that will best blossom if I drop the idea of anything else.

"What do you mean, 'follow my teacher,'" I mutter.

"I mean support everybody! It's how you support everyone there. It's how you accord with the current conditions." He pauses. "It's a 'When in Rome' situation… You know each moment is a new Rome, don't you?"

"When in Japan," he adds, with a pointed chuckle that cuts against the poignance of the moment, "just follow your teacher completely."

---

"Mr. Roshi-sama is muchly enlightenment," the young Japanese monk Ejo-san tells me quietly in *Gendogo*—Gendojese, our temple blend of languages—as we walk together on a late summer takuhatsu, approaching a lunch spot via a long stretch of quiet highway.

I nod tentatively. It is clear that Roshi-sama has something special going on, but I am still warming up to the E-word that I have long been encouraged to suspect highly if not to avoid outright. My recent conversation with Keishi, the fierce American ex-patriot, has helped me to clarify that I don't want to hide from the concept, indeed I want to honor and profess "enlightenment" as my profound motivation and my unshakeable, compassionate aspiration. It's one thing to take a quick ride on the enlightenment bandwagon, though, and another to thoroughly shake off my many years of indoctrination in American Soto Zen.

Much of the Buddhist tradition can be read (especially in Western translations, some scholars report) to emphasize enlightenment as its goal and purpose, but the Soto Zen sect in general tends to downplay the idea. In our school, the concept of enlightenment is observed to function primarily as fuel for more of the self-centered grasping and clinging that is at the root of the basic suffering that Buddhism aims to relieve. If the idea of a future perfect enlightenment is just going to confuse things, why not drop it and get on with the fundamental moment-by-moment practice of letting go into presence?

"If you're trying to drive to Osaka," a Japanese Soto Zen abbot once told me, summarizing the sect's view of enlightenment, "don't try to look at Osaka! Keep your eyes on the road right in front of you!"

In the American Zen of my religious formation, skepticism of the notion is widespread, and "enlightenment" is handled like a tenacious and crippling contagion. The set of naïve, dualistic, reality-fleeing ideals it implies makes it more an insult than anything else. Unless we're quoting scripture, in American Soto Zen the word is nearly always ironic, a put-down or a jab at somebody's narrow view of self-centered, distant attainment. *"Ohhh, he won't talk to us because he's trying to get enlightened…"* The immediacy of the present moment has no room for such abstractions.

Although "enlightenment" unmodified is taboo in my American temple, acceptable versions of the tem include "original enlightenment," and "practice-enlightenment." Shakyamuni Buddha's much vaunted awakening was just precisely his realization that all beings have from the first been awake, and that only by the veil of their delusions they have failed to see it. This original enlightenment is the foundation of Zen practice and doctrine—it is because enlightenment is already our immediate state that we can meaningfully practice meditation, especially non-striving, goal-less, "just-sitting" shikantaza. If we think of enlightenment as some moment in which we gain something that we don't already have, my American Zen teachers have drilled into me, then we are missing the basic practice of presence, and are missing the deep liberating point of Buddhism. Even if we acknowledge our originally awakened nature but hold onto enlightenment as a discrete and dramatic moment of seeing this nature clearly, still we are turning away from the alive and awakened moment that is before us no matter what or how we are seeing.

Here original enlightenment becomes practice-enlightenment, which is for Dogen-Zenji the key to the Zen school. The practice of Zen is precisely the enlightenment of Zen, and the enlightenment of Zen is precisely the practice of Zen. He insists that we do not practice Zen to realize awakening, but that our practice of Zen is our expression of awakening. Our enlightenment is evidenced, expressed, and fulfilled as our practice.

Ejo-san and I, walking towards our lunch break on a stretch of lonely highway with no house in sight to bless, let our begging bowls slump in our hands as we chat and trade praise of Roshi-sama and his great enlightenment. Silence is the rule on takuhatsu, but Ejo-san is senior to me and it would be inappropriate, implicitly critical of him, to not indulge the conversation. Our conversation anyway seems in accord with the teachings, and more pressing than the guideline of silence.

Once we've exhausted a first layer of our mutually patchwork Gendojese affection for Roshi-sama ("muchly enlightened," "first time of no one I meet life before," "how muchly luckful we disciple"), the conversation begins to veer into more murky waters. Gradually increasing in piety and vigor, Ejo-san starts expressing a certain sectarian line—that breakthrough into enlightenment, under the guidance of an enlightened teacher, is the only authentic Zen—and I start to get jittery.

On the one hand, if I still feel that "enlightenment" is taboo, how can I understand, much less talk about, Roshi-sama's deep charisma, deep power? I have an old and strong resistance to the way that Ejo-san is talking, but I can't deny Roshi-sama's presence and clarity, and in his presence the word "enlightenment" makes a new kind of sense, has a new kind of concrete reality. But where is this way of thinking going to lead us? And what does Roshi-sama's enlightenment have to do with our enlightenment? It strikes me that Ejo-san is missing something important by carrying on about enlightenment, Roshi-sama, and True Zen in this way.

I try, friendly at first but with growing frustration, to somehow convey my tenuous understanding of my American teacher's somewhat more clear understanding of the subtle teaching of practice-enlightenment, the non-dual and practical brilliance of Dogen-Zenji. Unfortunately, I'm not entirely convinced myself. After all, I learned the non-dual teachings from teachers who seem far less enlightened than Roshi-sama, who seems quite enlightened and is presumably the source of Ejo-san's more fixed understanding of the term. Despite my confusion, as I react to Ejo-san I glimpse again something very profound in the idea that understanding is not somewhere other than delusion, that practice is not apart already from awakening, and that the practice—this accessible, continuous zazen mind—isn't just a stage or a means to an end but actually the whole point of Buddhism and Zen.

"Buddhism is nothing if no Buddha enlightenment!" he insists, angry now. "Buddha's enlightenment is root! You are no Buddhist if no enlightenment teacher!" No one is practicing in the West, he implies, or in Japan, either, other than his dharma siblings and maybe a few dharma cousins.

I feel like I have been helped, at least, by teachers who wouldn't receive Roshi-sama's seal of enlightenment. I try to explain my hesitation with the on-off switch version of enlightenment, but Ejo-san shakes his head—I am not getting it—and descends back into his rant.

"Shut up and show me *your* practice!" I growl finally, exhausted by the theoretical usefulness or uselessness of teachers. The growing antagonism of our conversation is now suddenly full-fledged, and Ejo-san stops dead. I apologize but the conversation is over, and we fall back into the stretched-out single file that we never should have broken in the first place.

Why, I've been struggling to express impossibly in Gendojese, in my experience of various temples are the students in the assemblies of "enlightened teachers" apparently no more enlightened, and certainly no more mature, than those in the assemblies of "unenlightened teachers"? Who cares, finally, about the teacher's spiritual genius or ordinariness—what can *you* show me—what do *you* understand. A teacher's enlightenment is not one's own, and reliance on it perhaps just binds one, and blinds one to their own practice.

We stop for lunch at a Shinto shrine, and the upset of my conversation with Ejo-san lingers as I eat my obento lunch of soft brown rice and pickles. Is it his sectarianism, or mine? How can I be opposed to the way that he talked, if I have taken Roshi-sama as my teacher and abandoned the vague inclusiveness of American Zen in order to truly awaken to the genuine Way for the sake of all beings? How can I doubt the reality of complete enlightenment when I see what I see in Roshi-sama?

After eating, I wander around. Most of the dozen or so monks are napping, wide straw hats covering their faces, robed legs and arms splayed out in exhaustion. In a damp, shady corner of the *jinja* shrine, though, I come across my friend and roommate Genzen sitting in zazen under a mossy tree. My presence disrupts him, and he looks up at me.

"Sorry," I say.

Of course he is sitting zazen: it is free time after all. No matter that we did wake up at four a.m., sit for two hours, chant for another hour, and hike and shout all morning. No matter that we will continue walking and chanting all afternoon, arrive back at the temple after a meager half-hour rest on the train, set up for formal dinner, chant and eat, then wash dishes and finish just in time for the three more hours of zazen that close every day of the year except one. To Genzen, whose commitment alternately inspires and worries me, none of that indicates against spending the day's shreds of free time in meditation.

"Nice spot…" I say.

"Yeah," he agrees.

We are silent. I look at the lions carved around the jinja. Genzen cordially pulls a leg up out of his sitting posture.

"Is Roshi-sama enlightened?" I spit out. "And what does that *mean*?"

"You know, I think that he is," Genzen says, bringing his hands up energetically, explaining. "He trained hard, even after his first awakening, which happened at the very beginning of his first sesshin. You know, his teacher was hands-down the greatest master of the last century, certified a dozen disciples. I trust Rodaishi's *inka*, so Roshi-sama must be enlightened, or Rodaishi wouldn't have recognized him."

It helps to hear my friend Genzen say it, but I am still uneasy—I never heard of this Rodaishi before coming to Gendoji. Not that that means so much in itself, as my lineage is different and our view in its own way is just as narrow. It is natural that the names of teachers outside of our lineage wouldn't come up so often. But still, if Genzen's sole knowledge of the Rodaishi comes from his disciple Roshi-sama... well there seems at least to be some vested interest. Not that the enlightened would have vested interests....

I thank him and wander a little more, turning and turning in my mind, trying to shake the intellectual doubts that I know will anyway just resolve next time I'm face-to-face with Roshi-sama. I find my other roommate, the Australian Daishu, two or three years at Gendoji, leaning against the back wall of the shrine altar, looking blankly down at an overgrown, mossy ravine and sipping hot tea.

"Yup," Daishu answers without hesitation. "No one like him."

He raises up his steaming metal thermos cup and gestures towards his thermos. "Do you want some tea?" he asks.

"But the world is so *big*," I insist, to which he shrugs and sips.

First off, how can we know about anywhere else? And how did we get so lucky as to find ourselves in the assembly of the only enlightened being on the planet? Why isn't the temple overflowing with hundreds of thousands of devotees? Why aren't the disciples themselves instantly awakened by the power of Roshi-sama's awakening—why are we all so fucked up, if he is so great, and his greatness so critical? It just doesn't hold up; I can't wrap my head around it. But I also can't question the palpable aura of Roshi-sama, the way he meets me without fail in dokusan—beyond words—the way that he lifts up his tea bowl, hits a drum....


"*From now on enlightenment is your teacher, Buddha is your teacher, all beings are your teacher. Do not be fooled by other ways. This is the path of mercy for all existence and things,*" Lee recites.

We student and teacher sit on our heels across from one another in the barn-like meditation hall at our temple in the U.S., separated by a taut field of air and a low lacquer table that is cluttered with the cloth and candles of an ordination ceremony. The two abbesses are in attendance ("Not one abbot, exactly," I try to explain to other monks in Japan, "but *two*, and currently they're both *abbesses*"), and a scattering of other senior priests, as well as Dharma friends and family enough to pack the hall. The religious and institutional red tape that has led for years up to the event has been finally exhausted, and all that remains is the love-fest—the walls of my room are lined with congratulation cards, and the line to greet me with bows and hugs after the ceremony winds like a coiled snake through the Monk's Hall.

"All I got was a *tempura soba* dinner after my ordination!" my Gendoji roommate Genzen will say one day about his own Japanese ordination. Not quite such an exuberant celebration, and certainly no hugs.

Throughout my time in Japan, I will try to explain what ordination means at my temple in the States, how there, like in Japan, it marks the beginning of something, but that in the States it is also a fulfillment of something. Perhaps Americans can't help celebrating completion, while Japanese prefer acknowledging beginnings. Ordination in my lineage comes after no less than five years of training in temple life: waking up early, following the schedule, working in community, and frequently meeting the teacher. Since American Zen ordinations offer no traditional cultural opportunities, they are overwhelmingly the result of a genuine, personal spiritual intention. Gendoji, too, is off the beaten path—Roshi-sama refuses to ordain or certify young priests who only seek the credentials required to inherit their family's temple—but generally in Japan, ordination is rather the admission ticket to a few years of training, which is itself the ticket to temple property inheritance. "*Gonen ka?*" Japanese priests will often ask, "five years before you even ordain?!" By the time they complete five years of temple training, most have passed through the "higher ordinations" of *shuso*, head monk, and *shiho*, Dharma Transmission. In the U.S., that closure won't come for more like twenty years; and even once it does, not many Americans stand to inherit their father's Zen temple.

My body is rock-still. "*All beings are your teacher*" echoes in the hall. The room quivers with the Buddhas who don't know they are Buddhas, all being ordained as my teachers.

Lee says the line a second time. "*All beings are your teacher. Do not be fooled by other ways.*"

I look at him with intense affirmation, but I say nothing. No response is scripted in the minutely choreographed ceremony that I have visualized dozens of times in my head—in fact, Lee isn't even supposed to have said the line twice. I nod, acknowledging the depth of statement and inviting him to continue; he is old and clumsy in some ways, and in our years together I've grown used to guiding him sometimes, as does any teacher's attendant, helping him to navigate the mundane.

Lee looks severely at me and raises his voice to a shout: *"From now on enlightenment is your teacher, all beings are your teacher. This is the path of mercy for all beings. Don't be fooled by other ways!"* He waits.

"Ok?!" he booms, finally.

"OK!" I shout—I mean it—Lee smiles, and the solemn witnesses in the hall burst into laughter.

It could be said that I will be fooled—that my future in Japan and beyond will be marked by my being fooled on that very point. Perhaps I will never cease to be fooled, and foolishly, always be half-looking for a teacher who might fool me completely.


"Roshi-sama," Genzen says at gyocha, after Roshi-sama has finished his demonstration of taiko drum hitting and his general exposition of the Way. We have all sucked down our tea and packaged sweet bean treat, and Roshi-sama has spoken briefly and invited questions. "Roshi-sama, it is likely that all of us in this room will outlive you."

The hall is electric; the question echoes. No bean treat wrappers rustle, no one coughs, no aching seiza legs shuffle. The taiko drum in its high alcove, the bodhisattvas and Buddhas on the main and side altars, the invisible portrait of Rodaishi in the founder's hall behind the altar: all beings in the hondo hold their breath and peek out into the stillness to witness.

Though it is an understatement, it is rarely spoken in more than a whisper. Roshi-sama's age and illness is a quiet anxious rumble in the mind of the temple, but I have never heard it surface so bluntly, so raw. I don't think about it much; sick or not, to me he is the only Roshi-sama that I know. To Genzen, though, close to five years at Gendoji, and to others who have known Roshi-sama over time, his decline is tangible. And with his decline, the decline of the tradition, perhaps even the enlightenment, that he upholds and maintains—a dying man struggling to keep alive a whole world of Old Zen, a whole culture and way of life that will all-too-likely die with him.

He used to be at every single event on the schedule, and now he is often absent, a heavy emptiness in the seat that each hall reserves for him. He is rarely if ever at morning chanting, though he used to lead it every day, smiling and flowing through the hall with his incense and bows, the immense hara power of his quiet chanting. The weekly dokusans, even daily during sesshin, seem frequent to me, coming from a lineage that has fewer, longer formal interviews, but to his older disciples who recall dokusan held each day or two all year around, it seems like Roshi-sama is hardly meeting with them at all.

In the last few years, I learn, there has been a series of departures by the most senior monks, drawn as young men to Roshi-sama's fanatic, awake intensity and nurtured into middle age by his teachings. I've already witnessed it in my short time at the temple, when the monk Shogan-san, twenty-odd years at Gendoji, vanished without word one night, and all I heard said by the other senior monks was "I understand," and "Who's left anymore?" The seniors trickle away, as though they can't bear to watch Roshi-sama's decay, which is Gendoji's decay, and Zen's decay, and can be correlated, at least under the breath, to the temple's gradual infiltration by foreign gaijin, like me, and women. When each senior Japanese monk leaves, a supporting beam of the temple collapses, the Western proportion of the assembly increases, and Gendoji grows less and less like it was. As for me though, I feel like I've come just at the right time—early enough that Roshi-sama is still teaching, but long enough after his prime that I can handle his energy. I imagine that if he was any more healthy, I would have already have run away screaming.

Roshi-sama comes to nearly every period of meditation, in that he is unshakeable, but more often than not he sits upright for only a moment before slumping asleep at his seat in the hall. When it is my turn to be *junko*, to walk slowly through the zendo during zazen, carrying the kyosaku stick and wondering exactly how to know who I should or shouldn't strike, I watch him closely, praying that the next time he dips he won't roll off of his elevated platform and brain himself on the zendo floor. I wonder if that would qualify as "dying sitting up." Is that a noble Zen master's death?

He no longer eats with the community, but an inner circle of Japanese monks bring specially prepared "soft" meals to his room. It is food that he can eat, and the effort to get food into him has been intensified by order of his doctor. Earlier in the year, when about to undergo heart surgery, he ended up needing instead to spend two weeks building up his strength in the hospital before the urgent operation could even begin. The winter before, too, he was hospitalized, that time in a dramatic ambulance ride after a heart attack. It seems some days that he is hanging on by just a thread; as if at any moment he might drop. And leave us all alone.

He still surprises us with his incredible bursts of energy, but they are infrequent, and his recovery from them is long. He comes down from his room for the week-long sesshins, for example, rarely missing a formal Dharma talk and consistently calling daily dokusan, meeting the whole assembly one-by-one in what can end up being several hours worth of intense, brief exchanges. But after sesshin, Genzen tells me sadly, he virtually vanishes for a week or two, sometimes a month, resting and trying to build back the strength that he pours into us during sesshin. Occasionally still, impassioned, he jumps off of his seat in the zendo, wielding his kyosaku and shouting—but to me at least, he never again comes through with as much force as he did my first sesshin here, when his kyosaku hits left me terrified and in awe. Once or twice he will jump from his seat as though trying to relive a memory from his youth, but his hits on my shoulder will feel like taps—even weaker than my own, though perfectly placed. *Like a dead man might hit*, I will say to myself, sad but deeply inspired.

The community revolves around Roshi-sama. He built it—he is the main pillar. When he arrived fifty years ago it was in shambles, just the old hondo and tiny kitchen of a run-down, abandoned temple next door to the monastery where he had done his brutal and heroic training under his severe master. Every day as a young man after his appointment to the abbacy of Gendoji, the story goes, he went out on takuhatsu, begging for some money so that he could stay a step ahead of the carpenters that hammered away on the Kannondo, the hondo. The temple was his baby, his very body. His alms rounds birthed it.

Fifty years as abbot. Fifty years! When people ask for a vacation, for just a little time away, he offers gruffly, "How long have you been here? I've been here fifty years, and I've never taken a vacation!" (Anyway, where would one go on vacation? Gendoji is the place—if one cares about the Way, at least—the practice is here, the teaching is here. What is there to get a break from?) To be fair, he has been to India once or twice on pilgrimage, and sometimes does extended ceremonies in distant towns, but no one can deny that he has given the temple his whole life. Even the plaque by the mailbox by the gate has his full name, just like any other Japanese home. As though we are all just his house guests.

"I ask you, then," Genzen continues, with Shoryu-san translating, "when Roshi-sama is no longer with us, with whom shall we study; where shall we continue our training?"

It is well-known that Roshi-sama has no Dharma heirs. I hear that he has once or twice done the "Dharma Transmission" ceremony, the so-called "full ordination" of a disciple, but he is very clear that he has not bequeathed inka upon anyone, has not certified anyone's understanding to be on par with his own. He has produced no offspring in the lineage of Buddha-ancestors; he has not found the "suitable vessel" to whom he can transmit, mind-to-mind and beyond scriptures, the True Dharma Eye. Some lanky priest might inherit the grounds, the graves, and the Maibara parishioners, but clearly no one will inherit Gendoji's monastic assembly, and no one can claim themselves as the great master's heir. His disciples, then, will be adrift and teacherless after his death.

"That is a very good question, Genzen-san," Shoryu-san says, translating Roshi-sama's slow, solemn words.

"I know of no other teachers to whom you can turn. I know of no other teachers who have true understanding. There are people who have devoted themselves to zazen for decades—for thirty, forty, fifty years—but they have not necessarily awakened. Many people have practiced for a very long time but have still not come to true understanding. You should know that they are not awakened, but you should consider them good Dharma friends. When I am gone, I do not know a true teacher with whom you can train, but I know that you can help each other. Please, be good Dharma friends to one another."

There is a long silence before Roshi-sama continues. I think of Lee and the other American teachers I've known and studied with—truly I could call them Dharma friends, honor them as Dharma friends. Not enlightened, but sincere, experienced, and committed. They have been for me the *kalyanamitra*, "good friends," whom the Buddha also praised. Roshi-sama's words give me a new respect for them, a new appreciation of their value in my path, but also a new clarity about who they are: they are among those who have practiced for decades without attaining real understanding, real enlightenment. Even as I honor them, I renew my fervent dedication to the true teacher whom I have finally met, and with whom I may not have much time.

"I know of no other true teachers, and it is true that I have no Dharma-heirs, but I am still alive—it could happen still. There is *still* time, all of you still have the chance to receive my inka, if you are diligent, if you only don't look off from your practice."

Roshi-sama pauses again, and looks with wide, inviting eyes up at Genzen, who sits on the tatami in seiza, like all of us, fiercely still.

"Perhaps, Genzen-san—perhaps it will be you."

I dart a look at my friend; his cheeks are streaked with tears.

My body becomes rock, its heavy, even solidity stretching far beyond the edges of my skin. Breath moves through me like slow, blue fire—

*And perhaps me*, I think. *Perhaps me*....

The deepest disappointment of the life of a friend of mine, she once told me, was the opportunity she missed to let her teacher kill her. He was a martial artist and Zen master, and he called the disciples training in his European temple one day to assemble in the adjoining martial arts *dojo*. He announced that he knew a technique whereby he could kill and then resuscitate a person.

"Have you really given up yourselves to me?" I think he must have asked, gazing at each robe-clad student in turn. "Can any one of you step forward?"

I imagine that there was fidgeting in the hall, clearing of throats, people growing suddenly dizzy, suddenly needing to pee.

*I would, I would step forward but suddenly I need to pee. Next time I'll do it—it's really nothing I wouldn't do, I mean everybody knows that he has my total devotion and faith—it's just that right now I have to pee so badly that it wouldn't be right. It's just not the right time to let him kill and resuscitate me.*

My friend didn't tell me what she thought or didn't think, but she did say that she was unable to step forward. She had the chance to offer her life, and she didn't. She had not leapt: her greatest regret.

I want to live without regret. I want to be able to leap, as each Buddha ancestor has leapt, as our kind Roshi-sama leapt himself, into the abyss of the teacher. And I decide that I will leap. There is nothing else that I need to do now but to follow Roshi-sama; nowhere else that I need to be but Gendoji.

There is more at stake in this than just my practice and my personal dedication to Roshi-sama. Zen as a practice, a way of life, an enlightenment—real Zen seems to be dying with Roshi-sama, coughing as he coughs, pushing out its last breaths, its last fierce invitations. It is my responsibility to follow his awakening, to learn his awakening, to carry his Zen into this new and decadent age. If I cannot, if none of us can, then the ancient wisdom will die with Roshi-sama, the whole lineage, the whole world of Old Zen. Even the American expatriate Keishi can appreciate the freshness of American Zen and the sincerity of its students, but without anyone to receive the enlightenment that Roshi-sama sits prepared to transmit at any moment, how can Zen continue? It will be preserved, as Keishi predicted, as only a "religion," a set of empty forms and doctrines, while the generations of real, awake Zen will vanish into history.

I will do this: I have nowhere else to go and nowhere else to be. Roshi-sama's presence and teachings and the steady, whole-hearted Gendoji practice have broken through my vague ideas and plans, my various doubts. It no longer matters that I came to Japan with an idea about practicing the most formal practice and living the most pure monastic life, and that here instead the monasticism is chaotic, dotted with women, dinner, laymen, the occasional monk in a tee-shirt. I am no longer bothered that the cultural immersion is softened by some English speaking Japanese and a handful of Westerners who dilute the austere Japanese experience with a low but detectable dose of that Western "support" I'm habituated to—on the contrary, the Western presence seems even like a cultural boost that can free up some energy to just deepen the meditation that is the ultimate reason I'm here. It is ok that the ceremonial forms are lax and that the yearly Zen liturgical cycle is largely ignored. The ceremony hall roof is the right shape, but beyond that the grounds and buildings are unimpressive and randomly designed—it isn't the archetypal temple I've been dreaming about, but I no longer care, because Roshi-sama and his humble temple have razed my expectations. I know that I have found what I really came for: the Way of True Zen, not the formal remains of a vanishing religion. I can trust this place in a way that I haven't been able to trust any of the many temples that I have lived in and visited in the U.S. Here at last, perhaps, I can sink in and come to something, finalize my seeking vows, fulfill my practice.

I remember and at once understand a comment a nun in the U.S. once made to me, a nun of many years who had never even visited a temple other than her own. "When it hits you on the head, you don't go looking!" she reflected, remembering her late teacher and the vibrant early days of her monastery.

It has hit me on the head—I am no longer looking—and right after I get back from the couple of weeks I need to take for a promised visit to my old friend Jido-san, I will return to Gendoji and give myself completely. Overflowing with devotion, with my sincere commitment to live as a monk at Gendoji for at least as long Roshi-sama is alive, I go into the narrow room behind the ceremony hall to see Roshi-sama. Sitting before him, overwhelmed again by the kindness of his still body and his lowered eyes, I tell him of the confidence I have found that his temple is my place, and that he is my teacher, and that once I get back from a short time away, I will stay, become his disciple, and, should the fruit of my ancient vows ripen, become his Dharma heir.

"You come to me, tell me *your plan*?! Do you see?!" he scolds. "*Dame*!" he shouts, "no good!"

I grow very still. He bores into me with his voice and his wide eyes.

"When I young man, I meet master and I follow—Just!—master's teaching. Yes! Completely. I only follow him teachings—nothing else—and I become *free*! This is how must practice! Do you see, your way and mine? You walk in here, *tell me* your plan!"

I am stunned—my resolve wilts and my posture deflates. It is true, I don't really need to see Jido-san, although he's expecting me and I've promised it to my American Sangha. It is not a casual visit, exactly, and it has felt important to see him, but it certainly isn't life-or-death important. Even before I knew I would be traveling to Gendoji specifically, I made arrangements to see Jido-san, a sweet and precocious young Japanese monk who spent a few years in my American temple and made many friends and contacts there. I've been given gifts and messages for him, even some business to do with him on behalf of people in my temple. I am as much going as an emissary and representative of my American Sangha as I am as a friend. It has never even occurred to me, until now, not to follow through with the plan to visit Jido-san at his country temple, Komyoji. It certainly never occurred to me to ask Roshi-sama's permission to see my friend.

But if I am so sure of the practice here, so sure of Roshi-sama, why can't I just hand over my life? Why not just hand it all over right here and now, starting by turning over to him my plan to visit Jido-san? Do I think I can give myself to Roshi-sama later? Do I think the Great Way is about later commitment, later devotion? He is giving me a chance right now to leap, as he leapt with his teacher, into the ocean of Dharma.

Suddenly again I'm not ready. I watch in horror as I scramble, tentative, to justify my idea: "People are expecting me... arrangements all in place..." I stutter, not half-truths exactly but neither unsurpassable obstructions. As usual in my life, all the doors are still a little open, no commitment is so firm that I can't bow out from it. "These things are all in place... I will come back, afterwards, and practice like you say...."

I know that everything I am saying, my excuses and plans, are all just deflections of the leap, just personal ego, but the words nonetheless flow out of me. All the things I think that others are depending on me for dissolve—I see my obligations all as just me depending on me to do what my own ego-plan has laid out. Roshi-sama stands by a door or a cliff, showing me that everything I am saying and doing is one-hundred percent ego-driven and saying, in his vast compassion, "Come! Come leap!" He stands by the gate of the Dharma, inviting me in, but I cannot leap.

I am laid out naked before both of us. Directly facing the Dharma, I just wiggle, wobble, make excuses, look backwards, look away, and stammer ego-plans somehow claiming that myriad sentient beings need me to follow through with my tiny delusional ideas. I have the opportunity to lay down my life to Roshi-sama just as he laid down his life to his Rodaishi. All I would need to say is, *"Ok. I am no longer in my own hands. Everywhere I look is only ego-plans, please guide me, give me something greater that I can orient towards...."* But I cannot.

Perhaps, I think, perhaps even though my ego does seem to pervade everything, this situation may be more complex, or more simple, than the poles of "ego" and "Dharma" that we've set up. The two, the Wrong and Right, Deluded and Enlightened, maybe don't in such a trite way just diverge into a yellow wood, the patiently less traveled one whispering its invitation amid the noise and clatter of the other, egotistical ensemble. Things are more complex. They are more complex, I assure myself. Anyway, Roshi-sama is wise, but he's not omniscient, how can he see the many factors, the thousands of conditions of my foreigner's life? How could he possibly know if it's better for me to visit Jido-san or not? How can I just give my choices up to him, my plans, when he can't know the background? Can't I—shouldn't I?—give my Dharma life over to him in a deep way without letting his cultural conditioning confuse my own conditioning, my real needs as an American?

*"Dame!"* he shouts, and he clangs his bell ferociously, infuriated, and I skulk out through the curtain in a dark cloud of shame.

# 5   The Temple Priest

Adam, a friend who has recently left our American temple, has different problems than I do. While I'm obsessed with monastic life, complaining about the lack of it here in the States and imagining how fulfilled I will be once I finally get to Japan, he is a priest looking out. He thinks he is well-trained enough to go into the wider world as a Zen priest, and it drives him crazy that our American Zen culture isn't helping him with that project in the least. Despite all of his years of religious training, he is learning that he needs to do still more training before he is even remotely employable. His latest attempt is to enroll in a hospital chaplaincy program, but he's on his own—the temple certainly won't pay for that, much less feed and house him while he does it. He admits that he has probably spent too much time with Christian clergy—their talk of seminaries, degrees, and parish assignments have spoiled him.

"Two years, M.Div., and you're out the door, taking over a church!" Adam tells me on a visit to the temple, over a mid-morning tea break in the hot and busy temple summer. He throws up his hands, almost losing the peanut butter and jelly sandwich he holds in one of them. I understand the frustration: two years at our temple doesn't add up to much. Technically, it adds up to nothing at all. I am pushing five years, myself, and I do at times wonders if I'll ever have anything to show for it.

"People want it!" Adam insists. "There's huge demand, but these training temples infantilize people, hold onto people, don't empower them to grow up and move out to bring the Dharma into the world. It's always, 'You're not ready, you're not ready,' like you have be a realized Buddha before you can open your mouth about Buddhism. And meanwhile, out in nearly every town in the country, people are flailing trying to establish a practice and study the Dharma without any guidance at all. 'More training, more training'—as if your practice would die instead of grow if you were in the position of guiding others.

"All I hear about are that there so many 'creative opportunities' for priests in America, but it's a buffet without food. Give me some *letters* people, I need some goddamn *letters* after my name. ZP, OZB, I don't care, make something up, just some damn *letters*! I can't even get a chaplaincy job: 'You're great,' they say, 'really first rate... but you know, with no M.Div. we can't really...' I've been sitting sesshins, getting up at four o'clock in the goddamn morning for thirteen years, and these 24 year old M.Div.s, bless their tiny hearts, get whisked past me because they've got the letters!

"What's the temple doing to support us to fill these 'creative opportunities' they're claiming exist? Where's the training *program*, where's the certification? I'm not talking about thirty years down the road... I'm talking about how do we get the Dharma on the streets *now*, with what me and you already know, to the people that are crying out for it? A buffet with no goddamn food.

"Look at yoga—yoga figured it out. They've got storefronts in every state in the union, every backwater town. Why? Because they aren't afraid to certify people. They empower people to get out and teach. But we're not even close... we just hold on and hold on, 'more training, more training,' until we're so old we don't care anymore and we might as well just stay in the temple until we die."

Adam settles down for a moment and eats a little more of his peanut butter sandwich. I nod quietly. What are the opportunities? Where is the support? Even if there were letters we could sign after our names, how long would it take before the culture at large knew what they meant? American Zen clergy find ourselves in an awkward transition between a monastic model, where the training in a very real sense goes nowhere, and a pastoral model, where trainees are given tools and sent out to do good. In Japan there is still deep confusion about the two models, but at least there is a system in place—a few priests stay in temples as monastics, maybe eventually monastic teachers, while the vast majority are sent out after one, three, or at the most five years of intense training. They return to the vast network of small, parish temples where they will be head priest, probably with a family, and probably in succession of their father. They'll live out their days ministering to the births and deaths and in-betweens of the congregation. Granted, as traditional Japanese culture declines, more and more Buddhist priests are needing to supplement their temple income through worldly work, but still there is a shared cultural understanding and support of what a priest outside the training monastery can offer.

In the U.S., though, there is nowhere to go, because there is everywhere to go, a vast field of unturned soil. A buffet without food. There is no temple for a trained priest to succeed to, only maybe a temple to create. There is no recognition in the culture of what a Zen priest has gone through to become one, or what he or she might be good at, or able to offer. So it's logical that so many of even the senior priests at my temple who have put in the long decades necessary to receive certification as teachers just stay at the temple, which has adapted to support even families to live indefinitely in a semi-monastic system. Going out to make a life as a Zen priest in the culture at large is too scary, too wide, and perhaps simply impractical.


"I pick you up tomorrow!" Jido-san tells me over the Kyoto Eki phone I call him from. I'm out of Gendoji—temporarily, I remind myself—to fulfill the commitment I made, before coming to Japan, to spend time with my old Japanese priest friend. Being out of Gendoji is a mixed relief, and the thought of my imminent return there is a great weight and a great inspiration. It felt so very good this morning in Kyoto to sleep.

Jido-san is in his thirties, the junior priest of a temple that has been in his family since the de-criminalization of clerical marriage in the late 1800s. Jido-san's father, technically the head priest of the small temple and its congregation of old ladies, is a high-level Soto-sect mucky-muck who is more often then not in Tokyo on business, leaving Jido-san the de facto head of the temple. The details of his father's job, unbelievably to me, are neither known nor seemingly cared about by Jido-san. "My job temple," he tells me, and that is that.

At eighteen, as a matter of course, he went to the monastery where his father and grandfather trained, spent three years, and received "Dharma Transmission," the permission to teach that takes twenty or thirty years to receive at my American temple. While most of his peers then returned home to take charge of their family temples, Jido-san, because he liked the life and because his father didn't quite yet need him at home, went on to spend a couple more years at the monastery, Eiheiji. All along at Eiheiji, he told me, he was impressed by the sincerity and depth of the foreigners who would occasionally come to practice. After five years there, he asked permission from the monastic administrators and elders and was sponsored to visit American monasteries, a trip that ended up lasting another five years. His time in the U.S. culminated in a post with the Japanese Zen U.S. headquarters, an institution that sees itself as governing "American Zen," but which the convert Zen community tends to look on more as a quaint and occasionally useful resource. Whether Jido-san was in the U.S. infiltrating as a covert missionary operative, or whether he had just sincerely been seeking new, more vital modes of practice, I will never quite determine. His work at the headquarters leads him to sometimes refer to himself as a "missionary," but in practicing day-to-day with him, I felt like he was just another trainee, genuinely open to receiving the teachings of our style. He was sweet and open-minded—necessary qualities, I've noticed, for Japanese priests who aspire to participate in or understand at all the non-rigors of American Zen. He seldom offered the "in Japan we do it this way…" sort of "education" that lesser monks with Japanese experience are prone to, that I myself will struggle with when I finally return to American Zen and try to make sense of and somehow share what I learned in Japan.

Jido-san's practice, although in a sense circumscribed by his family heritage, was from a young age intensely sincere, and he visibly inhabits the unanswerable, enlivening question: "Who am I?" Suddenly serious, suddenly laughing, he doesn't seem to hold any part of himself too tightly.

When I ask him what he thinks he was doing in the States—missionary or trainee—he refuses to say anything definitive. In his characteristically Japanese and delightfully Zen way, he makes the question somehow vanish, or transform into another question altogether. I drop it, eventually, realizing that I don't know myself how I would answer the question, especially given the Bodhisattva Vow to work for the liberation all beings. Am I just in training in Japan, or am I a self-appointed American Zen missionary? Or maybe Jido-san and I are both just bees, mindlessly cross-pollinating our two strains of Zen.

Jido-san takes the train out from his rural town to meet me in Kyoto. We go to Kiyomizudera, one of the biggest tourist temples in the city, where high multi-tiered halls, steep slopes, dramatic city views, and waterfalls draw daily crowds of thousands. I am dressed as befits my station, formal black samue, and expect to take advantage of the monastic garb to gain free admission to the tourist temples, but Jido-san, in a Tee-shirt, jeans, and a baseball cap, seems to prefer to blend in when "off-duty," and pays for both of us at the ticket window outside the main gate.

We wind our way through the vast tatami-floored chapels and moss-covered pathways, stopping now and again to admire paper sliding doors painted with exuberant austerity, and statues dating to the first years of East Asian Dharma. The scale of the temple reminds me of the great cathedrals of Europe—though the grandeur has a different flavor, the expansiveness and gravity are equal. Arriving in the main hall, presided over by a giant seated Buddha statue, Jido-san throws a few yen into a box in the main hall, as do most of the other visitors in the mob we move with, and takes a stick of incense for each of us from a tray that rests beside it. The visitors ahead of us each light and offer the sticks in a cauldron-like incense bowl directly across from the statue, with the same mix of reverence and chatter that I noticed as we passed a waterfall where guests helf ladles out to catch sacred water, wash their hands in it and sip. The devotion impresses me, although it seems a little empty or mechanical, like the way a non-observant Catholic might, out of some remnant sense of propriety or accidental instinct, cross themself.

I ask Jido-san, as we stand before the silent, ancient Buddha, what the incense offerings and water purifications means to the throngs of laypeople.

"It doesn't mean anything to them," he tells me, slightly disgusted, and we deposit our own incense with equally little piety, and continue on through the complex.

Jido-san's several-hundred year-old family temple, Komyoji, is in Shin Maiko, a small town on the shores of the impressive Lake Biwa, and we arrive there after an hour or two on the train out of Kyoto. As we ride along the lake, it appears on the horizon as a sea within the island of Japan, and Jido-san tells me that he hopes to take me to the island that is in the lake's center. We will never made it to that island—apparently there is a Shinto shrine, some birds—but I will imagine it once, in a *Hua-yen* mirror moment, drunk on the infinite interpenetrations of the all-in-one and one-in-all (and perhaps a beer too many, hours earlier at the low, round dinner table) falling asleep, picturing a pond on the island, and a rock in the pond, and a puddle on the rock, and a leaf in the puddle, and a drop on the leaf....

From the moment of our arrival at the train station, nearly all of the passersby wave or greet us warmly. It is obvious that Jido-san is well-known and loved by the people of Shin-Maiko. He is the village minister, and ably fills the role: vocal at town meetings, speaking at mayor's office functions, coordinating children's' festivals—wherever there is a community event, Jido-san is there. As long as I am with him that means that I will be there too, as his exotic guest, trying to say the right things to the mayor, to find a vague but satisfying way to explain what I'm doing, and to get the young girls to stop teasing me about my oversized nose and my strange Japanese. Not many foreigners have cause to stop here, and I am an honored if awkward guest who confirms Jido-san's status as an international sophisticate.

At night we drink beer and eat fish. During the day we weed and run errands, visiting *danka-san* parishioners for any of a thousand reasons. "*Shugyou*," he tells me, grinning, "Temple priest training!"

"Yes, Jido-sama," I call him, using the ultra-formal suffix.

"No! No!" he screams. We weren't so close at our temple in the U.S., but at Komyoji we carry on like old friends.

After beer and dinner is bath time, startlingly formal. First I bathe, being the guest. Then Jido-san's father, if he is home, then Jido-san. Then grandmother, then mother. After the bath, upstairs for translations. Full of beer (later, when I visit in winter, the preference is whiskey with hot water), we pore over translations that he is working on of old Zen poetry he wants to share with a group of Americans who are coming to tour Japanese temples with him. It is fun, but I have my doubts about the benefit of the light-headed hours we put into the project.

At the end of the night, Jido-san invariably announces "*Hosan*," the traditional ceremonial proclamation that cancels the next morning's zazen. He insists that he sits nearly every morning, and I believe him; but although we do sit together once or twice, during all my time with him hosan is the rule, relieving us both of the early wake-up. I assume he is canceling zazen for my sake, or because his mother told him to for my sake, as I am just out of Gendoji and need some time to recuperate. I even wonder for a moment if, in fact, he is secretly doing zazen in the morning while I sleep. But more likely, there is just no particular gap in his mind between saying he sits every morning and announcing hosan every evening.

The night I get there, Jido-san consults me about my dietary needs. I don't really eat meat or fish, I tell him. We go into the kitchen and he conveys my restriction to his mother, who seems to understand. Or rather, it isn't exactly that she doesn't understand, or that she won't accommodate. Somehow, in spite of the feeling I have that she both understands and is accommodating, at dinner the main event arrives as a large platter of seafood tempura. Thick *udon* noodles are mounded in a bowl in the center of the table; a rich dashi broth steams in a pot.

Vegetarianism, like restraint from alcohol and celibate vows, has fallen, too, through the wide net of Japanese Buddhism. It seems outright fanatical to most Japanese, even the staunchest monastics, whom I have known over *sashimi* and *Asahi* beer to hold forth about the unbroken orthodoxy of their practice lineage, the mind-to-mind seal transmitted directly from Buddha and down through generations of ancestors. Even at purist Gendoji, fish and even meat sometimes appear, and it is only the Westerners who are vegetarian.

"You like these, right?" Jido-san's mother says, looking at me, pointing towards the crisp outside and soft inner flesh of the once-swimming tempura.

"Really, anything is ok," I stammer. "Any food, no problem… I mean, I love it, yes… I really like tempura. Yumm, thanks…."

From then on, there really is no problem. Each night is a foray into the corners of Japanese cuisine, the culinary education that I would not have chosen, but nonetheless appreciate.

Although zazen is cancelled by hosan, and late, tipsy nights are the rule, life at Komyoji is less of a rest than a shift: each day, between the various errands and home visits, I am expected to join Jido-san, his mother, and sometimes his grandmother in hour after hour of tireless weeding of the temple grounds. My head aches from the sun. Late in the afternoon, once the weeding is announced finished, I go to my guest room for an hour or two to study Japanese before coming down to dinner, another alcohol-drenched animal feast lovingly prepared by Jido-san's mother. Then baths, and inebriated translation efforts: intensive shugyou training indeed.

When he introduces me to the pleasantly amazed parishioners that come by, he always says the same thing, "*Kozo* desu!"

"What does that mean, kozo?" I ask him. It seems vaguely patronizing, always gets a laugh. *Boy priest*, reads the dictionary. Later I read another definition: *temple errand boy*.

"It means young priest. It is a good thing. I am also kozo." He laughs and laughs.

"Does he know how to bathe?" Grandma Komyoji asks Jido-san.

"Sure he does, Gran…"

"Well, then, how does he bathe?"

"Just like anyone, Gran. He bathes just like we do."

"Ask him how he bathes," she insists.

"Well," I muster in Japanese with some prompting, "I wash off with soap under the shower. I rinse off—really well, mind you. Then I get into the bath. I soak. When I'm done, I get out and maybe rinse off again. That's it."

"Hmm…" she says affirmatively. "How come you're so good at chopsticks?"

"Oh, I'm not so good!" I say. "But it's practice, I guess. Years of oryoki meals."

"Hmm…" she says. She likes me.

When I will visit Komyoji after my visit to Hiroshima, I tell Jido-san, "I'm sorry."

At the dinner table, he tells his grandmother that I am not like usual Americans, feeling *I'm sorry* at Hiroshima. I guess I think it is a pretty natural American response: we did evaporate a city after all, to win a war already won, to prove some budding Cold War point. Was it 80,000 dead in the first days alone? I guess I think that most Americans I've met would feel pretty damn sorry.

But he seems to need to tell his grandmother that—"She lived through the war," he explains. She doesn't seem extraordinarily moved by Jido-san's account of my apology; I think she nods. Someone spins the center table to reach another condiment; someone takes another bite out of their pancake-like *okonomiyaki*. There is a new silence at the table, each gesture slower, significant.

At Komyoji, between periods of weeding, I start reading "The Sword and The Chrysanthemum," an American cultural study of Japan, and I try explaining to Jido-san how fascinating it is to me, how it has helped me to understand some aspects of my Japanese experience. Though one of the first, it is still a standard book on Japan, written by an anthropologist, Ruth Benedict, who was hired in 1944 by the U.S. government to help them figure out how to wage effective war against the apparently insane Japanese people. As it was wartime, she obviously wasn't able to go to Japan, but by widely studying the language and literature, and extensively interviewing Japanese people in the States, she put together a brilliant and open-minded, if hopelessly 1940's, analysis. I am amazed to see laid out so clearly what I am feeling so concretely, the depth of our cultural conditioning and how it permeates if not dictates every way of thinking available to us. She points to some deep themes in Japanese culture that, though somewhat cliché, are newly relevant to my experience, despite the fact that the old Japanese values she describes are rapidly declining in the face of Westernization. I feel that I am starting to understand some little interactions I've been having with people, in the temples and in the city, wherein by expressing myself in perfectly natural and reasonable ways, I am met with offense and frustration. I then get frustrated and offended, but even aside from the language gap, I am left with no way to address my frustration, no way to talk it over, no "check-in," as it were, because the conflicting values each party is coming from are so basic that they can hardly be spoken.

"The Sword and The Chrysanthemum" doesn't make any of those situations go away; in fact, it makes me at some points quite hopeless about ever coming to understand anything about Japan, and renews my lack of faith at the prospect of trying to understand or apply Japanese Dharma teachings. It does, however, give me more of a context by which to interpret my experience, and helps me to understand some of the subtext of the various interactions I am having. I take comfort, then, in my new understanding, but am finally in the same place that I have always been, the only place we can really ever be with each other—just trying to meet across great unknown chasms. Trying, in zazen, as zazen, to meet another's zazen: our common humanity, common being. And failing, trying again; failing, trying again.

As we weed one day, resting from the usual silence, I start talking to Jido-san in Japanglish about the book. It is, I venture, a description of Japanese culture so that Americans can understand it. It points to the conflicting sets of cultural ideas. It helps Japanese ways of being make sense to us. "What is the book like that in Japanese, about *Amerika*?" I ask.

He looks at me as though I were from another planet—indeed, I am. "No," he says, dismissively. "No book like that, I think."


Just before I leave Komyoji to return to Gendoji, via a long detour through Hiroshima and Nagasaki that I take as a personal American Zen pilgrimage, there is an annual inter-temple event that involves taking a bus to Mt. Hiei, home of the austere Tendai "marathon monks," and the famous "warrior monks" of medieval Japan. Our destination is Soto-sect founder Dogen-Zenji's ordination platform—he was ordained as a child in the early 1200s in the Tendai school, and the site of his ordination is tucked away in an unvisited corner of the Tendai monastic complex on Mt. Hiei. The idea is that we would, as the parishioners do every year, offer the ubiquitous Zen devotional practice of weeding on the grounds of this sacred spot. I naturally assume that a certain reverence, solemnity, introspection, and religious sentiment will underlie the gathering, and I accordingly look forward to it.

In the loud cafeteria on the mountain, where our charter bus deposits us, I start to have second thoughts—we six or seven priests and thirty or so laypeople from Shin Maiko and some nearby villages sit eating fish from lunch trays, drinking beer and *sake*, and carrying on. After we spill, stuffed and tipsy, out into the brisk mountain air, the bus carries us to a lot a short walk from the neglected ordination platform. We spend half an hour or so weeding and sweeping boisterously, then gather together for a short chanting service, reflect quickly on the great Master Dogen, and walk back to the bus. In the hot bus, on a day that seems to be getting progressively less "spiritual," we drive the long way down the mountain into Kyoto to stop at a famous tourist temple, in the back of which, cordoned off by a chain link fence to which someone produces a key, is apparently Dogen-Zenji's cremation spot. There is a little platform commemorating the event; we offer some incense, get back on the bus, and drive home, laughing and chatting the whole while.

Dogen-Zenji, it seems to me, has been nowhere to be found. A social gathering, I reflect spitefully, but even a church picnic would have more spiritual content. I feel a jolt of the much-discussed decay of Buddhism in Japan, but I know that part of it is that I haven't understood much. I haven't been able to chat as much as the others; I haven't known so many people....

Anyway, what did I expect? Did I think we would all be reverently meditative, reflecting on "turning words" from Dogen-Zenji's masterpiece, the *Shobogenzo*, waiting for him to materialize from the trees, haloed by light, two feet from the ground, pronouncing: "You should know it is also like this"?

# 6
# Notes from an A-Bomb Tour

Nothing happens in Hiroshima. Nothing to remember, *moningu supeshuru* of eggs and coffee, tears at statues' feet, and rain. Nothing much of note: the green, statue'd memorial an island in the urban sea, the love hotels. I'm a Zen monk after all, and don't—I swear—call any of the numbers underneath the naked women pictures plastered on the phone booths when I try to call home saying, "Listen, I've spent the day in tears but *nothing happened* in Hiroshima." Nothing of note: schoolgirls giggling, eternal flame.

    One considers calling. I, for one, consider calling: daisy in a burnt field. *No, no, don't even think, just dial home, just don't look up.* Television in the hotel room, *Amerika no EMU-TI-BI*. Haven't seen pop stars in a long time. We're dropping bombs again; the girl-stars seem even younger than before, the he-stars seem more violent, uglier somehow. Perhaps it's just the context—was the dead child in the mother's arms, or child in dead mother's?—MTV does not address these questions, and it's sweltering and damp and all the bread and chocolate I eat won't satiate my temple-riced intestines.

    Something happened in Hiroshima so terrible that I cannot maintain my gaze. I could say something: tens of thousands, flesh and bone *evaporated*. Einstein's tears, bureaucrats move paperwork from files "active" to "inactive," geopolitics unfold, Buddha's body pulses, children wail beside mothers' melting skin… I could speak, but Hiroshima escapes me. Eggs and coffee. Tourists, businessmen, some school kids, and rain.

    As for Nagasaki, something happens here: I see a giant turtle. An enormous turtle building with a Buddhist statue, Kannon—Mercy—on top. I forget already why it is a turtle. One gets cried-out, you know, and has to just move on. The whole city here waiting, alive.

    With my oversized red backpack and my undersized black monk's clothes—*gaikokujin* in samue—streetcar to the adult part of town where children roam with lustful eyes. A few stares; some giggles. The city pulses. Go to where the rooms are cheap, you know. Don't watch the women.

    I can't say about the children. Little children at the hypocenter. A huge black column marks ground zero. Next to it, a piece of wall from the bombed-out Catholic church, with a little sculpted angel perched on top. Largest cathedral in East Asia at the time—Mass was in session when the bomb… Little toddlers wearing orange caps. A pre-school must be near here. We all need to run around somewhere. Can I tell you how they play around the smooth stone monument? They kiss and waddle, fall and squeal delight.

    Is there something more? Shall I pin my eyes open or have lunch—an overpriced baguette, convenience store cheese. Breath lingers in my chest, my head hurts. Sick from crying, I stop. I'm in a park, a bus rolls by. A mother and her child cut across the lawn; old woman leans against her ice-cream stand. A gentle rain begins.

    "Good morning—welcome back," my American friend Erin whispers to me at Gendoji. Meditation is over, but breakfast is delayed. Waiting for the meal bell, we linger at the row of six *Jizo-sama* statues with their smooth heads and their monks' staffs. Saint of travelers and children; saint of hell. We have just offered them their morning bath with ladles full of water, intoning, "*Om kaka kabi samma e sowaka.*"

    Her eyes are damp with tears.

    "The bombs are falling," I whisper back. She nods.

There is a dog outside a nearby house—we pass him sometimes, on alms rounds or exercise. He is tied in a cement patio. Sometimes his shit is next to him: he scoots as far away as his short leash allows. In meditation we sometimes hear his howls. I wonder if I should get up and go to him; or after meditation if I should slip out the little door beside the closed main temple gate, and go to him. Stroke his mangy white fur, weep with him. I know that if I were a saint, I would rise from meditation, let the dog go. He would lick my face, then run into the hills—I don't know—cavort with monkeys and raccoons, live happily forever after.

Harold the Brit goes to the library and looks up cricket scores. I guess it's a real game—I don't understand it although outside the meditation hall he once tries explaining it to me. Wickets are involved. Along with cricket, updates on our progress: nearing Baghdad.

Our abbot says, "Right hand, left hand," and sighs. Who wrote about the loneliness of a Zen Master's grief?—it's that their eyes see beings flailing in flowers. He says, for us it's just to realize the Truth. That all is one. That all is peace.

I want to know what that will do. I want to know why I can't bring myself to slip out of the gate and go to that white mangy dog, and weep with him. I want to know how we got it in our heads that we could save the world if we just didn't do anything at all. When did we start to think that if we sat still enough, it would all stop hurting?

In meditation, the dog howls. We sit silent, eyes resting on the clay wall. I can't hear the bombs from here—a sweet potato vendor's truck sings out its looped recorded jingle. Rain pounds on the tin roof, slaps against the windows.

# 7

# Days of Work, and A Day of No Work and Good Eating

*A day of no work is a day of no eating.*
—Zen Master Baizhang

Sesshin, Gendoji.

Twice each sesshin, the third and seventh nights, we have tempura and noodles. In winter we prefer thick udon; summer, thin buckwheat soba. Tempura also varies with the season: *kabocha, fukinoto, satoimo, rinjin, tamanegi*. Even apple, if the cook wants. "For sesshin tempura, any-ok," the sometimes veggie-stingy head cook Yushin-san says, *"nan demo ii yo."*

Tempura night the cook starts just after lunch. Once per sesshin, it is my turn. When I get the seventh night, it is easier: I just cook hard all afternoon, then crash, as there isn't much left of sesshin to save my energy for. But the third night shift is trickier, a sort of sesshin intermission: how can I keep the mind sharp and clear, maintain the focus of the "snake in bamboo tube" through oil smoke and deep-fried splatter? Tempura day by lunch already I have spent two or three breaks—the night before, the morning of—prepping vegetables instead of extra sitting, extra sleeping, graveyard wandering, or just lying still on my back amazed by breath, fatigue, and wonder. *How did I end up in Japan?*

Just after lunch I need to start the frying; I am slow. The big wok teeters with hot oil. The oil is generally recycled; after frying we, like housewives all over Japan, strain out all the non-oil through our oil-strainer set-up. Usually, though, for the first tempura of sesshin we use new oil. What a difference! The tempura comes out white those days; Yushin-san says it's not so heavy then, tempura with fresh oil. So we can eat all the more...

Afternoons start with the long-cooking sweet potato; then, as dinner nears, the instantaneous slivered carrots. Mushrooms lose too much water: we cook them last or in the oldest oil. They will—we all should know—ruin the oil, make it splatter with the foreign mushroom-water.

"Good, you understand" the tempura master Yushin-san said the first time I tried my tempura hand. "You understand, no problem," and he left me all alone in the cement-floored kitchen, frying for the massive sesshin crowd.

The first event following the after-lunch break is the formal tea and sweets. The tea crew spends the break in the kitchen, brewing tea and arranging sweets. As the zendo fills for zazen, the tea crew follows, loaded down with teapots of dark green tea and trays of over-packaged Japanese or Japanese-Western-style sweets. Vegetables are at Gendoji sometimes scarce but sesshin sweets invariably abound. And what sweets they are that spring from Japanese minds! My all-time favorite delighted me to out-loud laughter through the formal silence of my first Japanese sesshin, though I think that the people around me thought I was crying with nostalgia to see a Western cake. It was a Western-style raisin pastry of sorts, in two or three plastic wrappers, with English printing naming it: "High Raisin". High raisin. (*Talking to a raisin who occasionally plays LA / casually glancing at his toupee.../ Oh, it's so California.*) Another favorite is "Pie Manju," the butter crust with sweet-bean filling that brought real tears into my sesshin eyes, to taste how truly East and West could meet...

The tempura cook of course cannot be in the zendo, and misses tea. Shortly after tea is served, the tea crew comes back into the kitchen to wash up and fill thermoses with the leftover. Just before dokusan is called by the loud and clangy bell—and just as the zendo practitioners, tea-satisfied, sit expectant, vibrating with sugar and caffeine, preparing for the coming dokusan by focusing on only now, with nothing coming, only green tea-fired *now!*—just then green tea thermoses are set out in front of the kitchen by the tidying-up tea crew. In this way the tempura cook does not miss tea. I fill my cup from the lukewarm tea thermoses, and know that momentarily the frying should begin. I am at this point fueled, invested with the green tea-courage to begin to fry.

Tea without sweets, however, is dismal. Usually the head tea-server, knowing this, astute, not head tea-server for nothing, more-or-less discretely deposits a tea sweet or two on the long prepping table as an offering to the lone and occupied tempura cook.

I look up gratefully, "*Arigato gozaimasu.*"

This sesshin's head server, Ankai-san, a former kitchen monk himself, spills five or six traditional sweet bean-bun manju on the table. "Tempura," he says, smiling.

"Tempura? Yes, I am making tempura." *You should know! You see the flour is out and my vegetables are all lined up and the wok is teetering with oil; anyway we always have it on* sesshin *third night and you have been here quite some time, you know....*

He shakes his head. "Manju tempura," he clarifies, "very *oishii.*"

Dokusan begins: monks and laity clamor from the zendo, passing and surpassing one another in the dive to meet the master. Safe in the silent kitchen, I open up a manju, peel it from its esoteric packaging, and drop it in the oil. He said it was oishii, delicious, and he should know. The bean-bun sweet sinks momentarily then rises (sign of perfect heat)—soon darkened. I reach the webbed wire paddle in and lift out the golden manju. Some sesame seed sprinkles fall off into the oil, but otherwise there is no trace, no evidence of the sesshin indulgence. I raise my lukewarm thermos-filled green tea cup in *kansha*, the offering of gratitude; I take a short sip, and pop a hot, darkened manju in my mouth.

*Oishii yo!* Tempura prelude: sweet deep fried sesshin, the taste that I alone know.

The dokusan bell clangs madly, student after student. I spill a batch of *kabocha* squash into the crackling oil.

○ ○ ○ ○

> *All my ancient twisted karma,*
> *From beginningless greed, hate, and delusion,*
> *Born through body, speech, and mind,*
> *I now fully avow.*
> —Repentance verse from Soto Zen liturgy

I walk with my friend and roommate Genzen, shit-bucket dangling between us on the bamboo pole we carry on our shoulders—*All my ancient twisted karma*. We strain under the bucket—just as our eyes, my eyes at least, strain to catch the lovely Sakura-san glide her way to service—(there's always someone)—*From beginningless greed, hate, and delusion*—negotiating our way from the toilets to the far field.

I like the work: it has precise technique and a certain rhythm. Carrying the pole, I quickly learn, is not unlike receiving strikes from the kyosaku stick in zazen—the shoulder must relax. Relaxed, it takes the weight. Furthermore, I notice, if I stay in hara there is more than enough strength there to haul away a world's-worth of shit.

*Perhaps I'm home*, I write to my parents after learning that at Gendoji we use monks' shit as fertilizer. Shitting into water has always struck me as so thoughtless.

That day with Genzen, my first time, we haul from the septic pit behind the kitchen. To get from there to the field we're fertilizing, out past the graveyard at the very end of the temple property, we start by crossing the lot of the neighboring Shinto shrine, the neighborhood jinja. The jinja shrine is humble and stays pretty quiet; it is essentially just an empty lot marked off by the usual red Shinto torii gateway. Its two tall, thick columns stand imposingly at the entrance, connected by two high crossbeams. One crossbeam, about three quarters of the way up, spans between the two columns, and the second, resting on top of the columns, extends out over both edges. Just inside this red formal gate is a basin with water and ladles for purification; further in stands a small, covered stage, used once a year when a Shinto priest comes with a scattering of townsfolk to offer a ceremony. At the back of the shrine, against the mountainside, a bell hangs on a long rope in front of a large, closet-like deity altar. Pulling the bell is said to awaken the deity, bring it forth.

"They say that when you pass through shrine gateways, torii, you are purified," Genzen tells me as we cross beneath it.

The stench rises from our bucket, the fumes of the shit and piss that rock and splash up the sides of the grey ten-gallon bucket that hangs suspended by a rope from the bamboo pole that rests on and digs into our shoulders.

    Every week or two, we haul. Shit dangling, we look out at the autumn hillsides. Unforgettable Christmas, hauling shit through icy air. Carrying through rain, snow flurries; trudging buckets through packed snow.

    There is a way to carry shit, accordingly there also are varieties of shit mistakes: snapped ropes or overfilled, splashed buckets. Smooth hauling is not simple; it depends upon a subtle rhythm between lead and rear shit-carriers, a shit-carrying communication, a *je ne sais quois*. The hauling harmony—although involving speed and step—is not so much of physical determinants, but simply harmony. It is reflective of a deeper principle: shit-carriers' accord.

    For example, with my friend Genzen I can carry shit—oh, how we carry shit!—the top stays level, undisturbed by our walking; the buckets so light they seem empty. If silence perchance breaks, we speak of California Highway One, or sometimes women, LSD, the Dharma—such a warmly carried bucket with my friend, in rhythm and in harmony: the shit, it scarcely ripples.

    With my Italian acquaintance Freddy, shit splashes and rolls. Shit rises and crashes back on itself like great and uncontained waves, like stormy seas.

    "The void!" Freddy insists, explaining his path to me. "Practice is like sports, you have to be a little crazy. To make it you have to go the whole fucking way. You have to say, 'See that wall, I'm going to fucking crash through it!' No other way to get enlightened!"

    It's that our personalities are not so complementary: I'm somewhat reserved, and anyway I practice shikantaza. Just look at walls, that is. The shit between us ripples, crashes, and invariably splashes the gravel graveyard ground.

    Height is a factor; I confess that height is a factor. I am taller, he is shorter; perhaps Genzen is closer to my height. Still, I say it is a matter of mind as much as body, of carriers' accord.

    Carrying with Shoryu-san, the monk with the scarred hands and the ears, is to carry his compact intensity—not rage, exactly, although possibly a kind of rage—intensity of vow, that breaks into obsession, breaks some days to anger. When I lead with Shoryu-san, I don't know how fast to go. He is so small, so broken, but his energy is inexhaustible, he charges forward, locomotive, endlessly in overdrive. My legs are so much longer—I am so much taller—*I too have energy; how fast should I go today?* Front person pulls, back person pushes, bamboo pole communicates the pulling, pushing—total intimacy—shit and sun and rain.

Some wear raincoats, rain pants, and we all are told to wear our rubber boots, as splashing, though we try our best, is just a fact of shit-day.

"Don't wear such nice samue," Genzen tells me my first day. It seems to me that we should wear the monk outfits called *work clothes*, during work.

"Please, use mine," Ejo-san says that first day as I rifle through the free pile of old shoes. I thank him and I try to press my feet into his undersized rubber boots—I try to squeeze myself into Japan.

Carrying with Genzen—buckets always balanced—we cut through the jinja shrine so that we don't have to pass the kitchen where the vegetables sit unrefrigerated, growing older daily just outside the door. There is an admonition that we not walk by the kitchen with our shit, and although we are simply taking it to pour on other vegetables—albeit those as yet unharvested—I agree there is a difference and happily we take the long way through the Shinto shrine. Shit splashed anywhere in the temple or the shrine grounds is clearly a transgression, but the kitchen most of all; sacred space is sacred, but food is far more holy. Or perhaps just that much more ordinary: susceptible to shit.

We cut through the jinja, but it is hard to say exactly where temple ends and jinja starts. On *koikumi*, "thickness-carry" day especially, through the stench that fills the air, all borders blur. The temple and the jinja have no clear distinction, like the temple and the graveyard, like the temple and the town, like two shit-carriers in perfect harmony, accord.

In the blend of things as I carry, my mind—the sky and ocean merge—I sneak a bike out of the shed and ride across the water out to San Francisco, where I visit my old friends and lay my head upon the lap of a particularly dear, particularly old friend, crying, *It is so hard, it is so hard; I am so tired, I am so tired; It is wonderful, it's so wonderful*, and then bike back furiously over ocean to Fukui-ken, our small town Maibara-shi, to the eki train station and from there return in time for banka, evening chanting.... I look up just as we pass beneath the torii of the Shinto shrine, snapped back to the stench and rhythm of our pole and bodies.

A question is always whether to carry one bucket or two: there are many factors, including but not limited to knees and backs, fatigue, the time of day, and the level of the shit in the many shit-reservoirs beneath the temple toilets. All these things factor into load-size assessment, as does the speed of the shit-scoopers. *Are they scooping fast enough? Too fast?*

Returning to the shit-pit with two empty buckets after a run with Genzen, we come to our sweet and quiet, somewhat sad third roommate, the Australian Daishu. He sits on a stoop looking out at the sea of buckets he has filled. He has been alone to scoop while the haulers worked from one of the other pits, and though he took his time, he has run out of buckets and sits waiting for some empties.

"Are you doing zazen?" Genzen teases, as we string two full buckets on our bamboo pole.

"I'm doing mu," he nods, smiling.

I wonder if he is really doing mu. I hope he is, but I also feel that he needs rest from all that scooping, although it is in some ways easier than carrying: just smellier, sometimes a little difficult to breathe. He needs to rest and I am not sure if he rests on that stoop or cries into it. I do not see mu open him, but see him rather hunched under its weight, the weight of the ways that he still has not, still has not, still has not understood, has not yet become the Great Joy, has not yet become—as under mu he could only become—a pudgy and elderly Japanese Zen Master with a temple, an attendant, a flock of devotees, a potted lotus.

"I'm doing mu," he says smiling, and we smile back, and hoist up our double-bucket-bowed pole.

We set out through the jinja, trying not to splash the shit and scampering down the sloped part at the back, by the Shinto deity's altar. On slopes or stairs, the front person generally raises up the pole a bit, or the back one lowers it by crouching or slipping the bamboo off the shoulder for a moment—but sometimes when there is truly harmony, on the days when the shit stays dead still—those days it seems somehow that there is no need to raise or lower to account for slopes, but just naturally continuing, there is no problem, not a spill.

My first day is like this. We pass through the jinja, around the shrine and the hanging clangy bell where Genzen will one day teach me to clap and ring to summon the spirits of the place. I will find it a little creepy, but I will feel that the spirits like the summoning, they'll seem to come forth gently greeting us.

On our way out of the jinja, Genzen says, "They say that when you pass through Shinto gates, you're purified."

I pass beneath it, rear man on this shit-haul, my eyes fixed on the still surface of the buckets, and I feel that. Yes, I can be born anew, indeed have just been born anew right now, completely purified. Newness washes over me: new consciousness, again.

"Does it work," I ask, glimpsing the possibilities, "to walk back and forth beneath it? It would be like scrubbing—would that work?"

I ask because I too seek purity, though perhaps I'd phrase it in some other way. I want to be born anew, to have my shit—*From beginningless greed, hate, and delusion*—hauled forever-more away. I want some crew to haul it each time my reservoir begins to fill, especially before sesshin, or if I'm expecting guests, if anticipated use is high. Can it be done by walking? Can I pace back and forth beneath the double torii that upholds the jinja gate? Can I pass back and forth, like breathing, washing out my mind and body in the gateway, scrubbing away all that sticks to me?

"Does it work?" Can it be like scrubbing, or is it just a one-time thing? Once purified, that is, how soon again will new shit stick; how soon can we re-purify? What if, I wonder, I were just to stay beneath the torii; bring my bedding, camp out? I can even—if it would work—sleep under the stars, blanketless, exposed. Perhaps at night—for fantasy impurities, even in sleeping, stick—I can roll back and forth under the jinja entranceway, purifying. In the morning, then, I can rise and walk slowly back and forth beneath the gate, each time renewed, reborn continuously.

I will bother no one, I propose to myself. Sure the children will come sometimes to play in the playground just outside the torii, and maybe, drunk from playing, ecstatic or enraged, will wash their hands and faces in the basin, purifying further with water the purity of having crossed beneath the gateway, atop the purities of being children, playing. The neighbor might come now and then to his work shed just outside the torii, run his table saw, fix things by cutting others. Maybe once a year there will be some shindig and I'll have to lay low, but for the most part I will bother no one, camped out here to purify.

But perhaps it's not practical. If not, if I need shelter, food, tea, to chant a bit or speak with someone, I could just live next door. Anyway the borders blur—what if I were just to live next door at Gendoji? I could sleep in the Kannon Hall, perhaps have roommates. While there, I could just go about a temple life—it is just next door and anyway the borders blur—temple life will be a way I can support my life beneath the jinja gate—a context for my constant purity.

Of course, I realize the danger that I might forget that I have come to walk beneath the jinja entranceway and purify. I might forget, in the midst of my temple life, that I've moved to the temple to be near the jinja gate, and just instead walk back and forth through the monotonous temple schedule, walking underneath myself and cleaning others, pacing under others to clean myself, wandering back and forth, beneath or through the porous boundary of teacher, sky of zazen, through the sounds and liquids that ascribe themselves to day, each thing passing through me, me passing through each thing—mutually purifying, mutually purified. Perhaps I will forget that I have come to live beneath the torii, seeking to be purified, and perhaps will just be working in the kitchen, cooking even through the stench of koikumi shit-day, or, even if carrying, might find a shorter way to haul and then never pass beneath the entranceway at all.

I might forget the jinja and remember only temple; that is, forget my vow. I might forget to purify, to pass beneath and through things, and remember only tiredness, my grumbling, how far away from home I am—because whatever life, however pure or vowed, so soon becomes our life again—just life again—and we forget.

We set the buckets down in the far field, next to a vine of chile-like *tongarashi*. Genzen slips the pole out from the buckets, careful not to let the slackened ropes fall in. I pick up one of them, and tilt the bucket slowly onto the base of a tangled vine. It comes out in sloshes and clumps, speckling my tight and borrowed rubber boots.

○ ○ ○ ○

In Japan in the winter, we eat daikon. Monks eat a lot of daikon. It's in the soups, in the side-dishes, in the *takuan* pickles that we crunch with rice and use at the end of a meal to clean out our bowls.

"Tomorrow, daikon," the disciplinarian Daiko-san says to me, shoving my shoulder.

"What?"

"Ejo-san, Ankai-san with. Big daikon truck. Big work." Daiko-san scowls at me and wanders away. He will not condescend to speak Japanese with me.

Daiko-san, Roshi-sama's attendant, is the most senior disciple in the temple. While the rest of us wear the required monks' work clothes, he wears a black bomber jacket—"like a thug," the British layman Harold observes as he gently wrings his tea bag out into his mug. Daiko-san doesn't walk so much as storms places, grumbling under his breath as he moves.

"All the miso is on the bottom, you moron!" he screamed one day at formal lunch, as he ripped the ladle out from the terrified hand of a new Japanese aspirant, and flung hot soup and metal in his face. It's true the young man hadn't stirred it first. That really is annoying. Miso soup needs to be first stirred, then served. All the flavor sinks to the bottom. I mean, it's never that Daiko-san lacks justification. It's just that he's the kind of person to throw ladles full of miso soup at newcomers.

Today he's cornered me. I can't distinguish a particular mood from his base-line gruffness, and I can't tell if my assignment to the daikon trip is punishment, reward, or chance.

"Leave early to daikon!" he says later the same day when he sees me, before storming off.

I find Ejo-san and learn the details: another daikon harvest, this time a three-monk team. My shoulders sink. It will be the second time that I will harvest daikon, and I can't shake the body memory of the first time: a dreary, endless, stormy day of field work. That day the donation had been a farmer's sweeping arm gesture, "Here is my daikon field, take what you can," a sort of daikon shopping spree, all-you-can-pick day of daikon. A cold, muddy, exhausting day's work, and that had been with ten or twelve of us.

This time we borrow a huge (on a Japanese scale) flatbed truck from a parishioner, and get on the road just as formal breakfast begins. Before leaving, we three young monks, Ejo-san, Ankai-san, and I, eat together in the office, quietly preparing for our big day. Though it is clear out, the morning is bitter cold, promising a stiff-fingered, brutal day for us to pack the enormous truck full of daikon.

We set out driving, shoulder-to-shoulder in the warm cab of the truck, and very soon we stop for cans of hot coffee and convenience store snacks. *We need the energy*, I reflect, sucking down my sweetened milk coffee and crunching on a chocolate *Pocky*. We drive on, chugging along the coast, winding through mountains, snacking, and chatting in the characteristic Gendoji blend of Japanese and English. *Gendogese*, we call it, *Gendogo*.

After two hours or so, we come to the city of Miyazu. It is midmorning, and I expect that we have at last arrived at the farm. Our nice road trip seems to be over, and it is time to hit the fields for our daikon. After some deliberation between Ejo-san and Ankai-san, most of which is lost on me, they park the truck at the train station. We go inside, buy a couple of cans of hot coffee, and ask the vendor for directions. She points us on our way.

We drive to a nearby parking lot and walk to the base of a chair lift. Ejo-san buys three tickets at a booth, and we all ride the lift up the mountain. As we climb, I turn my head back and see the city shrink and the ocean grow wider. It is lovely, being so high, but I can't quite establish its relationship to daikon—it seems strange that we have had to cut through a tourist attraction to get to the fields, and anyway, how will we get all of the daikon from here into the truck at the foot of the mountain?

Ankai-san tells me that we are at one of the National Scenic Spots of Japan: a land bridge, an elevated sand bar that seals off a bay from the ocean. It is a thin strip of land, covered with trees, that spans a mile or two of bay and connects the opposite shores. From the particular mountainside we are on, one is encouraged to look backwards between one's legs at the land bridge. When one does so, the clear ocean water seems like the sky, and the tree-covered sand bar indeed like a "bridge of the heavens."

Eventually we ride the lift back down to the city and walk to the truck. We drive on far past the city, stop for some more cans of coffee, and pull over by some rice paddies to drink them with *okashi*, sweet rice and bean treats we brought from the temple. It is getting warmer out, a beautiful day is emerging, but I am getting increasingly worried about what the remaining hours will hold: we still have this truck to fill up!

After our snacks, we drive a few more minutes and stop at a farmhouse. Ejo-san puts his long travel robe on over his work clothes, and we are welcomed and directed to the family altar, an elaborate alcove with statues and plaques, all lit up with tiny candles and lamps. While our hosts watch and Ankai-san and I follow, Ejo-san leads us in a short service, chanting and bowing to the Buddha and the family's ancestors.

Now, tea. We eat sweets and chat about Roshi-sama's health, the weather, and whatnot; the farmers take a picture or two. I drink single-mindedly, preparing myself for the coming hours of furious daikon harvest that, at this rate, will probably go on into the night.

Finally we go outside, and the farmer opens up a storage shed. He gestures towards the clean and orderly stacks of daikon: "It's over there," he says.

The three of us spend about twenty minutes, with the farm couple's help, loading the truck in manic Japanese monk style. We tie a tarp over the top, say goodbye, and drive to the beach, where we run around, jumping and playing and screeching like kids. Ankai-san gives us a demonstration of the martial art he is forbidden from practicing in the temple; Ejo-san "finds" a cigarette on the ground, and we sit together watching the water while he smokes. The waves crash in and we sing *Simon and Garfunkel* hits until we are just too hungry, and then drive off to a restaurant for some noodles. Farther on, we stop at McDonalds for a drive-thru dessert—coffee and apple pies—and chat and sing our way home.

"Jiryu-san, everything that happened today is secret, ok?" Ejo-san says on the way back, as we pull out of the gas station where we've thrown away our coffee cups and apple pie cartons.

"Ok," I say, "It's a secret."

When we arrive at the temple, the assembly leaps out from evening service to greet us and unload the daikon with the requisite sprinting urgency. As we run back and forth from the truck to the kitchen, there are murmurs of praise—everyone is impressed at the load that three guys alone seem to have picked in a day. I try to look tired. An American monk with whom I am cordial, Nengo, shakes his head in wonder: "Wow, must've been a hell of a hard day?"

"The weather was good," I respond, and it is not untrue but I can say no more.

After the daikon is all unloaded and the crowd has dispersed back into the buildings, my friends Ankai-san and Ejo-san climb into the truck again, to return it with a token crate of daikon to the parishioner who lent it. The cab seems so empty, with just the two Japanese monks inside.

"Do you need me?" I suggest, leaning on the truck.

"No thanks," Ejo-san says smiling, pulling away. "You are done."

Standing in the deserted parking lot, I realize that I will only ever be a guest here. My usefulness is sporadic, soon exhausted. The cultural door might crack open, a warm breeze might blow through, but sooner or later it springs shut again, and I am left standing alone in a lot.

I go back to my room and get dressed for dinner. The deep evening bell rings through the temple, through the walls, through my body.

# 8

# You Do Not Call Winter the Beginning of Spring

*You do not call winter the beginning of spring,*
*nor summer the end of spring...*
—Dogen-Zenji, *Genjokoan*

I don't mind sweating in the California desert summer. It is painful, torturous even, bugs crawling into my ears, sweat dripping down my cheeks, rolling between my neck and three robe collars. It doesn't bother me so much; I just don't move. Mostly. My teacher Lee encourages me.

"Don't move at all," he says. "Feel each of the insects' little legs, each drop of sweat as it pearls and cascades…"

During a lecture, while I sit upright and rock-still at my seat, something lands on me. It lingers between my shoulder blade and neck. After a few stiff minutes of forced equanimity with the tickling tingle, I reach my hand to brush it away. But rather than buzz away, the soft, wet insect body just crumples at my fingertips: the sweat-drowned corpse of a fly.

I am happy about this, for it is as it should be. It is good that summer is hot, and that summer is buggy; the ancients also practiced like this. When it was hot, the monks of old were just hot. When it was cold, they were just cold. If we don't understand this, if we don't practice this, how will we engage with the Buddha Way, the Way of our life?

*When breathing in a long breath, know that you breathe in a long breath, and when breathing out a long breath, know that you breathe out a long breath. When breathing in a short breath, know that you breathe in a short breath, and when breathing out a short breath, know that you breathe out a short breath.* This is the basic teaching of the Buddha. Short breath is not something to make long, long breath is not something to strive for. Just completely meet your life as it is. Completely know your life as it is. If you stray even a hairsbreadth, manipulate or try to manipulate even a particle, right then you plunge again into the abyss of separation and suffering.

If we think of hot, then, as something to wriggle free of, to control, and if cold is something to conquer and avoid, how will we ever touch the pure reality of our life, unconstructed and uncontrolled? If we let our minds lead us ceaselessly from hot towards cold, from cold towards hot, how will we ever grow still enough to know the first thing about hot or cold? If we can't even bear hot as hot and cold as cold, where will we find the presence to face the deepest truths of mind and being? Without that, how will we learn the way of compassion? If we just follow our ideas of comfort, we can never become free of our minds; enslaved to our preferences and views, the simple fact of this one present moment will be forever inaccessible.

I know this, I uphold this, so it is not the heat in itself that bothers me as I sit stewing in the zendo, wilting and tensing, tensing, tensing in my righteous rage. It is not the heat itself, it is the heat in winter. A stuffy winter zendo is far worse than even the hottest summer day, because it is an insult to the winter, it is an affront to the Way. It isn't that I seek comfort, exactly, although in some moments I glimpse the ascetic possibility of comfort in the discomfort of my comfort, but it is that the ancestors have always taught monks to be cold when it's cold. It is Mara the tempter, the scourge of the Buddha, who has descended into this American temple, manifest as sub-floor radiant heating. The creaks of the hot pipes are his laughter; I hear it! Each degree of his warmth is a measure of his victory, for he knows what we seem to ignore: disciples of Buddha must be cold when it's cold!

Outside I am very, very cold, and that pleases me, and I bear it. I am underdressed, because if I dress for the outdoors, for the walk down the hillside to the zendo, the morning sweeping period, or my cabin—which thankfully has not yet been "improved" with the insulation and heating that spreads through the temple compound like a virus—I will collapse when I return to the heat of the pampered zendo. That some rooms in the temple are heated and some cold is inconsistent, even irresponsible. It doesn't allow the body to adapt to the season; the opportunity for full cold is obstructed. So I must wear my thin summer robes deep into winter, anticipating the zendo heat, and brace myself for the walk down the hill from my cabin to the zendo, shiver as I wash my face in cold tap water and use the toilet.

Sixty-five degrees is what they aim for. Sixty-five! Some blissful days the heating system malfunctions—I too then suffer cold in my translucent summer robes, but it is a smug, self-satisfied cold. It is cold as it should be: reality honored over whimsical preference.

But most days I suffer from heat, the unnatural heat, the imposed heat, the there-is-no-Zen-in-America heat, the heat that the Buddhas and Ancestors ridicule, the Mara heat, the heat that proves the laziness of my teachers, the heat of the last age of Dharma. I crack open the sliding paper window above my seat for just a fleeting whiff of air, but my neighbor on the meditation platform instantly slams it shut, feigning a pained, protesting cough and wrapping his scarf more tightly around the neck of his robes. People wear sweaters, turtlenecks jutting up from under their formal robes—it is ghastly, appalling, unreasonable. It is the antithesis of Zen. I suffocate in my summer robes, longing for the cold. I scrawl desperate notes to the zendo manager: "Too Hot, Please Open Doors!" Outside, winter swirls, invigorating, unattainable. I desperately loosen my collars.

"You should have been here in the early days," my teacher Lee tells me, laughing. "Back then we were all trying to be Zen heroes like you! Glad that's over! I remember a guy who sat the December rohatsu sesshin in a T-shirt. Hah! He was going to outdo us all. For a day or two it worked, boy, he felt like Shakyamuni, or Dogen, or something, and we were all ashamed of our long underwear. But then days three to seven he spent in a sleeping bag with a fever! Guess he showed us!"

Lee smiles, full of love but unmistakably bemused. "Let me ask you a question: are you beating the horse or the cart?"

I can't contain an angry grumble. I get it, I see it, but it isn't so simple! Meeting our life as it is of course can only happen in our life as it is. And I know that our fundamental effort is that, to study our consciousness, our minds, rather than to manipulate our conditions. But I know too that the Zen tradition is fiercely committed to the preservation of the practice environment. The teachers of old all understood that there are conditions conducive to meditation, and conditions unconducive to it! We work with whatever we have, but critical to our path of meditation is that we at the same time cultivate the supportive conditions, and turn away from the unsupportive conditions. I hate it when they use Zen to try to get out of Zen. Attending to our minds isn't a free pass to be lazy with our bodies.

My angry mutter soon finds words. "The cart and the horse are one body," I tell him fiercely.

Lee nods affirmatively, but his bemused half-smile remains.

*When summer comes it will be so hot I can't breathe*, I tell myself, desperate, images of stifling summer swirling through my groggy morning mind like the licks of cold that blow in through the seams where the window frame behind my head can't quite seal against the thin Japanese wooden wall. I'm wearing a stocking cap, wool socks, long underwear, fleece jubon, and a thick winter kimono, and I lie in my sleeping bag, which in turn is wrapped in a pile of blankets: anything and everything to keep the bitter cold at bay. I poke my eyes out far enough from my cocoon to glimpse the fluorescent hands of my alarm clock: 3:47am. The wake-up bell will start any moment. Genzen's rustling must have woken me, I gather, as he put on his robes and rushed down the stairs to begin his bell ringing duty. In a moment, when he comes dashing through the temple halls, clanging, I too will need to leap up out of bed, peel off the forbidden cap and socks, slip into my koromo outer robe, throw my folded okesa robe over my arm, and dash off to zazen.

I roll over, pulling my sleeping bag impossibly tighter around me, squeezing out degrees of heat and seconds of sleep. The merciless wake-up bell begins just as I drift off again—the face of a girl I knew—faint as it starts in the hondo, growing cacophonous as Genzen takes a few steps up our stairs and rings furiously into the freezing loft room.

In the meditation hall, even though Daiko-san ensures that the windows stay open, my body's stillness can sometimes create a bubble of warmer air around me, buffering the freezing air until a gust blows in, or someone somewhere in the zendo stirs and instigates a network of air currents that break the skin of my insulating bubble. I live to find this stillness, this bubble, but it comes and goes, seals and cracks, and even at its strongest it can by no means keep me comfortable. Comfort is a lost cause, a category losing relevance, but still pulling at me desperately.

After zazen, we file out through the dark, cold morning into the hondo for service. No warm bubble can form even momentarily in the spacious, high-roofed hall, the huge sliding doors wide open along the long south wall. We sit on our heels, seiza, on the icy tatami mats, and endless strings of archaic syllables pour from our lips, scriptures taking shape as the mist of our breath.

Now and then to spice up the freezing morning, to give our minds something more than just "cold," we watch Daiko-san pull Shoryu-san, his immediate junior after the untouchable and distant tenzo Yushin-san, behind the altar to scold him enthusiastically about either nothing or something we don't understand. We hear him shove and shout while we chant the shorter Kannon, Compassion, chapter of the Lotus Sutra and reflect on the thousand ways that Daiko-san is getting out of control. *Should I walk out?* I sometimes wonder. *Or should I go back there and stand up to the bastard for all of our sake?* Even Roshi-sama, although he is so rarely at service or meals anymore that he doesn't witness nearly as many such episodes as we do, is noticing Daiko-san's increasing temper, but it almost seems out of even *his* jurisdiction. Who can throw out the disciplinarian? None of us step up—we just sit quietly, resigned, and watch our breath turn the sutras to ice.

Formal breakfast, in the dining room that is close enough to the kitchen to pick up at least imagined degrees of ambient heat, in seiza again—which is worst on the knees in the cold—we wrap our hands around our bowls of rice gruel, lukewarm by the end of the slow meal chanting, but still warm enough, warmer at least than the air. Daiko-san doesn't take any at all, but just sits stiffly at the head of line, seething with an anger that I hope at least warms him. For the rest of us, it takes rice gruel to urge some life back into our internal organs. We loosen our cold-stiff hands as we fumble with chopsticks, finessing our bowls clean with takuan, daikon pickles.

Just at the last bell of the breakfast ceremony, the kaishaku wooden clackers signal work. I am just up from breakfast, still in formal robes, but somehow I'm already late for temple cleaning. Monks mysteriously already changed into their work clothes suddenly bustle with rakes and rags, while I rush back up to my room to change clothes. Formal robes to work clothes, work clothes to semi-formal robes, everyday robes to high ceremony robes, ceremony robes to work clothes: constantly changing, the theme of temple life. I jump up and down, stripping and dressing as fast as I can, trying to slip into the new just as I peel off the old. I pull an arm out of my kimono and slip it into samue before pulling out my second arm, then balancing the heavy kimono on my head to preserve its precious heat as I pull up my pants. The cold cuts into me; any exposed skin stings. My hands hurt—they've hurt since November—and I rub them together as I charge back down the stairs, by definition late to temple cleaning. I grab a broom and, more for warmth than from devotion, vigorously sweep pebbles, stray leaves, and dust off of the wide concrete stairs that lead from the temple gate down into the town street.

  After the short temple cleaning, I generally go to the kitchen to work. All the vegetables we have are strewn on shelves outside the kitchen door, as there is hardly space for fresh food in the two heaving household refrigerators that hold the leftover food to be re-served, or re-re-served. In the summer, while our vegetables soften outside by the hour, the refrigerators vibrate and churn against the damp heat. But on winter days even the cooked leftovers are spread chaotically out overnight on the counter: the kitchen is colder than the humming refrigerators. In our joke, we huddle around the open refrigerators for warmth, their two or three degrees Celsius heating the freezing kitchen air.

  *I am fucking cold*, I think as I walk finally back to my room from the kitchen after lunch and lunch clean-up. In the kitchen, around the warming refrigerators, burners, and hot water, I momentarily lose track of the temperature, but as soon as I step out it hits me again, and my face and my hands revert to their throbbing.

  "Take care of yourselves," Roshi-sama says in his weekly gyocha address, over the roar of the two propane heaters—doctor's orders—that pump hot air towards his weak body and incidentally raise by a degree or two the temperature in the vast, icy hondo. "If you look off from your practice," he insists, "the cold will make you ill. But if you stay in your hara, what problem could arise, what sickness could come?"

  *It is fucking cold*, I write to an old friend, in a fit of inspiration during my short time off after gyocha. *But what does it matter, if I stay in my hara? Anyway, I'm here looking for absolute zero. Absolute zero! Remember the Kelvin scale? Our practice is all about that absolute zero: the end of all motion, absolute stillness....* I am flailing. If it takes metaphor, or pride, or hot caffeine to pull myself through the winter, so be it, because deep down I suspect that summer will in fact never come.

  Every night I shiver outside the bathroom under the dark night sky and electric courtyard light. Forcing breath through my teeth in defiance of the cold, I start to strip down to my kimono under-robes. The winter air slips up my legs from below, and from the sides it fills my wide sleeves. My stiff hands struggle with the ties on my outermost, formal okesa robe, and fumble with its corners as I try to grip and fold it. Finally I manage to get it folded, at least well-enough to go on to the next layer: the glossy, synthetic fibers of my koromo robe seem to draw the cold. The shimmering material is like ice in my hands as I wrap the sleeves around the body and drape it just so, in the way of the ancients, on the wooden bar next to the door. My thin shukin priest's belt without fail slips once or twice out from my clumsy, numb hands as I try to tie it around the hanging koromo.

*There is a way to do things—yes—and monk's robes should not to be defiled*, I say to myself, clenching my jaw to dispel the thought I am having again, the thought that I have every night at the bathroom break that I take between the second and third hours of zazen in the evening, the thought that I should just hoist my stack of robes up to my hips and relieve myself without the slow and torturous formality of stripping in the freezing cold. *No! Let me freeze at least with dignity*, I urge myself.

A visiting old Rinzai-sect monk stands beside me in the bathroom at the sinks. Most days I avoid the brutal and freezing gesture of wetting my hands at all in the bathroom. Tonight, though, self-conscious next to the imposing monk, I wash my hands. I turn the faucet on tentatively and pass my hand quickly through the stream. The cold water burns my skin. I immediately turn the faucet back off and dry my hands carefully on the hanging towel—which of course itself is never quite dry. I rub my hands on it nonetheless intently, remembering the advice that lingering water causes the chilblains that can grow into the huge blisters and scabs like the ones that cover Shoryu-san's hands.

The old monk turns his head to glance at me. Scoffing, he sticks his hands under a full stream of icy tap-water. He rubs them together, slowly and thoroughly—pausing an extra beat, just for me—before turning the water off and wiping his hands on the towel.

*If you try not to be cold, you will die*, his hands say to me, almost out loud. *Just let the cold become your body*. He walks by me out of the bathroom, head high, the force of his concentration—as concrete as the swirls of mist that linger around his nose and mouth—pushing me back up against the sinks.

*It's a great lesson*, I write in another desperate and secret letter, huddled in my sleeping bag, itself cocooned inside three blankets. *We learn so much from the cold. When we fight it, when we resist it, it just gets that much worse. Have you ever just completely allowed something unpleasant? When the cold totally digs into you, eats into you, somehow it's like you're free of it then. I've learned to give up that fighting....*

I stick an arm out from my pile of blankets, refresh my half-drunk and already chilled instant coffee with some glugs from my thermos, and take another sip from the warm mug.

"Of course, it isn't really cold until that pool is frozen," the young Japanese monk Ankai-san tells me, gesturing to the water gathered in a carved depression in a stone that sits in the small moss and pine garden outside the zendo. I am already cold—*"fucking freezing!"* I tend to call it—have already been *fucking freezing* for at least a solid month.

I am not alone; the other practitioners are cold as well. The lines of defense are already established in long johns, thermoses, "chemical warmers." I resist the chemical warmers at least, not because I'm not cold, but because the plastic packets that are rolled and bent to activate and then adhere straight on the skin are creepy to me, unnatural. Plus, the face of the austere old monk in the bathroom looms in my mind every time I consider buying a package.

*Cold kills the monk*, I remind myself, remembering the old Zen saying. *When it's cold, let the cold kill the monk. When it's hot, let the heat kill the monk.*

My depressed roommate Daishu lives layered in chemical warmers, and gives me one. "Try this," he says beaming, slipping it into my hand. "I like to paste them on my hara; it's great for zazen."

I stick it on my lower back, and heat radiates throughout my body. But it doesn't feel right, it is too much, too intense. It is somehow too cold for such warmth. The chemical warmers might keep me barely alive, but I know beyond doubt, from my burning ears to my numb toes, that my only hope is to die, to *let the cold kill this monk completely*.

The heat, of course, will be no different—brutal August, September. In an uncharacteristically practical gesture, we will spread out bath towels on top of the zabuton cushions on which we sit in the zendo, to keep from staining them with our sweat. The pragmatic consolation, however, ends there—even at the height of summer, though the robe regulations relax and the full body okesa is replaced in zazen with the bib-sized rakusu, we ordained are still left with a minimum of three layers of clothing: jubon, kimono, koromo.

There is a zone where the heat is just how things are—this is a zone we touch now and then. Our tear-drenched dreams of February mingle with the drops of sweat that are absorbed by the towels beneath us, hours passing in over-heated, sleepy dullness, but sometimes, on awakening a little, we look up and see in our shadows cast on the clay wall just how still our bodies have grown. The sweat pours off of us, but we are completely still. At this place, in this zazen, the heat is just heat. Heat is just how things are. There is nothing to *do* about heat.

Here, heat and cold touch. There is just as little—the same nothing at all—to do about cold. And we glimpse it sometimes, amidst August fantasies and the cones of our frosty breath, the icy winds gusting from a door opening, or from anyone moving at all. The aching hands, the stinging ears—from this too we on occasion wake up. Freezing, but still; aching, but still. We see that there is nothing to do about heat, about cold.

Heat, as just heat, is the monk. Cold, as just cold, kills him—that is, cold is victorious. Cold is the only one that's left standing, all to be found, if there's anything at all, in this still, silent swirl called I.

We haven't seen the sun for weeks. It lands outside the gate on the townspeople but our mountainside shades us—our snow won't melt and we only see sun if we're working, late morning or early afternoon, in the furthermost vegetable plot. Nengo, the other American-trained monk in the temple, confesses that he goes to that plot sometimes, walks out there after lunch for medicinal sunlight.

"In the winter, I made a list," he will remember with me the next summer, as we sit by the ocean, saying goodbye. "Each day I would check it—had a parent died? Nope. Roshi-sama died? Nope. Medical emergency? Nope… Everyday I thought of going home, but my rule was that I only would if one of my list's conditions were met."

We all do whatever we can.

As for me, I make no lists, but just cry. I cry every fucking freezing night. Why are doing this? What are we trying to prove? How do my freezing hands support meditation? Indeed, doesn't their burning distract me from it? The Buddha taught the Middle Way—he knew the ascetic path, but was enlightened upon renouncing it. So why can't we at least close the damn zendo windows? Sure "comfort" is a slippery slope—I saw that clearly enough in the States—but can't we let the practice be about something other than just fighting off cold? What would we lose from just a tiny humane gesture of warmth? What have I gained from this misery? No warmth, no insight, just my mind-boggling weakness. Huddled under blankets, or stripping for the bathroom—hot tears turning icy on cheeks.

But a flash of hope dawns one winter day as I walk back in towards the main gate with Genzen, the Englishman Harold, and a couple of Japanese laymen, after an afternoon of building a new bamboo fence around one of the garden plots. As we walk, Shoryu-san plows towards us with his ever-present intensity.

"*Mite!* Look!" he shouts, catching up to show us an awkward flower he has found. It is a slightly unfurled, enormous green bud, bright against his white cotton gloves. I know the blisters and raw flesh beneath those gloves—I almost see them through the cotton as I gaze at the young blossom in his hand.

"Smells like spring," he says, delighted.

"What is it?" I ask, jumping at the word "spring."

"*Fukinoto*," Genzen says authoritatively, staring with us into Shoryu-san's hands. "It's great; makes really high-class tempura."

"Spring!" Harold says, chuckling. "Yeah, winter's behind us."

Is it? I don't know much about the Japanese seasons: sure, based on the pictures I've seen of snow-covered temples, I figured that it would snow a bit more, but it has already been fucking freezing, that I do know. I've felt like I've been dying since that day in November when it hit twelve degrees Celsius.

"It's the temperature *changes* that kill you, not the temperature itself," Genzen informed me that November shikunichi day, as we soaked up desperate heat in the weekly ofuro bath. "In March when it's twelve degrees we'll be dancing in the streets!"

I didn't believe him, of course—I'd be damned if I'd ever celebrate those twelve measly degrees. But now, at long last, it is over! Is it over? It is cold, but the blossom is incontrovertible—Shoryu-san said "spring"—is the tide turning, buds opening towards summer?

Genzen laughs. "Umm huhh," he says, "glad that's over!"

Shoryu-san giggles, his mouth so wide it nearly reaches his splitting, cold-cracked ears, and I catch myself. It is not even January; winter has scarcely begun.

So I have no choice but to come to coffee again.

I didn't mean to start, exactly, but it is just so damn cold. I don't know how it happened, I just found myself with a mug one morning, and it all somehow unraveled from there. Green tea doesn't boil the blood in the same way, and anyway instant coffee is more readily available: guests and parishioners bring huge jars of it as offerings, and even the ascetic and cruel Daiko-san, who incidentally likes his cup of Joe, can see that it is silly to stockpile it in Roshi-sama's room. Things get lost up there anyway, like the thirteen year old, top quality matcha powdered green tea that Daiko-san recently excavated from some corner and threw onto the kitchen counter, demanding that we "make a cake or something."

*Most pleasant duet by Brazilian coffee beans and Columbians*, reads the jar of my favorite brand, *"President."* I understand that my attempts at Japanese are as ridiculous as any Japanese person's English, and I have been in the country long enough to be more weary of than amused by absurd *In-gu-ri-shu*, but somehow that slogan strikes me. It is poignant and accurate, in a way, and as I sit huddled in blankets drinking my hot coffee and looking out my high window over the graveyard and town, I reflect that, what with global economics, I can in fact be said to be drinking ground Colombians.

The coffee makes me further wax, sometimes, nostalgic about my old apartment in San Francisco—so many years ago, so young—drinking coffee in the mornings, listening to music, settling down before a day at the office I worked in during my short and ill-fated life in the mainstream. But memory betrays experience: I watch myself sink into it, believing the charm of that old coffee and stereo, but I remember so clearly at the same time the acute misery of those days. That I'm by all accounts happier now doesn't seem to interfere—at least not while I'm drinking coffee, going around and around in my head, wasting precious time better spent in meditation—with the way that in some part of myself I long again for that life. Is it too late for me to just have a normal life?

Like memory and longing, mundane desires too unroll from idleness, and with coffee, I naturally want sugar. I have finished the pink, clam-shell shaped, plastic-wrapped sugar packet that I took from a box of twenty or so that someone left out for the monks, and a few days ago I began to seriously consider the possibility of going to town to buy my own stash. I see that it's a slippery slope—my shopping for sugar might easily unroll into nuts, would certainly spill into chocolate. More tea? Under my desk in college I had a plastic-bottle bar of sorts—whisky, rum, vodka, tequila—and between my futon and my window in my room at Gendoji I have a large tin full of tea, and more recently, instant coffee. My tea bar, as I think of it, reminiscent of my desk bar and comparably illicit. The tin can still accommodate some rations—perhaps at the *Seiyu* department store I will find that I need dried apricots, or granola. Hot chocolate is readily procured.... *Remember the wildflowers that day I hitchhiked to the mission at Ft. Hunter-Liggett...* So it goes—the mind and sweetness. Being alone.

In the same way that I snap myself out of indulgent memories and idle speculations, so too I snap myself from my lust for sugar. What business has a monk with his own stash of sugar? It's not a moral question, exactly, just a recognition that monastic life is based on forms, standards. I've committed to them in order to observe my mind's machinery. I'm through just following my every whim—nothing I crave, and sugar least of all, will quench the beginningless craving. Tomorrow I'll probably even cut back on the coffee. My path is meditation, my path is renunciation.

Time goes on, however, and my palette refuses to adjust to the bitterness of even the smooth *President* brand. I reason again, now more carefully, less idealistically. My practice is not in a vacuum, not disconnected from the facts of my life, my real needs, real joys. The old teachings of the Buddha were to shun the world, but the Mahayana, the Great Vehicle includes our life as it is: we are not just calming the lake, we are surfing the ocean! As with the monk who dies in cold and dies in hot, when lusting for coffee, for sugar, am I not just complete lusting, just complete coffee, just complete sugar...? I don't need to fight with myself. I must not fight with myself! Is not to do so adding delusion on top of delusion, compounding delusions of self with delusions of control?

And anyway, I am doing neither myself nor the Way any favors by not enjoying the coffee. Couldn't it be said that indulgence without enjoyment is a greater fault than mere indulgence? Also, the coffee—well, it has become a sort of friend. And the Buddha and ancestors have all taught, and I concur, that we must care for our friends, nurture our friends, support them to become the best that they can be... As a gift, then, to the coffee, I go on shikunichi bath day to the department store.

Oh sweet sea of sugar! The grocery store in the *Seiyu* basement, by no means large, has nonetheless an entire sugar aisle: black sugar, blocks of sugar, brightly-colored animal-shaped packages of sugar, cones of sugar, individually wrapped cubes of sugar.... I am a monk, though, so I will keep it simple. I look around the aisle for the plainest of plain sugars: white, granulated, in an indistinct clear plastic bag. I feel a little bad, dressed in my black monk's clothes and my white head towel, buying a kilo of sugar with cash that Roshi-sama distributes a few times a year for personal necessities. Even the cashier looks at me askance. But I just need to survive the winter. Besides, it's for the coffee—I mean, it's a gift.

The giddy morning after my purchase, in the minutes between soji cleaning and samu work, I brew myself up a strong mug of *President*.

Racing back to my room while the mug is still steaming, I crouch over my corner tea bar, tear off a corner of the bag of sugar, let a good gush of it out into my cup, and stir it with the small kitchen spoon that I've pilfered in preparation for this moment. I raise my mug up in *kansha*, a formal, tea ceremony-inspired "cheers," and I sip.

I choke, cough, and spit, all over my futon, a mouthful of salty coffee.

Sugar may be optional, but except in midsummer and in desperation, coffee requires hot water. Temple sensitivity around hot water is a theme throughout my time in Japan, a theme I've been little prepared for in the States, where at my root temple, for example, a huge samovar with three nozzles, piped straight into the water supply, keeps an endless supply of nearly boiling water for sixty, eighty, one hundred and twenty people. At Gendoji, though, the twenty or thirty residents are all served by a single electric two liter water pot that takes eight or ten minutes to boil. Kitchen old-timer Dogaku takes it on himself during the coldest months, diligent and generous monk that he is, to keep some additional thermoses of kitchen-stove heated water near the electric pot on the table that supports the shelves that hold our ordered teacups. Even when Dogaku's big thermoses are offered, though, each resident's hot water use is closely, if informally, monitored by the Sangha. I haven't had the preparation of living without hot water, but I have lived in community: one comes to recognize, eventually, when one is out of step.

"*Ookii, na,*"—"Big…"—the slightly crazy Japanese ex-Navy man, Tanaka-san, mutters under his breath, watching me pump water into what I consider my modest-sized thermos.

"I don't mind that sort of thing, don't mind it at all," the Englishman Harold tells me, looking at my suddenly enormous thermos as we both stand near the teacups after morning soji cleaning, the short work period before the longer samu work time, waiting for the steam to explode from the top of the hot water pot suddenly, and the little light to shift from the bottom characters to the top ones (*bottom: not-done; top: done*, I remind myself, ever-illiterate).

"People have flasks, sure. It bothers some people, not me though; don't mind it at all," he says, filling his big mug of *Each Day* brand black tea. "I'm double bagging today," he goes on to confess, kindly changing the subject.

"I don't really fill it," I try to explain, to his absent nods of, "Sure, sure…."

"I just want it hot to take up to my room; I'm not taking more than a mug-full…."

"Sure, sure," Harold agrees, sipping.

It takes me a long time to put it together that it is far better for Sangha harmony, not to mention my reputation, to just not use my thermos at all. The catalyst for the maturation of this insight occurs in a half-hour break between lunch clean-up and afternoon samu work, as I go to draw some hot water so that I can make tea at my clandestine tea/coffee bar. The floating level indicator in the public water dispenser starts out high, and drops gradually as I fill my thermos. Though the water level drops, I have by no means drained the hot water supply—enough remains for two or three more big cups at least.

I calculate, as we always calculate, the relative merits of leaving a bit of truly hot water in the pot for the next person, or refilling the pot from the sink with cold water. The latter decision, while putting in place the causal conditions for abundant future hot water, will quite possibly leave the next hot water-seeker—who likely doesn't have more than a five minute break—with a ten minute wait while it heats. I look at the level indicator, weigh it against my off-the-cuff assessment of water-usage in the next several minutes, bite my lip, nod to myself, and walk back to my room.

The temple-overlord Daiko-san hammers away at a wobbly shoe rack nearby, while Shoryu-san fills vases with donated flowers, his thick and misshapen gloved fingers clumsy with the delicate stalks. It isn't work time, exactly, but senior monks, equally in Japan and the States, tend to just work all the time they are present, and just disappear when they need a break. As I walk off, Daiko-san, completely ignoring me, shouts in caustic Japanese to his junior Shoryu-san.

"Hey, idiot! Fill the water pitcher!"

Shoryu-san sings a *"Hai, hai…,"* apologizes profusely to Daiko-san, puts down his flower arranging meekly, and carefully refills the water pitcher.

Walking back to my room with a heavy thermos and drooping shoulders, I realize the efficiency of Daiko-san's sometimes sideways discipline, and I know that I will never use my little flask again.

Three days have passed since I bought the salt and today, finally, I've summoned up the courage to take the kilo bag to the kitchen. What else can I do? In my head I've gone through countless scenarios: dumping it in the hills, digging a hole behind the garden, pouring it into the open septic system…. It is bad enough, though, that I bought it—I can't bring myself to compound the transgression by wasting it. As I quietly suspected from the start, my only real option is to take it to the kitchen.

After the night bells, I go back to the zendo for a period of night sitting. I'm just trying to pass the time until the temple settles and I can deposit my bag of salt discreetly in the salt bin in the kitchen, and I'm embarrassed to be joining Genzen, Shoryu-san, and Sakura-san, all sitting if not out of pure devotion, at least with more subtly twisted motives than mine. After an hour or so, when only Genzen is left in the zendo, I get up and return to my room above the Kannon hall. Moving quietly to not disturb Daishu-san, whose shadow sits wrapped in a blanket, still but droopy, inside the thin walls of his sheet-tent, I hang up my koromo outer robe and put the salt bag surreptitiously in the wide, deep sleeve of my kimono under-robe. I walk softly back down the stairs, and as I leave the Kannondo on my way to the kitchen, I come across Genzen walking from the zendo. He looks at the ground, pretending not to notice me—though I'm sure he is suspicious—still concentrated or at least maintaining the façade of concentration from zazen. I can't help wondering if he is finished sitting now because something in his body told him to get up, or just because there was no one left to compete with—he won first place meditator yet another night.

I switch on the kitchen light, almost knocking over a big jar full of spatulas and cooking chopsticks as I do, and creep across the kitchen to the ceramic salt bin. I take off the lid, pull the salt bag from my sleeve, and as I look to determine if the bin has enough room, and scramble to think what I might do if it doesn't, the light from the other side of the kitchen suddenly turns on, and the head cook Yushin-san walks in from the adjoining hallway he lives in. His ragged samue is open wide at the neck, revealing a sweatshirt underneath.

"Jiryu-san! Goo-to na-i-to!" he says cordially, looking at me standing in my thick kimono, eyes bloodshot, over the open bin of salt and the tell-tale kilo bag.

"What you have?" he asks, his kind wide smile full of broken and missing teeth. For the first time I wonder if he maybe really does have to go to the dentist as often as he claims, and that the appointments' correspondence with the busier kitchen times is, as he has always insisted, mere coincidence.

The plastic bag trembles in my hands. I quickly craft a carefully grammatical defense, but as I open my mouth, I spew only mispronounced, choppy Japanese: "Coffee... because cold, you know... And, sugar... Sugar—salt, you know? Use salt? Please thank you..."

Yushin-san laughs, and I wonder what he is doing up at this hour, why he is in the kitchen, why I see him most nights that I happen to be up late, rummaging in his things or walking around outside with mysterious buckets. "Not first time!" he says, laughing and laughing as he walks back out of the kitchen.

I try one more approach to hot water—I go back to *Seiyu* in a fit of desperation and buy myself an electric hot water pitcher. I've had it. To hell with these thermos police. I'll never use that public hot water pot again, but I need something.

*For the love of God*, I tell myself, *it's* unhealthy *to drink cold water in cold weather!*

On the second floor of *Seiyu*, above the grocery store where last week I bought the unfortunate sugar, I find just what I am looking for—a slightly smaller version of the electric pitcher that provides water for Gendoji. I feel a little greedy, but I am sure my health depends on it. Besides, I will share with Genzen and Daishu: it will make a nice secret addition to our loft room.

Ducking back into the temple through the cemetery entrance, the pitcher of water clumsily concealed under my arms, I realize that stashing the pitcher might be more problematic than I had anticipated. In the loft room, in consultation with a giddy Daishu ("Why didn't I think of this!" he exclaims), I try to find ways of arranging the room such that the hot water pitcher is most discreet. Senior Japanese monks don't often come in, but it does happen, and contraband shouldn't be left just lying around.

We try putting clothes over the pot, but that seems dangerous; we try stuffing it in Daishu's dresser drawer, but that precludes actually heating water. Eventually we find a way to somewhat conceal the pitcher with an old framed calligraphy—the Chinese character for "Gratitude"—that sits up against the wall at the top of the stair-ladder that leads into our loft. The calligraphy arrangement seems to work pretty well, although sometimes a senior monk, like Shoryu-san or even Daiko-san, will walk into our room, look straight at the pitcher, pause, and then go on with his business.

Genzen just shakes his head, keeps to his tiny thermos, and has nothing to do with the hot water pitcher that Daishu and I grow slowly addicted to. It is quite pleasant to have the hot water right there: no fuss with the communal electric pot outside, no hot water police standing over each drop... In short breaks during which before I was never able to make it to the hot water pot outside, I can now fill a teacup from our private pitcher and savor the hot water. If I am genuinely thirsty, I pump some into a cup of icy water from the tap, and enjoy the lukewarm refreshment. When a bumper crop of tangerines leaves more cases at the temple than we can possibly scarf down at tea, and a box of them marked *"take freely"* appears in front of the kitchen, I learn the culinary joy of tangerine-in-teacup. The cooling properties of tangerine seem to leach out in the steaming water. Slurping warm tangerine in a syrup of hot water, I wonder how I ever would have gotten through the winter without that electric pot, my convenient, clandestine supply of heat.

One day while I am changing from my robes to my work clothes, the young monk Ankai-san climbs up into our loft from his room alongside the Kannondo, does a slight bow, unplugs the hot water pitcher, and says "Not allowed" with a reprimanding superiority. He disappears with the pitcher—cord and all—down the ladder. The framed calligraphy that obscured it slides to the floor with a thud. Daishu, also witnessing the whole bizarre unfolding, just shrugs his shoulders.

"It was nice while it lasted," he says, and puts another arm into his samue.

"What? You're three years senior to that brat! He can't do that!"

Daishu shrugs, ties on his white head towel, and scurries down the stairs to work.

I will never be a good Japanese monk. Not because I don't try, I tell myself, but due to deeply conditioned cultural factors. As much as I try not to, I talk back to seniors. When someone tells me to do something stupid, without fail annoyance involuntarily registers on my face. It is sometimes painful and sometimes amusing, and no one will ever be quite sure how to take it. I try to be strict with myself and keep my reactions subdued, but this time in particular I am outright enraged. Injustice!

Not even reporting to the fields for work, I storm down the ladder and over to the room beneath us shared by Ankai-san and Ejo-san. In a corner, concealed slightly by a low desk, is my hot water pitcher. My heart pounding and my body convulsing with righteous rage, I rip the plug out from the wall and carry the pitcher back up to the Kannondo loft.

After work, Daishu sees the pitcher, and I tell him, seething, what happened. He tries talking me down.

"Maybe this isn't the best way…" he begins.

I start to calm down, start to see the "nowhere" this can only lead. I reluctantly unplug our pitcher, pick it up again, and carry it back down the stairs to their room. I shove it on the floor of their room, defiant, and stare up at Ejo-san, who has just returned from the fields.

"You can't do that!" I say in Japanese, flushed, through clenched teeth. My intensity knocks him back a few steps, off guard: it wasn't him, he says, he is really sorry. Aggression from a junior is so rare in Japan, I have learned, that it can be truly terrifying. *This guy has flown off the handle!* Japanese monks seem to conclude. *These people are downright dangerous!* Ejo-san emphatically, nervously insists that I take it back to the room.

"If you want use it," I say, guilty at how much I have rattled him, but happy to take him up on his offer, "just come in here and get water." I set the pitcher next to the top of the ladder, dispensing with the flimsy obscuration of "Gratitude," conspicuous and available for Ejo-san and Ankai-san to take from as needed.

The next day Daiko-san comes into the loft to demand something of Genzen, sees the pot in its compromised, easy-access location, and is outraged at our lack of discretion. He has seen the pitcher before—I am sure of it—but to have it set up so obviously is an outright affront to the temple regulations.

"You can't have that!" he shouts, ripping the pitcher out from the wall and flinging it down into the Kannondo, where I hear it bounce and crack against the wood borders of the tatami floor.

As the cold deepens, Daiko-san heats.

Just a few days after the pitcher incident which, though he demonstrated great restraint towards me, has put me high on his disciplinary interest list, I see his favorite strategy repeated at the weekly gyocha gathering. This week it is my turn to assist in the whisking of the tea, and my gyocha job instructors Shoryu-san and Ankai-san explain the position in and out, and both independently inform me of the special process for Daiko-san's "tea": no tea, just hot water. *No tea, just hot water*, I repeat to them, nodding, and again to myself. I consider that I am doing it for all of our sake; I can imagine what the caffeine might do to him, the way he has been storming around—it might literally ignite him, or start him on some killing spree....

The ceremony begins. As assistant tea-whisker, I am relieved of the heavy responsibility of whisking for Roshi-sama, and I am instead to whisk for the practitioners sitting on the south side of the hondo, headed by the senior monk Daiko-san. *No tea, just hot water*, I remind myself, grabbing a tea bowl from the table of more or less identical empty bowls. I look at the tin of sifted, powdered green matcha tea: *no tea, just hot water*. Resisting the impulse to add tea, I splash some plain hot water into the bowl—not too much, not too little—and set it out to get carried to the disciplinarian. I am proud to have remembered the critical detail. I scoop some tea into the next student's bowl, pump in some steaming water, and whisk vigorously. I studied tea ceremony for a time at my American temple, after all, and I know how to whisk up a good bowl of tea.

As I whisk, Ankai-san, who is serving the tea, comes back to my table. His face is pale, and he holds the tea bowl, still full, in his hands. My eyes bulge—did I inadvertently add tea? I look up at the bowl, but it's just hot water.

"What is it?" I whisper.

"That was Roshi-sama's bowl for seconds..." he says.

*Ooohhhh shit...* I gasp, sucking a quick, quiet apology through my teeth. I grab another bowl—nearly upsetting the one I am currently whisking—pump in a splash of hot water, and hand it back. The trembling server carries the new bowl to the disciplinarian.

As I look at the tea bowl that has been returned, I can see its subtle difference from the others. Roshi-sama's seconds bowl is more delicate, lighter, and its design is slightly more refined than the others. Ankai-san might have noticed, and I might have noticed, I muse regretfully, if I had paid closer attention. But it hardly matters—the important thing now is to face the consequences which, given Daiko-san's mood of late, will be by no means painless.

The morning address drags on and on, as I sit distracted in anticipation of my punishment. I brace myself the minute the assembly rises—I am ready for the worst. The *no tea, just hot water* mantra can't help me now. Just as I dread, as soon as Roshi-sama is out of sight, before the closing bells have even finished reverberating, Daiko-san storms to the tea crew table at the back of the hall. I jump to my feet as he comes: "I am very sorry about the tea bowl," I announce loudly, weak-kneed, in my best Japanese.

"It isn't your fault," he scowls, waving me away. He glares at Shoryu-san, who'd had nothing at all to do with my transgression, and punches his arm—hard. Then, with both hands Daiko-san grabs him by the cheeks and shakes his face. "It this idiot's!"

I walk, after zazen and service and breakfast, back to my cabin, straining under a armload of cookbooks. It is summer, and I am a cook at my American temple, churning out gourmet meal after meal to feed the guests whose cash-backed love of the cabins, the landscape, and the food keep my home temple, and her sister temples, afloat. I work hard. Very, very hard, and I am well aware of it. I don't, of course, know how to cook. They needed someone, and I suppose that I'm generally competent. When I'm not dicing onions or torching crème brûlée, I pore over cookbooks, preparing menus that have integrity yet flair, preparing produce orders, prep-work sheets.

The tanto, a senior teacher a step down from the abbess, passes me, coming the other way on the dirt path through the temple's central area, on his way to the work meeting that has just been convened by the deafening sequence on the large taiko drum in the meditation hall. The tanto looks at me, cocks his head, and points towards the gathering place where a growing group of people stand waiting to hear community announcements and receive work assignments.

"Work meeting is that way," the tanto says. "Aren't you coming?"

I am enraged. "You guys gave me this job," I say, glaring back at the tanto and continuing on my way back to my room. The nerve! My kitchen schedule consumes every moment of my day, every ounce of my energy, and the tanto expects me to waste time singing happy birthday and hearing about lost socks at the work meeting? A little respect!

Another time the tanto says, "You have been sleeping a lot in zazen…"

I am enraged. "You gave me this job! It's not my fault it's destroying my practice. The deepest meditation I do these days is to walk from the kitchen to the bathroom! Do you want me to sleep in zazen or stop making the fucking food?"

These outbursts are exceptions; I am a mild-mannered young would-be monastic. I notice my defensiveness, and regret it, even if I am no less confident in the truth of my perspective. That the tanto's feedback is uncalled for, inappropriate, does not hinder my appreciation for the sentiment, the principle at least that a senior would call a junior practitioner's behavior into question. Monasteries from time immemorial have transmitted their rules and encouraged their assemblies in this way, the old forming the new, the new emulating the old. It frustrates me that feedback, correction, doesn't much flow through the weak hierarchy in my American temple. People seem to just do what they do, and no one holds them accountable, no one pushes them further or insists on the right way. I am very aware of the many things that could use correction, all the people who would benefit from active, on-the-spot criticism. I advocate, generally speaking, correction. I am sad that I can't, given the culture of this temple, offer the gift of feedback to others, and I sincerely wish that more would come my way. I fear that I might grow sloppy or lazy without even noticing it. Still I see clearly that the tanto, in these cases, has missed the mark, has offered incorrect assessments. I respect him no less for it, however.

My teacher and the abbess give me advice, sometimes strong direction, but there is no forum for the daily senior-junior feedback that is part of the hierarchical Japanese temple organization. This strikes me as an oversight; it plainly hinders growth.

"You know," I tell a junior student, during snack time, "in Japan it is different." I have heard about this difference. I have been asking, here and there, investigating what the practice is like in the mystic East, what integrity it has that we here are lacking. My aspiration to go there is budding, and though I am conscious that I am romanticizing, and that it won't be what I think exactly, the myth of Japan is nonetheless neatly addressing all of my disappointments and frustrations with American Zen life, that is, with *my* life.

"In Japan they give each other feedback all the time," I tell the junior student. "It's not just like here, you know, anything goes and *maybe* the tanto will mention something later. There it's like every move you make gets corrected!"

"Wow," the junior student says, biting into an apple that he has smeared with chunky peanut butter.

"Yeah," I continue. "So if you want to know... I mean if this were Japan, I'd be able to tell you some things about how you're doing..."

"Oh?" the junior asks.

"Well, I might point out, for instance, that during zendo meals you've got the procedure pretty wrong. I mean, whatever, it's not really my job. I mean however you do it can be meditative, right? So whatever. But it sounds like you maybe want to know the right way—anyway, the spoon gets washed first, then the chopsticks. You've got it backwards.

Spoon, then chopsticks. That's how Dogen did it. That's how we do it. Can you remember that?"

The junior student is silent, then reddens. "I know, ok?" he says, and with a somewhat violent bite of his apple, he gets up and walks off.

"Today Daiko-san almost strike Jiryu-san," the kind, broken-eared monk Shoryu-san tells a handful of us, gesturing towards me. We stand around casually, drying the last dish and wiping up the last kitchen countertop of the night. "It was exciting," he giggles.

I disagreed with Daiko-san over the details of a trip I need to take to secure my resident alien status. From what my foreign cohorts suggested, I thought that I needed a certain document from the City Hall in our town of Maibara—in Daiko-san's view, I could bypass that and just go straight on to Tsuruga, taking less time away from the temple. I stood my ground, which was foolish on several counts, not the least of which was that he turned out to be right. He was furious at my insolence. He shouted and raised his hand to hit me. If Shoryu-san had been within arms reach, he no doubt would have punched his jaw instead. As if in slow motion, his hand hurtled towards my face, but he pulled back just before hitting me. His pulled-back fist reminded me that I am still a guest in Japan. I have the dubious advantage that I will never really be "in."

As with the thermos, I felt instantly terrible, like I really deserved it, and therein lies another layer of Daiko-san's disciplinary strategy.

*Yeah, I'm such an ass, I should get hit.*

"We're not like them, we don't just take that kind of crap," Dogaku says to me in the kitchen after Shoryu-san has finished recounting the story and everyone has left. He cracks his knuckles and rolls his shoulders. "And I've told Roshi-sama, too. I tell you, if he ever touches me, I'll lay him flat."

Gendoji is fraying, coming apart at the seams. I let myself wonder, for a moment, if I really want to secure my visa after all. Daiko-san is so damn mean. Shoryu-san is so damn intense. It is so damn cold.

With no choice but to follow Daiko-san's instruction, on Christmas Eve—the 24th and thus a shikunichi day—I go to the city of Tsuruga to finalize my visa. I am excited to be going on a trip, although I am a little upset that it is shikunichi; usually foreigners are allowed to miss a normal work day to do their visa business, but missing bath day seems to be my punishment, in lieu of a punch in the face, for insubordination.

From the warm train I see falling snow vanish as it touches the ocean, and pile in drifts as it falls on the rice paddies and hills. I am delighted to be outside Gendoji's gate, but the distance also fills me with a great warmth for the temple. The struggles seem incidental, superficial. The snow vanishes on the ocean, and I drink a hot can of vending machine coffee and reflect on how deeply I love the Zen life.

It has been winter long enough for me to know that monks are not to wear jackets over their samue, inside or outside of the temple. I am learning the tricks to staying warm: long underwear and fleece jubon, white cotton towel scarf, white cotton towel cap. Before leaving I worried about getting cold while I was out—it is cold out, after all—but soon it struck me that nowhere I went could possibly be any colder than the temple courtyard, or my drafty wood-walled living space. I more or less live out, I realized, and the trick of going to town is rather how to cool off in heated spaces, how to slip out of long underwear on heated trains, for instance, while maintaining priestly demeanor.

The paperwork is quick, and I explore the city a bit. Christmas music blares from the stores and "Merry Christmas!" paraphernalia chokes the shopping district. In a department store *"patisserie,"* calculating how many pastries I can eat without getting sick on the train ride home, I shake my hips to "I saw Mama kissin' Santa Claus."

I call my brother from a pay phone outside the post office.

"Where are you?" he asks.

"I'm in a big city doing visa stuff."

"A big city? Are you in Tokyo?" he asks.

"Well, no. It's the big city, but it's not much of a city. Maybe it's like I live in Roswell, and now I'm in Albuquerque."

He pauses. "So you'd say you're in Albuquerque?" he asks.

"Yeah—" I pause too. I look through the glass phone booth door at the street corner draped in swirling snow, the red mail drop box, the snow-obscured kanji street signs.

"Yeah," I say, "I'm in Albuquerque."

# 9  Spring

> Then the Venerable Ananda said to the Blessed One: "How, Lord, should we conduct ourselves towards women?"
>
> "Do not see them, Ananda."
>
> "But, Lord, if we do see them?"
>
> "Do not speak, Ananda."
>
> "But, Lord, if they should speak to us?"
>
> "Then, Ananda, you should establish mindfulness."
>
> —Maha-parinibbana Sutta

She sits across from me and I drink *osake*, honorable *sake*, and eat and my belly hurts and I am light-headed, but I am no less a monk. My belly hurts, and I keep eating. Eating and looking across the table at the beautiful and silk-skinned Sakura-san.

Then the singing. At her turn, she stands and sings a haunting Japanese song, it must be a love song though I can't make out any words out beyond "festival" and "uncle," but the way she sings it must be about love, her full voice dancing up and down a scale I don't know, nearly too exquisite even to hear. I watch her, her eyes closed, her face drawn tight with singing, her rough cotton samue falling around her curves like silk, sheer silk, I imagine, her breasts pressing through thin fabric, the gentle silk slope of her skin, her navel, hard hara and soft thighs… My fingers quiver, imagining tracing the slopes of her skin, and her tracing my own hard hara and soft thighs, and she opens her eyes and she looks at me as she sings, and she smiles a little half smile and tosses her head a little half toss and I drink some more *sake*, it is the only night, after all, that we can drink, it is our great winter feast, the only night I will drink but I am so tired, my belly so bloated and I eat another piece of the quiche I myself made, with eggs I bought on my own at the *Seiyu*, with my own money, with a butter crust whose butter I bought of my own, with flour and salt from the temple… She smiles a half smile and closes her eyes again, but they are still on me, her closed eyes, her samue falling like slipping silk from her shoulders, her breasts, and I have some more *sake* and someone else sings.

And then I sing. I close my eyes and I draw up my face, tight with singing, overwhelmed with my sad, homesick song, the American Buddhist song that I sing to show them, to show them that my country has Dharma, has songs, that the Way there is underway, damnit, has its own rhymes and melodies, its own hymns and *dharani*, and just as I start I wonder if she is watching me, I think she is watching me, she must be, but my eyes are closed though they are on her and I sing and forget her, forget everyone even her and just sing while she watches.

"What this is?" she asks after everyone has finished singing and has resumed their banter, pointing to the couple of slices left in one of the pans I used for the quiche. The English slides, strange and beautiful, from her Japanese tongue

I swallow. Her smooth face, her cheek bones strong, her almond eyes, poker straight and jet black hair and I love her. I love her and I want to step over the low table and take her up in my arms and I drink another sip of *sake* and my head is spinning and a wave of quiche, rice, and tofu wells up from my bowels, spills into my chest and presses to break out from my mouth and I swallow hard, and I drink some more *sake* and try to look relaxed, try to look at her. She will be impressed if I look at her. I am a monk—I know how to look, and I will look at her in that way. I look at her the way I look at Roshi-sama; I look at her firmly and clearly.

"Quiche," I say. "It is quiche."

I poke at the crumbs and small mounds of food left on my plate, break a section of crust in two with my fingernail, and eat it. It is too salty, and not too crisp. "Quiche," I say again.

She giggles and looks at her friend Yoan-san beside her.

Roshi-sama is sick so I cannot play the harmonica that has hidden in the bottom of my bags since the day I arrived, narrowly evading the luggage check. This is the logic of Daiko-san, although Daishu also brought a harmonica and is mad that he cannot play it and doesn't until in a drunken flash of freedom he takes it from his pocket, but then suddenly before it gets to his lips Ejo-san grabs it from him and plays a couple of bars of straight up blues, straight up down home Chi-town blues, and I know he likes music and he did sing a Neil Diamond song with not too bad an accent at his turn for singing, but I did not know that he could blow on a mouth harp like that but I do not dare to take mine out, though I can blow right along with him, I swear, and Sakura-san would see and she would as from my firmly looking at her be impressed and would want me, with her eyes and her silky smooth navel, would want me to step over the table and take her up in my quivering arms. Take her in my quivering arms to the graveyard, and lay her out on a cold ancestral stone and breathe the night into her, breathe it through her, be whole together again. I take another drink of *sake* but I am aware of my breathing: I am no less a monk.

I am aware of my hara. I am aware of the rustling of people, the starting to clean up of people and the laughter and uproar around me and the gaping hole where Roshi-sama should be sitting, at the empty head of the table, but he is not here, and by Daiko-san logic that means that there will be not no but only slight reverie. I am enjoying the slight reverie and the silk skin of my love Sakura-san across the low table from me but I miss that I cannot take out my glistening steel or maybe aluminum though it should be steel, it looks like steel, or silver, my glistening-cold, silver-hard mouth harp and blow it, blow it harder, more fiercely, more Chi-town uptown straight up down home than Ejo-san did, could ever, for Sakura-san, my love, my true and desperate and silk-navelled love. I am aware of my hara and the hole where Roshi-sama should sit which is why there is no music but of course singing cannot be helped in Japan. He is in the hospital. In the hospital again. Maybe we will lose him this time. Maybe the world will lose him this time, and with him the Zen of a hundred generations. What will be left for us then?

I drink another sip of *sake* and refill my cup. I smile and tilt my cup towards Sakura-san, and she giggles and takes another sip of her own and I am quite confident that I will lay her out tonight on the cold ancestral graveyard stone but my belly hurts so incredibly and I see

Daishu down the line getting up, rocking, and he has been drinking *sake* and whiskey and beer, all at a fine clip, a damn fine clip if I say so myself, which may explain how Ejo-san had with such ease removed the mouth harp from his hands before blowing on it such sweet and down home Chi-town riffs though I confess now that his Neil Diamond had a pronounced accent even though he got all the notes rights and even the words, as far as I know, not being so much of a Neil Diamond fan though not by deliberation but simply circumstance. I am quite sure I will lay her out cold on the hard ancestral stone and breathe night into her, be whole again together.

How will I say this to her? People around us are cleaning up, her Dharma sister, Junsho-san, the blind former opera singer, has been taken back to the women's dormitory on Myojun-san's arm, though she does not need the arm, as she knows the temple as though it were itself her eyes and could of itself see, in that way she knows the rocks and moss and grounds, and she is also beautiful, but so immensely, too immensely powerful and strange. Sakura-san's friend Yoan-san is much less beautiful but sometimes from afar I have confused for Sakura-san and once or twice she has noticed me confuse her for my sweet love Sakura-san and she appreciates the gaze and takes it rather personally which has complicated our otherwise straightforward relationship. Sometimes I think briefly of laying her out on graveyard stone, on cold ancestral slabs but only quickly, tightly, as I do not love her but only sometimes in the distance accidentally confuse her with Sakura-san and those times she smiles, seeming to enjoy the accident and I look away. She too is rising, Yoan-san is taking dishes to the kitchen as she rises. There is singing from the kitchen. Ejo-san is singing. He is a very good singer. Now Bob Dylan.

How will I say this… "*Chotto...*"? Yes, it should begin *chotto...* or *Sakura-kun...*. Yes! My dear little Sakura, it should begin, whether or not it makes any sense… or *shitsurei itashimasu…* yes, please excuse my grave presumption, but… it should begin. *Chotto arukimashou ka?* Shall we a small walk? Let us, then, a small walk! She will giggle and within hours I will have her in my arms, her silky samue falling from her shoulders, the heat of her breath warm in the icy twelfth month night, the heat of her heaving breasts, breaking through the thin sheer silk of her samue, her mouth enveloping me, my longing and my pain, her tongue…

She reaches for her cup and drinks the last gulp. She looks at me again, with a half smile, I swear with a half toss of her straight and perfect night black hair, and looks down at the table, scattered with our feast labors and our feast gluttony, looks right and left at the table and back at me and giggles and I know this is my moment. How will I say this?

*Chotto*… yes, I will start with *chotto*… *Chotto shitsurei itashimasu ga chotto arukimashou ka,* and even maybe a *ne,* as in, *arukimashou ka ne!* which may or may not make sense but should, should make sense, should express what in this moment I desperately must express and with no hesitation, with no deliberation: Shall we, right?, let us then walk a small!

I clear my throat, another sip of *sake* and another wave rumbling up from my belly, through my chest and pressing at the back of my throat and I grab another crumb, a sizeable crumb of salty, soggy quiche crust and I eat it and it calms me though it sends new ripples down and through my chest and belly, my sides and even into my back. She starts to move, shuffling in her seiza sitting pose, sliding her beautiful and silky soft right thigh back slightly from the table, as if ready to get up…

"*Chotto*…" I mutter, taking another sip of *sake,* looking at her with accidental desperation, accidentally insane, not at all with the clear determination of a monk and the firm fierceness with which I look or at least try to look at Roshi-sama, but instead with a sort of desperate frailty, another wave uprising from my aching, gnashing belly. I look at her with a pathetic desperation and I know just then that she will never lay beneath me on cold ancestral rock, that my face is puffed with gluttony, my eyes poke out like light bulbs set back deep into dark sockets, sockets ringed with thick black bags of sleeplessness and deeper or at least more purely Buddhist desperations, my enormous nose breaking out from the chapped snowfield of my face like an obscene iceberg…

"*Chotto*…" I mutter, quickly drinking again, pushing down another wave in my belly.

"*Sou na!*" she says, smiling at me, standing slightly, her silk rough cotton samue slipping from her shoulder, gliding off her breasts like soft and deft tongues dancing on cold hard ancestral stone and heating up a frozen twelfth month night and I have wanted you for so long, I have wanted for so many desperate moments just to lift you in my arms and hold you, rock you, tell you everything and melt my own hardness with the tears you pull from me my love, my dear dove Sakura-san, and wail all my loss and longing and the Way that day by day seems to recede before me but that we can at once accomplish on the cold ancestral stone that puts to rest the prideful strugglings of seekers…

"*Sou na,*" she says, half smiling and gesturing, "Indeed!", but casual, informally as though we were old friends or even lovers and I want for a desperate moment to whisper "Sakura-kun," my dear dove Sakura into her silk crisp ear, gesturing as she speaks at the disarray of feast gluttony that spills across our festive though somewhat sad long table at whose end the gaping hole of Roshi-sama sits not, gesturing at all there is to do, and looking at me, and looking at her friend Yoan-san who is coming back through the doorway to bring more dishes to the clattering and singing kitchen.

"Much clean, *na*!" she says, as though she is agreeing… as though she is agreeing but I have not quite yet said it, have not quite said that to which she will, she must, agree, my *chotto arukimashou ka*, or even, more boldly, *chotto arukimashou ka, ne!* or even, desperately, "My love!" because she knows some English, more than she lets on, I know because of how she sometimes laughs when we are talking, and smiles as she laughs, especially to me, when I am talking, when I say something funny, when some of us are talking casually in English, and she laughs then at the right times especially at me, but even if we are not or not really laughing, or before we do, and so I know she knows what it would mean about all things when I say, "My love." "My love, then, my dear little dove, then shall we, don't you think, let us then a small walk?!" I have not yet quite said in any language but my desperate hollow eyes and she is gone.

If monks were just immune from fleshy love, the desert fathers would have had no need to amputate their hands; Ananda would not have pleaded on the Buddha's deathbed—*What, oh what, should we do about women?* If the carnal held no sway over the spiritual, the tempter Mara would not have sent his luscious, dancing daughters to distract the Buddha on the night of his awakening; the nun Eshun would have had no need to take a scalding iron to her face to clear her path of lusting monks. If the Buddha thought that celibacy came easily, he would not have dwelled on rule after rule about monks' deportment around women, and nuns' with respect to men.

As for me, self-appointed young American monk, I just follow helplessly—propelled by some uncanny force—a devastatingly alive seventeen-year old girl, daughter of a senior priest, up the creek that cuts a cold channel through the temple's mountain valley. We wade over rocks and splash under waterfalls, until eventually I return, hungry and damp and exhilarated and ashamed, to the kaisando subtemple to bow in self-imposed penance until my feet bleed.

The air is thick with incense. The shadows flicker from the single candle on the altar. Down: forehead touches sweat-damp tatami, palms raised by each ear, toes extended so the tops of my feet lie flat against the floor. Up: toes rolling back under, rubbing flesh and tatami, torso lifts, palms together. Down again. Up again. Toes sliding back and forth on tatami, mind flashing with her face and her cheeks and the chance, the great, fragile chance for awakening. Down, the smell of tatami. Nothing matters but this. There is nothing but this devotion, this prostration, this surrender to Buddha. Up again, toes curling, skin scratching tatami, both wearing slowly away.

This cycle can only so much be repeated, but still I draw a good two years from it. In its larger phases, the relationship consists of a week, or even several weeks, of walking up-creek, flushed, warm skin, everything newly crisp and alive, everything poems again. Then, mysterious, unbeckoned, and inevitable, a sudden crashing realization of spiritual doom ushers in another week or two of pristine and repentant re-monkhood. But I cannot for long resist her late night, cupped-hand owl hoot outside my window, and eventually it without fail compels me down the dormitory stairs to fade with her once more into the dancing, crisp moonlight, wide awake and blissfully drunk on my lover.

She knows the misfortune of loving a monk. When I feel unbound by doctrine and identity, I arrive; remembering my vague but incontrovertible call, I depart. The elders of the American Zen family roll their eyes and try to keep the damage isolated. It is a matter of policy that new students must refrain from romantic involvement for at least the first six months of their stay in the temple, but reality too often defies it. If there is blame, it is at the disruption, not the passion. It is all just part of temple spring. Zen students are human, the teachers know, and the Great Way can bear that truth whether or not the students themselves can. Buddha is right here in humanity, right here in lust and in romance. It is delusion, they teach, to think that the fundamental truth of life will only reveal itself in the purity of some monastic ideal. The truth is exactly in life, and the young men and women have no choice but to learn life in their life.

In any case, Zen slipped off of its monastic tracks a long time ago; it's not just something that has happened in the West. Zen's relentless emptiness teachings privilege formless, unconditioned reality over the details of moral discipline: teachings like "the One Precept" eschew the duality of "good" and "bad" conduct, and ground moral action instead in nondual awakening. As Gendoji's Roshi-sama often says, "Just awaken, and then do what you will." Once awakened to the interconnection of all beings, right conduct will naturally flow forth.

Deep teachings, but a slippery slope. If nondual enlightenment—which has no particular causal conditions, and no particular identifying traits—is the ethical standard, what basis is left to support monastic discipline? The precept schools, the Buddhist branches that embodied the truly monastic streams of India and, to a lesser extent, China, could never quite gain hold in Japan, and even the monastic orders that were established gradually softened their rules. Already by the eighth century a Tendai monk named Saicho convinced the Japanese emperor to allow Buddhist ordinees to take only sixteen ethical precepts, instead of the two or three hundred of the older traditions. "Don't be greedy" seemed to him a more useful framework for Bodhisattvas than "you may own only one robe and one bowl." It may indeed be more useful, but a dozen short centuries pass and the order ends up filled with monks who have four or five robes, not to mention some street clothes and a wife and a car, sometimes even a day job.

With the exception of the Pure Land Buddhists, who perfected and institutionalized a set of marvelous and compelling doctrinal justifications for the non-monastic path, the monastic ideal generally remained intact in Japan even as the lifestyle loosened. Most Zen priests, for instance, live with families, *sake*, and meat, while no less revering and emulating Dogen-Zenji, a die-hard monastic whose teachings drip with praise of the renunciate life. Apart from the occasional young idealist or purist abbot, these "monks" seldom seem troubled by the basic hypocrisy of their worldview. They are expected to be celibate during the year or few years of their monastic-style training, or at the very least to forgo sex while on temple grounds, but to continue the celibate discipline after their brief and intense training is unusual at best, more likely unacceptable. Still, rather than embrace the temple family lifestyle with elaborated doctrines or institutional pronouncements, for the most part the Zen establishment just buries the tension—resolved or not—in the rich earth of *just how things are.*

American Zen culture faced with the dilemma has adopted an understanding of Buddhism that takes the intimacy of romantic relationship as a model for the intimate interconnection of all things. Sexuality, committed relationship, and child-rearing are seen as positive paths and genuine Dharma gates, providing abundant opportunities for moment-to-moment zazen practice. The bedroom is seen as a Technicolor meditation hall, and each murmur of a child the call to meditation—no different than the mallet cracking against the han, the signal block that reads: *Great is the matter of birth and death. Life is fleeting, gone! gone! Everyone, awake, awake! Don't waste this life.* Those who would suggest that the sound of the han is more spiritual, more enlightening, more Buddhist, than the cry of a child or the touch of a lover are likely to be viewed with suspicion if not condescension in the Sangha. Relationships and romance have grown to seem not just important, but even vital on the path to spiritual maturity.

Most American Buddhist converts, then, must discover on their own the tension between the basic teachings of their new religion and the way it's currently lived. What at first seems natural to those with Protestant or Jewish backgrounds—married or even dating clergy—becomes problematic as they study the lineage of ancestors, most of them fiercely celibate, who are said to have passed their understanding (which absolutely included monastic discipline) mind-to-mind down the lineage to the married Japanese and American teachers. Students, would-be monastics sometimes encouraged to think of themselves as genuine "monks," eventually stumble upon the rigorous monastic rules that the Buddha himself taught, the tremendous admonitions of Dogen, the ascetic standards of the early teachers, or even the teachings of some traditionally-bent Buddhist teachers today. They see that, at least from a historical perspective, the whole Buddhist religion has centered on a community of monastics who have literally abandoned the home life. Only then do they feel the disconnect, and demand from their married teachers explanations and justifications that may or may not fall flat on their ears.

Disconnect or not, the American temples are breeding grounds, and most of the young would-be monastics eventually find themselves participating in the fun. And so it is that the young woman and I walk up the creek together, through the creek, cold water sloshing in our soaked and heavy sneakers. On a rock we kiss, a trembling seventeen year-old Buddha and twenty one year-old trembling Buddha, and for a moment it is clear that the Great Way can hold this. But as we push aside the brush with dim flashlights, exhausted, searching for the path back to the heart of the valley, the smell of incense that has merged with landscape overtakes me again, and I find myself alone in the kaisando founder's hall, pants damp to the knees, offering bow after repentant bow, chaffed feet slowly bleeding.

"Beautiful!" Sakura-san says softly, an exuberant whisper, her bright almond eyes dancing, looking back and forth between me and the window of the four-wheel drive Jeep that bounces over the stones and ruts in the road, engine revving fast to climb the steep dirt grade that ascends high before descending low into the mountain valley that shelters my—our—American temple.

I put my hand on her silky arm, and whisper close into her ear, "Sakura-kun, my dear dove, we are near."

It is beautiful. Ascending in the twilight, the wide central valley of California lies out below us; descending, the rugged green ridges ripple and overlap in endless distances, like our future, our endless future together, our bodies and paths overlapping, here at last in *Amerika*, land of the free, land of unobstructed love, where we can practice the Way with the same passion and integrity that we lived at Gendoji, but alongside one another, in one another's arms, teaching and following one another, sitting, walking, working alongside one another, opening. Hearts, minds, and bodies together open into the fullness of the unlimited Way.

Rumbling down the familiar and strange road back into the heart of American Zen, where the Path is not proscribed but dynamic, where love is not an obstacle, but, as the Tantric schools have always insisted, an unequaled Dharma gate—I whisper again, "My dear dove Sakura-kun, we are near…" She clutches my arm and lays a sweet soft kiss on my cheek, her faded and baggy black samue draping her like a gown of the finest silk, pressing close against my own loose and worn monk's clothes.

The sun rises, the sky brightening as we ascend, and gaining in ferocious high desert strength as we begin our steep descent.

The light grows brighter, brighter, and brighter as the kyosaku cracks down against my shoulder, exploding stinging waves of wakefulness through my sore, cross-legged body, rocketing me back into the clay-walls and cold dawn air of the Gendoji zendo, at my place in the long line of monks, Roshi-sama's rocking, aged body hunched in the center of the room, Daiko-san prowling the aisles with the kyosaku warm from use, and Sakura-san in her seat, out of sight across the hall, thinking of nothing and least of all me.

From the window in my section of the loft above the Kannon hall, I can see a piece of the graveyard, the main gate, and the low wall that separates the temple from town. A sprawling cherry tree—I wake up swearing it is snowing again, the spring day its blossoms begin blowing through the air—stands between the graveyard and the path that leads to the main gate.

From the graveyard—and I have tried it—from a certain cluster of memorial stones, especially at night when it is dark outside and a light is on in the loft, one can see up through the window into my section of the room. Day and night, when I return to my corner for a moment or a transitory night of rest, I sit by it, looking out at the distant world, the close graveyard, and the blossom-speckled cherry tree. In doing so, innocent, I have observed a ritual. Indeed I have become a player in a what has grown to be a nightly ritual, a silent, nocturnal dance with my silky, slippery lover Sakura-san.

The night bonsho bell begins it routine, last in the cycle of bells and blocks that has dismissed us from the final period of meditation. The young and proud monk Ejo-san chants blessings into the night as he crashes the hanging log against the thick potential of the waiting bonsho bell. The bonging continues as I make my way across the courtyard to the Kannon hall, offer a low bow to Kannon-sama, and climb the flimsy stair-ladder to the drafty loft. I take off my koromo robe and carefully hang it up, preparing for sleep in my grey kimono under-robe, but for a moment before spreading out my bedding, I sit on my folded up futon and gaze out my window at the reverberating night.

Sakura-san, on schedule as every night in every weather, steals into the graveyard and stands beside the cherry tree. She looks up and around, looks to my window, and looks at me behind my window, in my grey kimono under-robe, backlit by my dim lamp. She looks up at me and smiles her devastating half smile, tossing her silken black hair in cascades over her black sitting robes and purple laywoman's rakusu. She stands, looking at me and then suddenly away, as if it is too much, as if I am too much to keep looking at, but, as I her, can be taken only in sweet sips. I watch her too, my heart clenching, the shape of her face pressing against my chest from within. Something deep and not quite lost within me cries out against her silken cheeks, her night-black hair. I cannot maintain the gaze, but continue the façade of bed-time preparations and slowly lay out my futon as she disappears into the shadows of the cherry tree, from which she can slip through the graveyard to the back door of the women's dorm.

Each night we dance this dance. In the mornings we sometimes steal a glimpse, but just as I see her face, I see her look away. She blushes slightly, avoiding my eyes in coy denial of my seeing her see me, and she glides off. Genzen tells me that she was a dancer—he is the only one of the monks who actually speaks to her, as the two have rapport, the clarity of platonic respect. I know that his heart belongs to Erin, so I am not jealous.

"Roshi-sama loves her tremendously," Genzen tells me. "He spends hours and hours with her in dokusan."

But Sakura-san and I don't have the luxury of private hours together, so we improvise our intimacy, stretching and shrinking it to fit whatever space we occupy. Outside the kitchen, for example, in the courtyard where we take our tea and daily sweets, we slip and slide around one another as though in a ballroom. I reach for my teacup and she slides back three steps; I sidestep to the hot water, and she turns and walks two beats away; I bow slightly, smiling—but inward, always inward and always smiling, like any dancer—I pause a beat, then sidestep again, turn, four beats back and she slides in, two sidesteps for the hot water. The air between us is electric, our changing distance is our closeness, the gap is our connection and we push and pull against it, fondling each other through the taut field of air.

Our eyes seldom meet, but sometimes when we are alone, when we seem to be alone, I hold my gaze on her firmly, boldly. I look at her, let myself look at her, let her see the way I look at her, let her watch me drinking her, and she looks too at me but just a moment—she is shy and dedicated to Zen decorum. She looks at me for just a moment before dropping her head with a demure smile, half tossing her silken black hair and sliding away, as though off stage, exeunt through an invisible door that has just opened next to her. Or sometimes she turns her head, flushing, just turns her head as though denying everything, as though it is too much, I am too much to even sip. I know how she must feel because I feel it too, she is sometimes too much even to sip, even to start to open to for fear she overtake me and already I'm consumed. So sometimes I act as though I do not see her either, my hands in shasshu—I am not a bad monk—my head upright and eyes straight forward and downcast, in my concentrated, serene bubble, in my cocoon of internal effort, in faith that it may serve to liberate all others, and I don't even know if she has passed or not.

Tonight warm rain falls in cascades. Drowsy and nostalgic in evening zazen, my mind wanders from silence to past, passes momentarily through future, drifts again to silence, then back to the past.

I think of my American ex-girlfriend, the days many springs ago when we would chase each other up the creek, laughing and splashing in fleeting but sincere love. I replay each time we broke up and got back together, only to break up again. I'd had the Way to attain, after all, and could not be bothered the next morning. Finally, after a weeklong retreat in which my teacher demanded unconstructed presence and railed against the righteous "Zen stink," I was temporarily cured of my monastic pretensions and realized that what I really wanted was to live with my lover, to practice meditation in the world, in the bed, in the streets with her. What joy! The Way could hold it, the living Buddha did not care if I wore priest robes or overalls, if I shared my bed in damp, exhilarated purity or lay alone, kimono-clothed, on my right side, palms together under my head in devotion. I resolved to leave the temple at the end of the next three-month retreat period, and to move with my lover to a quiet, coastal town.

She was—or seemed at least, to my ringing ears—delighted, and she looked for a house for us. She found one, a carriage house in the middle of a backyard garden with lemon trees, two blocks from the beach. I counted the days of the ninety-day retreat. Eighty-eight, eighty-seven, eighty-six. But on the sixty-second night, when I called her from the temple's single phone, after the lights-out signals had faded into the vast sky and the last monks had returned to their silent rooms, she informed me that she was dating someone else. She had to make a decision, she told me—she was eighteen and had to decide something—and she couldn't choose me.

What future can a monk offer a young woman? I tried anyway to preserve some dignity, to proceed undeterred, and I abandoned the retreat and went to the town we would settle in, where she too was living. I moved into the carriage house under the lemon trees, alone, and I waited, and waited, for her to come to her senses. Three weeks of lonely beach walks later, I returned, head hanging, to the temple where I belonged.

Her face haunting my meditation, I resolve to call my ex-girlfriend. Tomorrow is shikunichi and we have an hour more of sleep in the morning, a chance at a nap in the afternoon. I will slip out tonight after the night bells and call her from my faithful payphone at the Maibara Eki. Tell her hello, life is hard here, but pure… maybe tell her, try to tell her, that I am in love again. I have a lover again—her skin is silk like yours, her mouth a bit smaller, her eyes more oval, darker hair, but the same exploding inner passion, the same grace, the same pressure in my chest, incurable longing, incurable pain approaching fulfillment… I will call her after the night bells. I owe it to her. She should know.

I run across the courtyard after zazen, rain pelting down, splashing me as it bounces off the ground and blows under my umbrella. I climb the stair-ladder to the loft and change from my muddied robes into samue. I will have to wait until things have settled before going out into the stormy night to the eki payphone, wait until the night sitters are established in night sitting and the rest of the assembly is settled in bed, except Daishu, who I can expect will sit in his tent in our room, but who won't mind in the least if I'm up to strangeness. He's always slipping out himself on mysterious errands, and I've never pressed him about it—we have an understanding. When the temple is still again I will sneak out through the graveyard, across the narrow walkway that runs along a neighbor's rice paddy, and out onto the neighborhood streets that spill onto the Fushihara highway by the churning dark mountain tunnel.

I sit on my futon and look out the window while I wait. The rain thunders on the roof of the Kannondo, shakes the wide branches of the cherry tree, puddles and splashes on the memorial stones of named and nameless ancestors. Soon, small under a broad umbrella, Sakura-san materializes beneath my window, looking around before glancing up to my window, half smiling, her head half tossing it's dark halo of hair, her black sitting robes damp with rain and splattered with mud. She makes her way to the cherry tree and stands there, looking around and looking up at me, getting wetter and wetter in the thunderous rain.

I sigh deeply and look at her. Her devotion to our secret, silent rendezvous amazes me. She peers up at my window, I look down, our impossible and pregnant bond in the celibate prison of temple life—the impossible passion to which history is eternally witness.

A white figure, ghostlike, catches my eye across the graveyard from the cherry tree, emerging from the back door of the Japanese monks' rooms beneath the Kannondo. The rain blurs everything, but I can see that it is Ejo-san in his white kimono. Having finished ringing the night bonsho bell, he is walking in zori monk's sandals, no umbrella, getting drenched as he quickly crosses the graveyard through the torrent back towards the bell platform. Has he left something there? No, he is walking towards the cherry tree.

Sakura-san glances around nervously, then looks up at him coming towards her. Her body extends, leans towards him, her hair falling as it fell the day I met her—"migi," she said to me, leaning and giggling—her silk hair plummeting against the angle of her body, her chin leading out, and she takes a step towards him and disappears behind the cherry tree. Glancing around nervously, he speeds up, half-running the few remaining steps to the tree, until he too disappears behind it, and I roll away from the window, crumpling onto my futon, my cheeks suddenly damp, my chest suddenly convulsing. They are in love. In love! It has not been for me that she each night in desperate devotion stands beneath the tree beneath my window, waiting.

I lie dead still in a ball on my futon, a restless, chilled, unsleeping pile of monk. An hour or two pass before I finally pull myself up, descend the stairs, slip out of the Kannondo, and walk out of the temple through the side of the graveyard, my flimsy umbrella blown inside out by the storm. I see no sign of the lovers, and I wind my way through the neighborhood streets to the eki phone booth, where I dial my ex-girlfriend, just as I intended.

She answers, and I tell her nothing. What can I tell her? Can I tell her that I've penetrated Roshi-sama's saying about enlightenment: *The way you thought things were, you see that they are not. The way things are, you never dreamed they'd be.* And that even that wasn't what I thought?

Can I tell her that I've seen the source of all the Buddhas—and that she's making out with Ejo-san (of all pretentious monks…) behind the graveyard cherry tree?

I tell her instead that my inspiration is unequaled, that my practice is finally for the first time underway; that I am near, perhaps quite near, the great awakening, and that in the face of that all obstacles—if there are even obstacles—are only pebbles on the road. Yes, pebbles on the road. As in, the pebbles that make up the road. Which is to say, it's nothing like you think it'd be, before you're walking on them. No obstacles at all, I mean—just pebbles.

"Pebbles?" she says. "I guess I'm okay too. I hope you come home soon. I'd like to see you. I love you."

Why does she always say she loves me?

And the next morning, across from Ejo-san in service, chanting truth in syllables that no one understands, with incense that is only burning wood, bows that are just bodies falling, tears pour down my face, my sobs trying to time themselves with the great bell that it might absorb them, Ejo-san glancing up, and Genzen, Daishu, no one looking, exactly, but everyone noticing and Ejo-san as we process to the next part of service looks up at me, at my red and tear-blistered cheeks with great understanding, great concern, and great compassion, and I never look at Sakura-san again, nor go near to her, nor let a thought of her enter my mind without wrapping it in chains of grief and shame, and flinging it back to the muddy ocean.

# 10  Breakings Through

*If you set out to accomplish it, you will accomplish it.*

—Gendoji's "Roshi-sama"

The day I lost my faith I look out from my window at a cherry tree, a graveyard, village rooftops, green rice paddies. I look out at the distant department store sign, "*Seiyu*," the chaotic patterns of the coastal sky, mountainside and highway, the low wall that encloses the temple and excludes the town.

From the window in my loft above the Kannon Hall, I can see the shed that houses some garden tools and a few dump-salvaged bikes. It is shikunichi, bath and rest day, and through the partly opened door the shed looks empty: the bikes are all in use, though Roshi-sama says that we should not go out. He at least had not gone out in the long years of his own training, especially not biking into town for ice cream or to swim in underwear in the Wakasa bay, the way I do, alone or with Genzen, some shikunichi days—though not today—bike out, dive in, and see how far I can swim, roughly homeward, before growing exhausted and remembering that I do not want to die in water, but in breath, to the Great Way, and paddling back to shore.

A young Japanese monk—Ankai-san, it must be—climbs to the top of the shed roof and lies there, basking in the sun. He deserves a moment of rest; it is shikunichi after all. Resting in the sun, oblivious to everything. I sink into my futon, furious and heartbroken.

How can he rest? What is he doing? I hate that he is resting, but not because I know what else he should be doing. What does rest have to do with anything? What does effort have to do with anything?

What are we doing?

I think again of the old boxer monk—his stooped shoulders and rocking head have haunted me since dawn. He is an older Japanese monk who comes by to visit Roshi-sama now and then. I don't know his name, but in my head he is the "old boxer monk" because that's the way that Genzen described him to me once: "He looks like an old boxer, hit one too many times."

When I first saw him, a few months ago, from the same window I sit looking out of today, I saw it too: he walked like an old boxer. His shoulders were bent over, and his head hung forward and rocked back and forth with his steps. It seemed like he didn't quite know where he was or where he was going. He lumbered along like a drunk, looking at the ground, lost in the rocks and moss as though they were speaking to him, bore for him some secret message.

In temple legend, it is said that he had once been the best of monks, destined to be heir to Gendoji. As tenzo, he ran the kitchen impeccably, but his responsibilities never pulled him away from zazen. Between kitchen shifts and formal zazen, he would sit informally in the zendo—just like I do some days with Genzen, Elaine, Shoryu-san, and Sakura-san, who do most days. Regularly sitting far into the night—having firmly set out, not looking off, continuing *Just!*—the old boxer monk's *joriki* spiritual energy increased gradually, unmistakably, until eventually he passed beyond the human need for sleep. I expect his need for food too faded—perhaps he ate a bowl of rice in the morning, another small bowl at noon? In temple legend he had been the perfect monk, and everyone looked on expectantly, awaiting his confirmation as sole heir to Roshi-sama, and the inevitable blossoming of his brilliant Dharma career.

He opted one day, instead, to run out of the temple screaming, run onto the highway and into the narrow tunnel through the mountains.

Sometimes I see myself too, running on the highway towards the tunnel, screaming. Sometimes I see that option before me.

Since then, Genzen says, sometimes the boxer monk tries to come back for a sesshin or to join the regular schedule, but it never lasts: during zazen he starts talking to himself, or screaming out. Roshi-sama and Daiko-san ask him to leave again, and no one hears of him for another couple of years, until he tries to come again for a retreat. I will never hear him screaming—only watch him walking, dumb—but I know the feeling of that scream, the scream that might at any moment burst out from my hara. To leap off of that final place, screaming as I fall. Letting go—breaking through—into madness.

I wonder, as I stare out my window at the relaxed, reclining young Ankai-san, what the old boxer monk saw the day he lost his mind and ran into the highway tunnel screaming. Did he drop that last shackle, "sanity," that keeps us lesser beings bound? I have felt that feeling, that I can drop or snap that last thin strand of bondage, that last tie to the living. I have known the feeling that to dive off of the "hundred foot pole" in that way, with no hesitation, no regard for so-called sanity or madness, would be to manifest the metaphor of the last hair shaved in the ordination ceremony—final renunciation, the irreversible plunge into Buddhahood.

"This last hair is called the *shura*. Only a Buddha can cut it off. Now I will cut it off. Do you allow me to cut it off?" my teacher Lee recited, razor readied, three times in the breathless hall of my ordination. "I will," I said, three times—"I will!"

Beneath that dramatic dropping that I sometimes dare to skirt in zazen, that total renunciation not ritual but physical, witnessed not by humans but by Buddhas, I feel that there lies a universe-shattering scream. It is a scream from which I would not return, separated forever from the illusions and delusions of being as I now know it. It is "Enlightenment"— to become as the Buddhas who do not engage in the karma of controlling mind or body, who have dropped the last ties to the living. Perfected shikantaza. But if I let that last thread fall, pass through that gate of "no control" into the realm of the vast scream, will I run too, insane to the world, out into the highway tunnel?

Roshi-sama is not angry with me exactly, but he is severe. "*What?!*" he shouts in dokusan.

"I mean that I get to this place in zazen where if I take one more step I think that I will go completely insane. But if I step back from it, I feel like I'm backing out of the Way, sliding back into my ego-control of things."

"What?!" he bellows. "Step forward? Step back? That isn't my teaching! You do shikantaza, right? Only *JUST!* No forward, no back! Stop making things up in your head!"

Roshi-sama mutters, as though to himself, "*Isshokenme*, wholehearted, sure, but he makes things up in his head!"

"I guess your teaching about breaking through confused me," I say.

"I don't teach breaking through!" he yells. "Only here! Now!"

"Before satori," he continues, "I was like you, grasping things. Now I do shikantaza, grasping nothing!" He is talking out both sides of the Dharma—if he doesn't teach breaking through than what does *before satori* mean?—but I trust everything again. My panic deflates.

I breathe deeply. My feeling is still real, in a sense, but I see that I am making it: I am creating a precipice that will create a fall. I am making up "forward-and-back" in my head. In soft strict shikantaza there is nothing like that, Roshi-sama is saying, we are not pushing, breaking forward into anything, but simply allowing all things to be, *just*. All things simply as they are, released. Not necessarily released in some explosive bright light, in some dramatic, penetrating madness. That is not his teaching, no matter what his disciples imagine.

Roshi-sama is reminding me that I have another feeling, another meditation. It is a subtle feeling in the chaos of my grasping mind, but as he reminds me I realize that I trust it intuitively far more than "forward-and-back," than "breaking finally through." That feeling I really trust is that I can *relax* out of the precipice that I've excited myself to dive into, *relax* to the sounds of the sweet potato vendor's truck on the road, the children next door at the Shinto shrine, my sleepy zendo neighbor's rocking body, my own body and belly, softly, naturally, filling and expelling. *Just this* in the "just this" sense, not as some cosmic *JUST* beyond this, or underlying this. *Just this*: total appreciation, dedication, relaxation, joy.

The old boxer monk walked around the grounds, swaying his lowered head, looking at the big rocks that cut a path through moss and water.

His walking has long haunted me—today's loss of faith is not sudden, exactly. It is acute, but it has been building with the heat of my second Gendoji summer, mirages or oases of doubt. Only a few days ago I met Roshi-sama in dokusan and coughed out my doubt yet again.

"Roshi-sama," I muttered, tangled in my words, "this place… I'm not getting it! Do I even believe in this path anymore? I just see myself getting tired, and then hard inside, bitter. Is this what it feels like to be Daiko-san? I snap at people, hating myself, discouraged all the time. This practice isn't working, Roshi-sama. I'm not becoming what I've come to become. It is time for me to go."

He nodded gently, knowingly. "Stay, go—this battle, common. But for us, only *Just!*" He pushed a belly-full of air out forcefully, his small round body hanging totally relaxed, completely energized.

"If you really want, please go. But somewhere else, same problem. Here, with me, maybe you see how no problem anywhere. Maybe you see, and *smile*." He kept his eyes downcast as he spoke, but he looked up, suddenly and intently, eyes wide open, on the word "smile."

Everything was suddenly new again.

"When I meet my great teacher," he continued, "I only stay with him. I follow him *Just!* and one day, great smile!"

We were silent. The possibility, the faith, slowly and unmistakably welled up in me again. *I can! I can find the great smile he has found! I have no other choice, no other desire. For this and only this I have become a monk and have left home.* It was irrevocably obvious again, and a "*Hai*," "Yes, I will!" filled my belly, its heat rushing through my body as it burst into the room, not a scream of madness but an eruption of concentrated vow.

"You—" he cried, delighted, "only leave after great smile! All the time, only *Just!*" He struck his fist against his abdomen, his hara center. "Continue!" he belted, and his little hand bell hammered me out of the room.

It will never cease to ring in my ears.

How could I do anything but stay in the temple? Lack of faith is only a function of thinking, I reminded myself, it holds no truth beyond that. My mental and emotional confusion wouldn't defeat me, wouldn't lead me to abandon Gendoji and my great teacher. Walking from the interview room into the courtyard, renewed, I applied myself once again to my practice. Walking, I just walked. Sitting, grounded deeply in hara, I only sat. Eating: only chopsticks, brown rice, jaw and tongue. I would not leave without a smile on my face. *Only Just!* I demanded.

My jaw was clenched, and I vibrated with concentration, moving as though on the bottom of the sea, as though encircled by a force field that pushed against everything within two or three feet of me. My confusion loomed at its edges. When my mind would drift for even a moment, doubt would crash back through the paper walls of my concentration.

"There is *nothing* here for me; I don't *believe* in this!" a silent voice would insist. I would exhale it away, with all the strength of hara. I exhaled it out—tape on the paper wall—and continued.

But already today the vibrations have settled, and my concentration has gradually faded. It always fades, the high after dokusan, but these days especially it fades each time more quickly. From the window in my corner of the room above the Kannon hall, everything I've lived at Gendoji rearranges, shifts, and takes new shapes like the fast, colliding clouds that form and evaporate above our temple graveyard and the narrow streets of Maibara. I think of the old boxer monk, and I think of my own practice, my own mind.

Closing my eyes and leaning back against my folded futon, I remember—as if for the first time able to remember—May sesshin, the fifth day.

I had spent the day with some equanimity, deep enough into sesshin to have relaxed the panic response that long sitting, or the prospect of long sitting, can engender. My body had loosened, as my mind had, into the hours of zazen, and the physical pain was at most simply discomfort. Intently concentrated, I was at last settled. Breath and body; hara and mind. I was of course exhausted from the relentless schedule, the sporadic night-sitting I'd been doing throughout the sesshin, and the speed and stress of the interspersed kitchen shifts that clogged the few breaks in the sitting, but that evening, during the after dinner periods, my hara was on fire with energy, and fits of inspiration kept me alert and awake. *Perhaps tonight!* Roshi-sama's promises—"You will marvel!"; "The way I thought things were, I see now that they are not…"; "Great smile!"—awaited their fulfillment. I pushed into my hara. Deeper and deeper.

Green tea after the night bells—then back into the zendo, where the clay walls darted with the shadows of the meditators who were throwing down their final cards like dawn Las Vegas gamblers with nothing left to lose. It was late in sesshin, after all, our concentration was established but our time was running out. The Great Opportunity danced in front of us, waving at us to step up, whispering seductive promises. We pushed and struggled, pried our eyes wide open to resist the drowsiness and fatigue; clenched our haras to divert us from our searing knees and burning backs.

The night wore on, slow and empty, the traffic noise subsiding to the night bird's cry, the intermittent roaring of the highway tunnel. One-by-one, sitters retired, bowing first to their cushions and then to the room before stumbling, sleep-dizzy, towards the dormitory. Of the few meditators left, some succumbed to sleep, rocking violently or gently in the discordantly bright, fully-lit night zendo, others doubled their torsos over their folded legs and lay their heads on the front edge of their sitting mat, banking on a few minutes of painful sleep to somehow refresh them. Some, firmly sitting, just continued like stone Buddhas, staring down the blank wall that held the final fulfillment of their vows, the end of all the problems of precarious and sorrowful *samsara*, birth and death. *Deeper! Follow through!*

I sat a long round of zazen, intense, alert and caffeinated. *It has always been just this. This old friend.* Breath, body, wall. Everything hanging, somehow, in everything else, indeed *as* everything else. After sitting, I stood up. Vibrating with presence, I walked out into the wide night.

I took up my favorite night-walking place, the sidewalk path from the main gate to the hondo, tightened up my hands in the shasshu standing position, and began the short slow steps that I knew would sustain my meditation far into the night. Just as concentrated as zazen, but impervious to sleep, *kinhin* is the best way that I know to plunge my night meditation beyond the bounds of my body's desperate pleas for sleep.

What is time in meditation—in anything? It expands, contracts, and wraps around itself. A bell rings and the meditator stands. Preceding eons vanish.

Did I walk for an hour? Four hours? Back and forth, from the gate to the hondo, back to the gate, back to the hondo. Slow, precise, tiny steps. Immune to sleep; laser-like awareness.

I stepped back into the zendo frozen in concentration. Dropping, dropping, dropping. Only three sitters remained, two hunched and one upright. Despite myself, I took attendance: sesshin frequenter Al, the upright one, and Sakura-san and Shoryu-san, slumped with sleep or sleepiness. Even adding to my calculation the one or two sitters I suspected were out sitting on straw *goza* mats and cushions in the graveyard or the fields, I knew that it had grown very late, or very early. By being awake still, I had qualified for the night's elite corps of sitters.

I sat down, dropping with some shame my pride and my comparisons, and pulled my legs into a sesshin-weary half-lotus.

Suddenly, as I settled into my posture, as though a volcano were erupting in my hara, an unmistakably white light ignited and flashed through my body. It was an inexhaustible energy. *So this is how they do it!* It poured through me; what began as a flash continued as a relentless flood. With that energy, what could ever be impossible? Would I ever sleep again?

Engorged with the white energy, I sat immobile, meditating with extraordinarily natural effort. I sat dropping. No thought but: *Drop everything! Deeper!* No fear. I would drop every tie, every "control," every link that held me chained to the mundane.

Something—only a memory now as I sit against my futon above the Hall of Merciful Kannon, the day I lost my faith—slapped me at my core. It was a shape, something like the shape of a body, my own body, but inexpressibly hollow. It was everything suddenly hollow. It was as though another body, without mass, had crashed into my own, had merged its emptiness with my weight... It was like something, but with everything missing....

My body lurched—nothing left of me—and it was obvious: I had arrived! Here was the other shore! Here the promises were not promises at all, but just the shape of things, the flora and fauna on this now immediate shore...

I did not scream. I did not leap off of my cushion and run out through the temple gate and down the winding neighborhood streets into the highway tunnel; I just sat on, fixed in concentration and white energy. Degrees of drowsiness and new arrays of mental states—vastnesses and darknesses, envelopments and permeations—passed through me, but the strength did not fade. The energy pouring out of my hara showed no signs of depletion. Indeed, it was nothing like a thing that could be subject to depletion.

I didn't get up again that night. Sitting effortlessly in full-lotus I uncrossed and re-crossed my legs only once or twice in the hours to come. As I sat absorbed in deep concentration, with all of my senses wide open, I noticed as one-by-one my fellow night-sitters groggily took leave of the zendo. I heard their robes rustle as hands came together to bow before rising; I heard their joints unlatch as they stood; I heard each soft footstep, just as it started, set, lifted; I felt the wind as their walking reorganized the settled zendo air. Then I was alone in the brightly lit hall.

Eventually the early morning sitters trickled in. These preferred to come to morning zazen one or two hours early, rather than clocking their extra hours in late-night sitting, although some of them, like my roommate Genzen, maximized their tabulations by practicing both. First entered a familiar Japanese laywoman who attended each sesshin and whom I would often see, when I came in or out of the zendo during night meditation, rocking sleepily in her place. It was somehow apparent to me that her mind was quiet. It was palpable as she walked in: a quiet, non-judgmental mind. She took her seat. She noticed me, but I sensed no particular reaction. Her mind was still.

After her entered the maternal and heavy-set Czech woman who lived in Japan with her husband, also Czech, a sculptor and Zen priest. Together they would attend most sesshins, and she would, after every meal, do full prostrations in the hondo for thirty or forty minutes. "This place brings you to your knees," she said once, praising Gendoji's relentless demands. As she took her seat near me in the early hours zendo, I felt her warm presence. Her attention rested on me for a moment, filled with affirmation and support. "Yes, yes," I almost heard her say, before she settled into her place and took up her focus on the wall.

Next Genzen walked in, stiffly upright, to sit for a while before he would need to stand and start ringing the wake-up bell throughout the temple. I had never been in the zendo early enough in the morning to have confirmed if it was his habit to sit then or not, but having often heard his rustling robes in our loft room long before it was time for him to get up and rouse the assembly, I assumed that it was. Early that night during my long walking meditation I noticed him returning to the room. Although he was one of the last sitters in the hall, I knew that it weighed on him to have to go to bed before the others, to have abandoned his effort so early, to have such weak resolve that he could not sit up all night, night after night. In part, I knew that he simply loved to sit, and was deeply driven to sit all he could, but I couldn't help wondering if the pre-morning sitting was like penance for him for having succumbed the night before to the obstacle (one of five, in the old teachings) of sleep.

"Shit!" I heard, clear as a cry. I jumped in my seat, realizing only after a delay that he hadn't spoken aloud at all, but was quietly walking, head high, to his seat. Eerie shudders pulsed through me: I was hearing his mind.

"He followed through! He followed through!" Genzen's voice bellowed in my head, my ears, a cacophony of his pain, his anger with me. "What I have not been able to do! He broke through, he followed through!" He melted into sobs, "Why will I never…? Why am I so…" His wailing distress tormented me, even as he was totally silent and still, and even as my energy stayed white and strong, my posture solid.

Clearly he had recognized, I imagined as I sat on the cushion, rather alarmed to be listening to his mind but taking it only as further evidence of my realization, that I had seen That Which Is To See, had fulfilled Roshi-sama's promise, met emptiness face-on, ripped through the veil of the mundane, shattered the ego, ascended to the awakening of all Buddhas… It was understandable that Genzen was so disturbed—he had been trying and trying for so many years, and I, a relative new-comer to the austerities of Gendoji, had succeeded where he'd failed. But the pain of it cut into me. In the Sangha we were not only friends but indeed brothers, walking the same path together, pursuing the same truth together—shouldn't there be nothing but support for each other? If he had true kensho, wouldn't I applaud him, rejoice for him? And yet here was only anger.

I could not silence his howls in my mind. His thoughts—harsh and accusatory, jealous and raging, self-pitying and depressed—resounded in my ears, pounded through the still and silent zendo air.

Soon after Genzen came Erin, inviting suspicion that they liked, or had even contracted, to come into the zendo at the same time, where they could share their intimacy, even if facing opposite walls and across the hall from each other, free from the view of others. Always pious, she walked briskly to her seat, and when she saw me, I felt her bloom into a giddy smile and lay on me a "*Yoosshhh!*" a favorite phrase of Roshi-sama's to say "Good!" Roshi-sama uses it when we show him our strength, when we shout with resolve, or shovel with intensity, or carry shit with real hara. Quickly becoming a little Roshi herself, Erin too would use it in praise, and though it was a habit that annoyed me, I felt her love in it, her recognition and joy at my obvious awakening. Beside Genzen's anger and disappointment, which still cycled through my mind, I was warmed and encouraged by Erin's silent, crystal clear, "*Yosh!*"

I then heard Al and a hefty Polish night-sitter, who preferred graveyard sitting, and who I imagined had also spent the whole night awake, whispering together outside. They exchanged words about my night of energy and breakthrough, offering praise and support in a sort of running commentary, not unlike a sportscast. It was a little disconcerting, both what they were saying and the fact that I could hear them, but that the minds of all the deepest, strongest sitters were responding to my kensho only proved to me that I had truly broken through.

As I sit recollecting, on the day I lost my faith, it strikes me that the voices were so incontrovertible, Al's from outside, and Genzen's even as he sat on the other side of the zendo from me, that it never occurred to me to question the reality of what I was hearing. I was convinced of my awakening, and that it had opened me—in what was surely a sample taste of what the sutras know as the Buddha's omniscience—to the thoughts and emotions of others. I had no room or impulse to reflect on whether that was desirable, or had anything to do with spirituality at all. Much less could I speculate as to whether the strain to see something beyond the mundane, coupled with the intense energy that had come to me that night, had ruptured my sanity, launched me into some psychosis. It was, after all, I reflect, leaning back against my futon and indulging a descent into Western analysis, a textbook case of projection. I was perceiving in the minds of others simply what I assumed about myself, the greatness of what I'd experienced.

"Crazy," I whisper to myself, new tears forming in my bloodshot eyes. Maybe I'd just gone crazy, and made believe I heard the minds of others in what grew to be a private hell. And what does that mean about my version of Zen? This is just the kind of shit that Zen is supposed to undermine, to go beyond. *Chopping wood and carrying water* is the essence of Zen, the concrete, grounded, present Zen that I've given my life to practice and realize. Zen is medicine for the so-called spirituality of distant spirits and the disembodied confusion left in the wake of astral wanderings.

But whatever my intention for a grounded, mindful Zen, I had indeed grown more and more distant and disturbed in the final days of sesshin and the week or so following; my mental landscape turned darker. The merit of whatever realization I'd had dwindled compared to intensity of the new skill that seemed to develop alongside it, interfering significantly with my well-being. It seemed to me that walking, working, eating, talking, wherever I was I could clearly hear the thoughts, fears, and perceptions of whoever was near me, or even those who weren't. People's minds grew gradually angrier, more judgmental, and eventually new voices, new presences emerged, new spirits and demons adding their howls to the psychic cacophony.

"What have you seen?!" Roshi-sama bellowed. He stared wide-eyed at me in the interview room, fiercely awake, fiercely interested. "I must understand what you've seen!"

I couldn't explain, though I ventured some words—"hollowness," "white energy," "everything missing from everything." "Terrified."

"But do you see that there is no need to grasp anything?" he growled.

My insight was exposed naked in it's falsity. What was emptiness, what was clarity, what was "seeing the nature" if not "nothing at all to fear"? How could genuine insight be haunted? How could the "no-self" be frightened? My fear was precisely my grasping, and my grasping was precise proof of the shallowness of the insight I was grasping.

Indeed, if I had seen emptiness, as I'd convinced myself I had, wouldn't I have seen that I didn't need to grasp at the thought-demons—the sounds and contents of everybody's minds—that were terrorizing me? Wouldn't real seeing of real emptiness lead exactly the other way, towards calm, accepting joy?

However deep or shallow an experience I'd had, by the time I sat before Roshi-sama my overriding feeling was no longer the clarity, the lightness, but the screaming chaos in my mind. Even as I described my insight to him, the openness was just a memory, but the demons who had slipped in through the crack were still very real. I abandoned my words and just shook and cried before Roshi-sama. I waved my hands in gestures of creatures attacking my head from above, and I cowered to show my body crushed below them.

"Jiryu," he mouthed, his kindness palpable, as he wrote the characters for my name and made a note to himself on a little pad of paper that he pulled from his robe sleeve. Of some ceremony he might perform for me, I imagined, a reminder to offer me some psychic assistance.

"Only nothing grasp," he said softly, his eyes cast down again, his body a wide and warm ocean in front of me. "Only *Just*. Only hara. Only here, now. Please, please continue…"

I nodded, offered my bows, and stepped into the days after sesshin armed with the one tool that could protect me, the one concentration that could quiet my mind.

*Namu kie butsu—I take refuge in Buddha.* From deep in my hara, only just in this one here and now, completely falling into the refuge of this. Completely relying on the strength, the demon crushing enormity, of the Buddha who is all and the foundation of all. *I take refuge in Buddha.*

For a week after sesshin, people's minds stayed wide open to me, kept resounding in my head. People's insecurities, dark sides, and judgments were laid out for me to read without effort. And it took its toll. I could hardly sleep. Mornings would start out manageable, but as the day would progress, the cacophony of others' minds would grow gradually unbearable.

One night as I pushed them aside with my hara, with my *refuge in Buddha*, fiercely concentrated, fiercely denying admittance to demons, I made some headway. I did not need to fall for this, I had a larger refuge, the ground of who I really am, of what I really am, apart from whatever suffering, whatever demons, whatever mind at all. Deep hara exhalations, deep hara refuge in Buddha. I gained the upper hand, the voices, the minds of others receded, and after zazen, as I followed Roshi-sama, and the Dogaku, and then Shoryu-san out of zendo, Roshi-sama turned at the bottom of the stairs and pointed to me. Dogaku and Shoryu-san stopped between me and Roshi-sama. Roshi-sama looked at me closely.

"Good!" he growled.

I nodded. Dogaku and Shoryu-san gave little starts of surprise, and we all returned silently to our quarters.

"I got through it barely that time, but then I just came back to the same kind of warped effort that got me there in the first place," I whisper to myself, sitting in my room sorting through the shards of my shattered faith. "What about the next time? Where is this going?" I close my eyes again and lean back against my futon as though I might dissolve away in it.

The next day, I slip out through a gap between two halves of morning service, go back to my room, and pack my bags. Enough is enough—this practice is leading nowhere but hell. I leave some clothes hanging from the bamboo clothes rod so that Genzen and Daishu won't notice anything, and to be discreet I throw more clothes over my bulked-up bags. The *umpan* bell rings for breakfast—if I pack in the stolen private seconds of the day, I calculate, I will be ready by evening zazen to escape unseen and unsuspected. While everyone is in zazen, I will walk to the train station, Maibara Eki, get a train to Kyoto, take the bus to the hostel I know, sleep for two days, and from there reassemble the fragments of my faith, of my life in Japan.

As I pack my bags in the storm of my doubt, Roshi-sama's face fills my mind. He looks calm but disappointed, sitting at his seat in the dokusan room under the huge framed portrait of his teacher.

Is there is too much at stake, I wonder, do I have too much invested to just walk away? If I leave in this crisis—if I ever leave carelessly—will I ever forgive myself? How can I walk out on Roshi-sama? Wouldn't it be exactly walking out on the Way? And yet staying is no longer an option.

I have one further recourse. Skipping lunch, leaving my luggage not-so-discreetly situated behind my folded futon, I slip out the side of the temple and jump on a bike that an anonymous monk, likely Genzen's fun-loving alter-ego, keeps leaned against a tree there for clandestine exits. I pedal madly to the train station.

I dial the long extension to reach the U.S., and punch in a California number. My American ordination teacher picks up the phone.

"Lee, I just thought you should know," I cough, "that I am about to get on a train and leave here."

"I see," he says. "Why's that?"

It is hard to explain—it hasn't been sudden, exactly, but I can't say it's been gradual either. As I look for my response against the blank static of the phone line, only one image comes to me, and although I know that it doesn't explain my lost faith and my packed bags, it is as close as I can come to expressing how it has happened that temple life has grown intolerable.

"There is a young American woman here, Erin…" I begin tentatively. "She isn't a good friend, but we know some of the same people at home… We've appreciated each other. We could be closer, but she's been practicing very intensely, single-mindedly, maybe like the ideal Gendoji practitioner…. Anyway, night before last…."

Her shouting breaks the night chant. It melds with the night bell. I cannot make out her words.

She steps into the zendo. The cycle of bells is building to dismiss us, ringing through Ejo-san's mournful closing verse—zazen is in it's final moments.

I turn my head—*I should sit still.* Just slightly. Her hair is wet. Her skin is glossy, even in thin zendo light.

Has she been swimming somewhere, in the river or the ocean? There, in others' sickness, we throw paper images of Jizo-sama, toss translucent paper squares into the water, chanting with each, furiously, "*Om kaka kabi samma ei sowaka,*" praying for health, praying our wonder at the water.

Is she wet from swimming prayer? Tossed off herself in prayer? Her shouting shatters zendo silence.

I face the wall, sit on.

She walks in, dripping wet and with great confidence, and she approaches Roshi-sama's platform in the center of zendo. She has awakened, she tells him. Zazen is done. She shouts and laughs, and she bows a deep bow to Roshi-sama—though awakened, he is dry. He scowls and stands up, severe but not off-center. "*Dame,*" he growls softly. "*No good. Now go to bed.*"

We file out of the meditation hall. I do not linger. I go to bed.

I have not awakened. On time off I sometimes swim the ocean, but I haven't swum the river. I dry off quickly, as I only swim in sunshine. It is night, her hair is long and wet.

I go to bed.

Drifting to sleep, I am awakened. The sound of muffled shouting rises from the temple graveyard.

Most everyone has gone to bed, but she is shouting—she's awakened. She is shouting songs I know, though muffled. She has awakened chants up from that other country in us, that it hurts to think about, whose songs it hurts to sing. *Amerika.* She shouts songs I know, the songs of those who live and die for redwood trees.

She too has lived in redwoods. It's not that she has lost her love of redwoods, being in Japan, just that she grew weary of our clear-cut, Western shores. Sought temporary refuge, to return to trees re-sapped. It's just that she was borne by some Japan-bound wind, had caught it west to East, where I at least have never seen redwood trees.

I scramble into loose clothes, stumble down the stairs. It isn't something that I choose to do, exactly: it's just I know the songs. I mean, it's just what anyone would do. She shouts the songs I know, and someone muffles her. I run to her, like anyone.

Everyone already is awakened, when I am—who can stay in bed? Everyone is gathered, dazed, outside the Kannondo, Compassion Being Hall. I run out through them towards the graveyard.

Freddy says, "Don't go! You're crazy; she's *beyond.*"

I find her on the ground. Her two Japanese women friends, Sakura-san and Yoan-san have her wrestled to the ground, and muffled with their hands. They too have been awakened by her shouting, and they just want silence.

*Are the neighbor's windows lighting?* They glance out past the graveyard wall, towards darkened farmhouses. *Will their windows light?* Her friends are wet with sweat.

*Silence!* speak their muffling hands. *Then everyone can just go back to sleep—we're all so tired—just let this be nothing. In the morning all will be as it has always been, and we will try again for our awakening. Just let us sleep for now. The very night pleads silence!*

I am horrified—she has her song, must sing it. Is it that they don't know redwoods? Don't they see that we can simply lock ourselves together in this temple graveyard, love, and sing soft songs of redwoods who've awakened, gone beyond?

"What help is silence?" I cry, pulling Sakura-san's desperate and thin hands away from her mouth and nose. It's been a long time since I've touched a woman's fingers.

I sing some quieter songs, and we are all relieved. Her friends learn quickly and softly with me sing the songs sung at the feet of redwood trees. Gradually she joins. Her hair is slowly drying, though her body trembles still. She is wild-eyed, awakened. On one side, as we sit and sing, the lights of Maibara bleed into the night sky. On the other, the dark slopes of our mountain.

"Mu," she says, looking intently—wild-eyed—and laughing. "Mu is broken."

She speaks from her awakening, for she has gone beyond. She's broken, mu has broken her—but something still is left. Those remnants then, she speaks. The redwoods, our other country's pain, the redwoods' friends, ice cream. All of these things well out of her. Her wet hair and her wild eyes.

She tells us how she swam. About a feast laid out, and colors. She had walked around Maibara wet—awakened, gone beyond—had seen but had missed the feast. Apparently there had been some confusion.

One of her friends goes to the kitchen, bringing back cold noodles. She speaks old pains of pepper spray, ten thousand other things. Dim stars shine over the graveyard. They're different, in Japan.

I go to bed. She has awakened though, and sits up still. Her friends sit by her side, and after dawn they take her to the hospital. I do not go. I go instead to meditation. The zendo air is sad. Walking meditation. Sitting meditation. Chanting. Breakfast.

Her friends say, when they return, through damp eyes, "*Chotto taihen datta*," "It was difficult." She shouted. She awakened clinic objects, throwing them through halls. Such things need no translation. The doctors gave her sedatives, and sent her back to us.

Her friends stand by her like police. It's temporary; it will pass. They hold her wrists tight, and they look from time to time into her wild and awakened eyes. They bring her to her small, shared room behind the ceremony hall. They try to get her to just sleep. *Just sleep; just welcome silence.*

Roshi-sama will not speak to her. He does not say a word. A rumor spreads that he had prior indications that her mind was slipping off. Her madness had been brewing in the dokusan room. Meeting after meeting, she would just mouth back his teachings.

"*Everything is Buddha*," the rumor says she'd say, "*endowed with Buddha-wisdom, Buddha-virtue.*" Roshi-sama's mantras.

"*Good!*" the rumors say he'd said. In Zen it is asked that people penetrate the meaning. Mouthing words is not enough. She'd mouthed them, he'd said, "Good!" Accordingly, she got to thinking maybe she'd awakened.

"If she had been practicing correctly, this would not have happened," Roshi-sama tells me. I am scared and look into his soft, wide eyes. "She went her own way."

"Will this happen to me?" I ask.

He sees that she has gone beyond, and will not speak to her. He sees that she is only shouting, is not hearing, but still I wish that he would talk to her. She's given up her life to him, I've watched it. I saw her come into the temple—I can't believe it was a year ago already—and give herself up to him. Surrender.

She arrived at Gendoji and instantly accorded with the practice. She scarcely looked up, scarcely spoke. She never shirked the schedule, and on her free time, most nights, she would meditate or weed the grounds. Always smiling enormously.

She totally immersed herself in Roshi-sama's teaching. She had all of his lecture tapes in a giant box beside her bed, and she knew them back and forth. She would recite to herself the English translations, and even some of his obscure Japanese phrases, intonations. It was utter devotion.

True, she's fallen into a bit of a love affair. They've been discreet; they scarcely speak. Keep downcast eyes. Only sometimes at night, they go behind the kitchen and whisper their sincerity and dream of children, travels, home. Not many people know.

I know because he is my roommate and my friend. He is now quite confused. Did he bring this on? Is it something he has done? We stay up late at night together, going over and back over again their conversations, secret promises. Will she ever be the same again? We get up for zazen the next morning. 3:50 a.m. as always. A swirling, dark wind rustles through the meditation hall, overturning mats and sitting cushions, breaking rounded hand mudras, slumping our straight backs.

They bring her from the hospital to the women's shared room behind the ceremony hall. Her two friends try to get her into bed, and the rest of us go on. For five days, we will just continue on—around, amidst, above her intermittent, gone-beyond sedation. We will go along as best we can, as always, waiting for her mother who will come to take her home. That is, we will go on resolutely to awaken. "*Muuuuuuu…*," our endless practice.

Sometimes she will shout. Other times she'll sit sedately and we'll speak the painful joys of redwoods, of our other country. We have some friends in common at home—we'll speak of them, on a bench outside the meditation hall. She'll be lucid; wacky but coherent.

"Yes, he is quite a character," I will say of a mutual friend.

"What kind of cake was it? Were you there that time?" she'll ask, but I was not.

We will awaken. We will all awaken so that we can be with her. She will awaken us out from our resolute and effortful awakening, our silence; awaken us out from our faith. She has awakened us with ocean water dripping from her hair, with songs of those who live and die for mu, for redwood trees.

It will be quieter after she leaves, after the day her mother comes to take her to that other country, where the redwoods are. I will not see it—we, the men, will be out on alms rounds. We'll be out shouting and awakening the village streets.

We'll be shouting out our alms round "ho" for pennies and the Way. And we'll be shouting too for her, and for the ocean that has wet her hair—her wild eyes—and somehow, somehow we'll be shouting in the Japanese streets, shouting out our call for alms, for redwood trees.

"And so—I don't know," I cough into the phone outside the busy station, reaching for my teacher across thousands of miles of ocean. "It's like this has let me, for the first time, open up my eyes and see what this practice *really* does. I'm next; I know I'm next. I don't trust it. I can't take another day..."

"Roshi-sama is amazing, incredible. I've never met anyone like him, but...." I choke on tears. Roshi-sama's round and deeply wrinkled face descends on me again—this time, he slowly lifts his downcast eyes and peers at me. His kind stillness, his fanatical encouragement. His total love. His unequivocal, contagious, and immense enlightenment.

"But maybe—I don't know—maybe he's just too old, too sick," I continue. "He's around less and less, it's like the temple is unraveling. It's like he's hardly teaching anymore. All of us, strung out on the insane schedule, are just getting depressed and bitter. We argue all the time—this isn't religious life! The kitchen is filthy. All of us are pushing, pushing for some opening in zazen, but it just won't open out, it's just not working, we're not getting it but just going degrees of crazy and I've finally opened up my eyes to see it. So I'm calling you to let you know that I'm about to get the train and get me the hell out of here. Maybe visit you in a week or two…"

"I see," my American teacher Lee says. The line is faint and filled with static. I stand inside the phone booth at the Maibara Eki. A familiar spot—I've spent hours here hollering English into the handset, reaching out for home, in rain, and sun, and snow. My hands sting from the cold some days; other times, leaned back against the wall, I prop the glass booth door open with my foot to disperse the stifling heat. Sometimes I get a 125 *yen* coffee or hot cocoa from the vending machine just inside the station doors, and drink it while I talk to someone, running up minutes on a phone card that my parents keep paid up so I have less excuse not to call.

But I hold no vending machine coffee today, iced or hot. Today is far too urgent.

"Now is, of course, exactly the time not to leave," he says.

My heart and head sink—I know. I don't hear much anything else he says, I know what he will say, what any teacher probably would say. Our decisions come from stability, not panic. The temple's chaos doesn't need the further disruption of another sudden departure. We do not, as Zen students, act when we're off-balance. We furthermore do not run away anywhere, to anywhere, from anywhere, ever. We stay and stand and witness. We breathe, consider, step. If we are truly harmonized, perhaps we simply and spontaneously strike—but neither he nor I harbor the illusion that I'm acting from such accord.

I mutter my affirmation, and I mutter my goodbye. The handset clicks into its cradle. I look out through the glass booth walls out at the train platforms. Schoolchildren and businessmen bustle. A train from somewhere pulls away from its platform, slowly at first, gaining momentum. A shrill, female Japanese voice—*train to Osaka departing*—wails out over the loudspeakers.

My heart heaves and I do all I can do, all any self-respecting monk could do. I bike back to the temple, sullen, and unpack my bags again.

# 11   No Coming, No Going

> *No coming, no going; no arising, no abiding…*
> —Zen Master Dongshan, "Song of the Jewel Mirror Samadhi"

One afternoon, more than a year after we met, the young American monk Nengo and I go to the ocean together. We have lived in the same place for a long time, but it seems that we have never really sat down with each other before. In the temple there is always something to do next, and even when there is some free time, talking feels out of place. We do, we all talk now and then, but it is never entirely satisfying. I, at least, am always glancing back over my shoulder, half expecting to see Roshi-sama charging down the stairs with his stick.

"It is very difficult here," he confessed to me a day or two after we'd met. He had been in the temple just long enough to realize what he had gotten himself into. It looked to me like he'd caught a glimpse—the glimpse I too was just getting—of how long a "year in Japan" might end up feeling. How long is a *kalpa*, again? How long does it take that occasional bird to wear away the cubic mile of granite? When are the rest days, exactly?

I had only been at Gendoji for a few weeks myself, and although I was glad to hear that I wasn't the only one having a hard time, I was committed to making the best of it, and was steeled against any doubt that might reduce my fatigue, aches, and stress to mere vanity.

"Yeah," I agreed, "difficult but good."

He stopped, reflecting for a second, before correcting me: "Just difficult."

What did you expect? I wondered silently, my head nodding. The veneer of my exhaustion—paradoxically all that was holding me up—was already making me a little tense, a little irritable on top of my homesickness and overwhelmed confusion, and I felt in his confession the impossible admission that it might all not be worth it. If I succumbed to that, how would I survive? Maybe I couldn't quite see the point some times, even most of the time, but my strategy was to not look too closely, not question too much, assure myself that it was all in pursuit of something much higher than me and my struggles.

"These guys don't have any respect for us," he continued.

I nodded again—it was obvious. My first of many conversations with Keishi-san, who bitterly dismissed Western Zen devotees and their watered down ventures, had been only a day or two ago, and I'd seen Keishi-san speaking with Nengo too in the same secret tone. "I don't usually tell people this, but..." I heard him say, going on to repeat his refrain.

"This crap about no Zen in the West, where do they get off? Who do they think they are?"

Of all the foreigners in the temple, Nengo and I had the most similar backgrounds; we both had trained and were established in Zen Sanghas in the States. Arriving in Japan, though, was for both of us like starting from zero, like being out at sea with no map, and no ship. We were being treated as though we had never heard a word of the teaching or sat a minute of zazen before in our lives, and I at least was starting to feel like it might well be true. The Dharma personas we had cultivated at home were now void—Roshi-sama, his magnetic wisdom and compassion aside, just berated us on our posture, and the monks, Japanese and Western alike, either totally ignored us or offered their unsolicited, candid assessments of "Western Zen" and "Western Zen teachers" (if even indulging the existence of such categories). The intense purity of the Japanese practice still held us enthralled, but the summer heat was wilting the edges of our fresh, bright aspirations.

It is summer again, a year has passed for Nengo and I, with all its tremendous ups and downs, inspirations and crises, and on the shikunichi day before his departure we take a couple of bikes from the shed outside the temple gate and bike together through town to the ocean. At the *Seiyu* department store we buy some espresso ice cream and jellied coffee. "It isn't…" he sighs, picking up a four-pack of the black jello-like substance. How can we resist?

"You're going back home!" I say, watching the water. I am sad and excited: sad for myself, and for our parting, but excited at the emerging possibility that there might be such a thing as "going home." That even kalpas trickle away. I bite off a piece of my espresso ice cream bar, and remember once in the States looking at the ocean with a Japanese monk friend, watching the waves roll in and slide back. He taught me the word *natsukashii*, like nostalgic, homesick, longing backwards. It had seemed right then that he could swim home if he wanted—I had seen him see that he could swim home.

"I'm going home," my American friend Nengo agrees. We sit on a concrete pier, looking out at the bay that opens into the sea. I imagine that I too might return, could just dive off the pier right now and swim home.

Why not go? What am I holding out for? It's not just that I'm homesick, though it breaks my heart to even think the word, it's that the whole thing has changed, my whole world has changed, my expectations seem all to have shifted, or vanished, or crumbled. My naïve hopes for the great gains of practice seem, from this pier at least, with these snacks and Nengo's confident, down-home sanity, just as empty and unrealistic as the adolescent fantasies of the fifteen year-old Australian boy who I recently walked from the temple back to the train station with his parents, a month or two after he had written to Roshi-sama about wanting to come to Gendoji.

Dogen-Zenji was fourteen or something, right? Eight? All the ancient masters seemed to have had their heads shaved at four, or six, or thirteen. So why not?

Some of us who heard about the letter thought it was a little weird, but Roshi-sama didn't bat an eye. Somebody even suggested that the child might be coming to take his place as Roshi-sama's heir. Karmic connections are mysterious, I admitted, but it seemed to lot to ask of a kid.

One day the Australian teen showed up with his parents and some luggage. They were shown the zendo, the hondo, the bathrooms. The mother was nearly hysterical. The father was collected and cool. The kid seemed distant, overwhelmed, just trying to figure out that he was really in Japan.

"Don't worry, we'll take good care of him," the Dutch laywoman Elaine told the boy's mother. She shot a horrified look back: "We're all staying…" she stammered. Elaine looked surprised: we hadn't heard about that part.

The boy's mother wasn't exactly suited to Japanese temple life. She was oppressed by the compulsory zazen, by the nerve of her roommates to insist that she get up when the wake-up bell rang. She couldn't understand why she couldn't sit next to her husband at meals, much less stay with him at night.

"We've been living in the bush," she told me. "The outback. It's pure bliss except when you have to go into town for something. Town is hell." She stared into my eyes, "A living hell."

The kid was involved in archery; he showed me his bow as I tried to help him get settled in the dorm room/dining room that he was moving into. "It was made special by a craftsman in Europe. I'm not sure that I can use it here," he told me. "It's alright if I can't shoot it, just as long as I can keep it." He started peeling the duct tape off of the long thin cardboard box it was in. "Will I get to meet with the Roshi soon?" he asked. "Is he going to give me a practice?"

I liked him. He was ready to get going on this Zen thing.

"My son got this idea of moving to Japan," his father told me, "and it seemed like a good one. He's a special kid, you know. A very special kid. So we said, alright, we're all going. We sold everything and bought a one-way ticket here. There are no real teachers in the West, you know."

"Yes, I know."

"Enlightenment is just realizing that everything is shit," he told me later.

"Yeah."

"Everybody here is so ugly," the boy's mother whispered to me.

"I know what you mean."

Two or three days after they arrived, the father took me aside as I stumbled, bleary-eyed, to early morning zazen. "It was good to meet you," he said, shaking my hand. "Do you know a travel agent?"

The rush to zazen was quickly over, and the four of us stood alone in the courtyard. An electric light above the zendo door cast our shadows on the ground.

We walked to the eki, loaded down with their luggage. On the way, I gave the kid a little Buddha statue someone once had given me. I thought maybe it would help him. He came all this way; he should have something to show for it.

The sun was just rising, morning light reflected in the glass doors of the deserted train station. We said goodbye.

"It's good we're getting an early start," the mother said. "This way maybe we'll get somewhere today."

On the concrete pier at the bay, eating espresso bars and saying goodbye to my American friend Nengo, I wonder if my own dreams aren't just as transparent, impossible, and ill-advised. At least it only took the boy and his parents a few days to see it, before they went home, cut their losses. How long will it take me? Am I expecting this life to somehow suddenly redeem itself?

Nengo tells me that he has been remembering what he knows about *Jodoshinshu*, Japanese Pure Land Buddhism. The way he says it, the way I too recall it, the sect started when some sincere monk way back hit the end of his effort, the edges of effort, and he saw that whatever he did, it was him. That is, it was karmic, his effort was ego. How could ego-effort go beyond itself, beyond ego? Nengo has been thinking about this, as we all race our dented, rusted-out body-minds down the Zen *Autobahn*, clutching the steering wheels with white knuckles, not knowing if we will spin out or arrive.

The boxer monk spun out, Erin, Daiko-san spun out. I've had some skids, some slips of the wheel. And who exactly has arrived? When am I going to see, in anyone other than the naturally graced Roshi-sama, the part where it all pays off, the part where we arrive?

I've had my moments of clarity, sure, of intense dedication, wide open meditation, the extraordinary and selfless power of the "Hai!" I offer to Roshi-sama in dokusan. The empty-handed bliss of takuhatsu. But I am also increasingly noticing a hardening, a "fuck you" I feel like I'm carrying through the world.

A former priest I met in the U.S. once told me about practicing at the Japanese Soto Zen head temple Eiheiji—not just the parties and porn, but at the gate, when he'd announced, upon ritual questioning, that his reason for coming to the monastery was *ahimsa*, "non-harming." At that he had received a look of total incomprehension that really set him back, an early blow that never went away, that never turned around, and he'd only made it for nine months or so before getting out of his priest robes and out of Japan. If it isn't ahimsa, he said, what *is* the point?

What is the point? Had Daiko-san seen it, after twenty some years in the temple? Did his outbursts express it? His fists? Did Erin find it, in her wet hair and wild eyes? The boxer monk? Me? Where is it exactly that we are going to arrive, when we arrive?

Nengo and I sit watching the water, coursing in the profundity and relief of the that ancient Japanese monk Shinran, that one thirteenth-century monk, at least, who had just decided to stop. He gave up, he jumped ship, and he threw himself into the merciful ocean of Amida Buddha. He just lived out his ordinary life, because he knew that by his own power he could never reach freedom, never reach the other shore.

We each slurp up a coffee jelly. Its gustatory resemblance to fresh coffee is unnerving. Who would imagine? On the beach across from our pier, a couple dismantles their colored umbrella and walks hand-in-hand towards their car.

"Why do we need to become such great people?" he asks.

# 12
# Three Days After Money Day

It's not that I haven't earned my *Obon* money. I worked hard during the Obon festivals—as hard as anyone else. I did *tanagyo* with the tenzo Yushin-san, full days in the rain going to house after house of parishioners, chanting at their household altars, trying to maintain the long and repetitive *Daihi Shin Dharani* with no book and only two people, keeping time on a tiny *mokugyo* drum while Yushin-san played bells... When he stopped for breath, I had to carry the chanting alone without hesitation, with confidence, while the laypeople watched, affording no slips, no mumbles, and that chant in particular that wraps around and winds on itself, the *"namu kara tan no"*s all looping, trying to snare me in an infinite repeat... And then having tea with the strangers in their houses and trying to follow the Japanese conversation, to smile at the right time, *"Sou desu, ne!"* at the right time, listening to the same old temple news, Roshi-sama's health, *"Oh, how your children have grown!"* Yushin-san repeating, and how about the weather, crops, the traffic patterns. And at each house, saying: *"Jiryu-san does not eat meat, imagine!"* and all eyes turning to me, everyone murmuring and chuckling at the awkward and devoted vegetarian Western monk... And I have worked my cold fingers in the kitchen, and sweated over the summer kitchen stoves, and I have followed the schedule, even when it has seemed insane, and done takuhatsu, not lagging, not complaining, hour after hour marching; I have joined in all the temple work, I built a fence around the squash patch, and even though I had to take it down when Ankai-san's promotion left the fields headed by a monk who didn't want the fence, still, the point is I've done my part, I've earned my Obon money. It would be foolish to just leave without it! How can I leave just before money day, turn my back on the offering that I have earned, and that will help me navigate the coming weeks through hostile, overpriced Japan...? But how can I leave the morning after money day? Even if I leave two days after, won't I be perceived as greedy? *"Good timing,"* they will mutter once they see I've gone.

But let them mutter. My time is over. I am leaving. This time really.

A monk more senior than Daiko-san, the long-time field boss and incurable night sitter Shogan-san, slipped out of Gendoji without making a fuss. So did the senior monk a few years before him, I hear.

And so too does Daiko-san, finally, although not without stray hints and rumors in advance. At the peak of his violence and rage, humiliated and reprimanded even by Roshi-sama, he finally leaves Gendoji—one morning he is just gone. Gone. Roshi-sama acts like nothing has happened, and suddenly the broken-eared Shoryu-san is in charge. Everybody seems unsettled: deeply relieved and strangely sad.

"You know," Genzen tells me, "he really helped me when I was going through some hard times. He gave me a pastry once, just when I needed it. He got a little crazy, sure, but he was good friend. I mean it: I hated him as much as anyone did, but he was a good friend."

"Once on takuhatsu he took us way out of the way so that we could see the autumn colors in the back valley," Daishu says. "I swear I'd never seen such a magnificent fall."

"He kept things together, that's for sure," the laywoman Elaine reflects. "I don't know how we'll manage without him. The practice is going to deteriorate."

"He has nowhere to go," Genzen tells me. "He's given his whole life to the training here, he really has nothing else. Once he told me that maybe someday he'd like to just do takuhatsu all the time. Live on takuhatsu. Maybe he got a car, and lives in it doing takuhatsu. He has no family, you know, he has no one now. I heard that before he left he asked

Roshi-sama if the temple would please take care of his grave, when he dies."

Daiko-san, like countless others in the long temple history, in his own time just disappeared from the temple. When I first arrived at Gendoji, this method of leaving struck me mildly irresponsible, accustomed as I was to the explicit, contractual, and endlessly articulated commitments at my U.S. temple. Over the months, though, I've come to appreciate the lack of fuss as a way to preserve the practice, to reduce the distraction of someone's leaving. Why involve the whole Sangha in somebody's personal plans or crises? If the teaching is that in ourselves we should endeavor to cut off the "mind roads" of past and future, it follows even more that we shouldn't drag others into our delusions of the future, our plans. Isn't the American Zen way, I come to wonder, of constantly chatting about our comings and goings, our plans and "needs," just a wholesale distraction from the real matter at hand? Such talk is not tolerated at Gendoji, and Roshi-sama refuses to engage with us in those terms. "Nothing exists above your hara; only *just now!*" he insists. One walks away no more clear about the future but more clear, perhaps, about the present. If we have some designs on our future, we can't involve him. Despite our pleas, he won't tolerate the possibility that our planning has anything to do with our real practice. If we insist on straying from the present, Roshi-sama will not follow us: if we must, he'll have us dig that grave with our own hands.

After these midnight disappearances the community is shaken up for a short time until a new order settles around the absence; it is all-in-all less disruptive than the before-during-and-after involvement that tends to surround peoples' leaving American temples. In the Gendoji myth, at least, we then hear no more of them, are left only to guess whether they ascended to the abbacy of an obscure and snowy temple or returned to the marketplace with gift-bestowing hands. In fact we do hear news now and again—Zen circles aren't so large, and people pass through Gendoji bearing rumors. Shogan-san, for example, is said to be alone in a mountain temple in a distant province, for his post-enlightenment "long ripening," it was suggested; a monk arriving for Gendoji sesshin tells us that Shogan-san cut down some trees there, planted some vegetables, and was passing his days in meditation.

The Israeli layman Illy, leaving after roughly a year, resisted the tradition by trying to share his plans and concerns with some of us. It didn't go well.

"I'm leaving," he sobbed one morning, as the rest of us suited up for takuhatsu. "I just can't anymore," he said, the tears streaming down his face. "This place is killing something in me." I nodded, sad myself, reflecting on what was thriving or dying in my own Gendoji life.

We embraced and I deigned to offer him my warm and understanding goodbye—Westerners may well need such sentimentality, I magnanimously mused. Returning from takuhatsu, I saw his silhouette in the kitchen window, surrounded by steam, straining long udon noodles out of boiling water.

I don't know how Roshi-sama took it; most of the rest of us were just amused, but Genzen was annoyed.

"Leaving forever?" Genzen mocked, "Should we save lunch?"

But Illy never really came all the way back, and before long he had again steeled his resolve and tearfully informed us of his departure. That time he made it as far as the eki before turning back around, walking meekly into the kitchen and just starting in on clean-up.

He couldn't bring himself to walk out on the temple, tantamount to walking out on the Great Way. I understand; I can't bring myself either. But still something in him—and now the same thing in me—was crying out for it.

Finally one morning I saw him from my window, bag-laden, passing through the temple gate for good.

I must leave too, that is clear.

My mind, crushed between the rigors of the schedule and the breakdown of the temple structure, Daiko-san's absence, Roshi-sama illness, is each day more chaotic and despairing. As much as I endeavor to be an island in the stormy sea, hoping to be a locus of Buddha-like gentleness within the harsh edges of the temple, in fact I too am hardening. I feel it in my iron jaw. I startle myself one day shouting "fuck off!" at the Italian Freddy. He quite possibly had it coming, but still I'm distressed by the ease with which the words slipped from my mouth. I try to push myself harder, more zazen, truer zazen; I invest more and more in the possibility that I will see something, finally, in my meditation, something that will irreversibly justify the strain and resolve all of the stress. The more I push, aiming for this special state, pulling myself through the jungles and cliffs of altered mind-states, the more the stress increases. My jaw grows tighter, my reactions sharper, and my doubt, corrosive and despairing, each day secures a stronger foothold.

A quiet observer, deep in me, shakes his head slowly; a quiet voice in my mind has already made a decision. Nearly obscured beneath my high ideals of ego-shattering enlightenment, I secretly know that my truest goal is nearer, softer. It is clear that Gendoji's austerity will not open my heart, and it is clear that I will any day now be leaving.

And it is clear, too, that I will not make Illy's mistake—I will leave instead like Shogan-san and Daiko-san. I will keep my silence. It is only a question of when to leave exactly, and of how to make my preparations and escape without inciting the suspicions of my brothers and sisters in the Sangha.

Shogan-san, I recalled, had left just following the monastic allowance day after the August observances of Obon. In the U.S. we call them "stipends," and they come twice a month to our mailboxes in the office—"A-D," "Q-T", etc. (Of course in Japan we don't have mailboxes, and any letter we happen to get is screened by the disciplinarian.) Stipends come to our mailboxes, and we pick them up just like paychecks. They are, in fact, paychecks: social security is deducted, and "federal," "state," Medicare, etc. The years I had a checking account, the stipend would be direct deposited, appear by electronic magic on my monthly bank statement. I appreciated the spending money—and others truly depended on it—but I would still rail against the practice from time to time in the U.S. The whole thing seemed an offense to the monastic spirit.

But in fact it is traditional, and no less at Gendoji where a few times a year Roshi-sama calls the assembly into the hondo, stands in front of the altar, and hands out envelopes with spending money. If the temple finances are thriving, the envelope is thick; if takuhatsu and funerals have been slow that quarter, the envelope is thinner. Obon, the great summer festival of the dead that draws even the most lax parishioners to the temple with their donations is a main source of the temple's yearly income, and, from what I have heard, the post-Obon money day will bring the thickest envelopes of all. Shogan-san had collected and vanished, but, though Obon is fast approaching, for me to do the same seems unforgivably tacky. The tempting possibility haunts me, though—it is time for me to leave after all, and it just happens to be Obon—and I turn it over and over as I consider how and when to leave, as I try to extract myself from a place and ideology that I've spent the last year plus trying to surrender to.

I don't know why Shogan-san left. I assume that he had deep spiritual reasons, and though I justify my departure over and over in my head, part of me still suspects that I, in contrast, am leaving out of weakness. I've just gotten worn out and lazy, lost my faith; my leaving, as Illy feared about his own, is simply turning my back on the Way. Do I really think the practice would be any more complete somewhere else in decadent Japan, much less the U.S.? Shogan-san left right after allowance day but he had been in the temple for decades, he had status and clout, and besides, after so long as a monk he was impoverished and without family ties—he had no *credit card*, for God's sake—and to leave meant to navigate his way through time and space to find his next arrangement. I am certain that no one thought anything of it to discover that he had left just after Obon money day, but for me to do the same would be greedy. They will all think it greedy of me.

Not that I won't also have to navigate my way through Japanese time and space: the secret plans I have been making on the eki telephone and the community center internet are sure to stretch my thin resources. But to hang on just for the upcoming money day at the temple I am intent on leaving is, if not transgressive of precepts, at the very least in poor taste. But to leave before the offering would just be foolish—how will I make my way through Kyoto, afford even my bus ticket to the Osaka airport? More guilty withdrawals off my parent's account?

The day before Genzen's birthday, we smuggle a couple of beers behind the neighboring jinja shrine. The beers have been staling in the outside refrigerator for a month or two since a Shinto festival that a few of the monks participated in, helping to haul a huge torch up to a mountaintop shrine and then drinking and eating with the townsfolk. Since noticing the smuggled-back, leftover beers that appeared in the kitchen refrigerator, unseen by most, Genzen and I on our joint kitchen shifts have been joking about popping the tops. Tonight, at bedtime, after evening zazen, as we stand around in the kitchen wrapping up the final cleanup of the night, we look up at each other and smile: it is time.

"Happy birthday," I say, as we raise the cold cans. We talk late into the night, until finally I cannot contain my goodbye, the news I've been holding so silent, so close.

Once I let the news slip with Genzen-san, I relax my security around the plan to leave. I decide, in fact, that although I will still slip out quietly, I owe it to my friends—who amount to the few Western men—to say goodbye. I bike around all day on the final shikunichi day before I plan to leave, finding some imported cookies and even chips and salsa from a liquor and health-food store in a distant corner of town. Getting back to the temple, I spread the word about an after-hours party (rare, but not unheard of), in a vacant room of those of us who had already gone, the American monk Nengo, and the young Dutch David.

Surreptitiously we gather after the night bells, giddy at the breach of discipline. I lay out my goodies and announce my departure.

"What about the rest of us?!" Freddy the boisterous Italian wonders as Daishu, Harold, Genzen, and I stuff Pepperidge Farm cookies into our mouths, reading the English packaging with great interest.

We all pause and look around: "I guess this is 'the rest of us,'" he continues, voice dropping. We look at each other in the curtained-off section of the downstairs Kannondo: the Western men of Gendoji, reduced, after the next day, to four; the life of the temple slowly leaking away.

The day before I leave, I request a final dokusan with Roshi-sama. Unlike my friends, he is not surprised. He has watched me going over and over it in my mind.

He is not disappointed; he does not encourage me anymore to stay, does not respond with any strictness. It seems to me that he appreciates my resolve to leave, that I have come to a stable conclusion, and he simply, after an understanding nod, asks "Some question?"

I consider for a moment, knowing it is the last time I will ever see this incredible teacher. What do you ask the Buddha, on his deathbed? What *is* the most important thing?

As though reaching into my future, over the sea to American Zen, I ask Roshi-sama about teaching and enlightenment. "If I go back to *Amerika*, it could be that I would be asked teach or offer Dharma even if I have not truly awakened. Should I refuse?" I ask, thinking of Keishi's harsh opinion of the unenlightened "teachers" in my country.

"No! No! Teach zazen!"

"What should I teach about zazen?"

"Three things," he says, animated.

But what about inka certification of enlightenment; what about Roshi-sama's lack of Dharma heirs, the strict standard for teaching? What about leading others astray, the blind leading the blind? Those concerns all seem suddenly tossed to the wind—were they ever real?—and Roshi-sama comes to life, ignited with the hope that the practice of zazen might spread epidemically through the country that had Atom Bombed his own.

"One: chin in. Pull tall here," he says, placing his hand gently on the back of the top of his head. "Chin out—*no good!* Chin in! Two: breathe from nose. Lightly, gently. Three, *point here!*" he pounds his belly-center with his fist, "Mind only in hara."

"Teach Americans *taiso* stretches, so that bodies become loose. Half lotus, ok, but full lotus is best. With *taiso*, not difficult! People start with a little bit of zazen, and slowly, slowly more, longer periods.

"New zazen person begin with counting breath. Like this," a new peace settles over Roshi-sama: his body straightens slightly and his eyes fall to half-shut. "*Hitotsu…*" he says slowly, drawing out the word, quiet as a whisper but completely suffused with the slow power of his hara, "One…." He silently inhales, then slowly, from deep inside, starts the new exhalation: "*Futatsu…*" he whispers, "Two…."

"Once person is *yooshh…*" he says, sinking into another long and slow exhalation, "with much concentration from breathing counting, teach them shikantaza. *Just!* Easy to say, but very difficult." A moment of silence, then he starts again.

"Shikantaza—Nothing bring," he begins, shaking his head, prohibiting. "No grasp. Mind: hara. Thoughts—no touch. No separation. One with everything." He sits still and silent for another moment, resting in the vastness he has brought into the narrow room. Then he continues, an urgency blossoming up from the stillness.

"Please teach zazen: correct posture, correct breathing, hara, grasping nothing. But you must also continue this zazen. Please!

"Eating, *become* eating. Study, *become* study. Bell, *just* bell. Pillar, *just* pillar. Become one with anything, everything. Slouched is *not* zazen! Chin in. Any thoughts, *don't worry*. Always natural."

As the tears well up in my eyes, he concludes: "Only… Mind… Great…." He signs an immense circle with his arms, as though to hand me the unspeakable immensity of things.

"Point here!" he shouts suddenly, pummeling his belly with his closed fist, and reaching for the bell that will for the last time and forever dismiss me.

"*Yarinuite!*" Go all the way through!

"*Continue!*" he belts, and the crashing of his hand bell overcame the room.

August 20th, an excruciatingly calculated three days after Obon money day, I leave Gendoji, straining under my bags with my accomplice Genzen, walking through the pre-dawn morning in thin streetlights to the Maibara Eki. Alongside the parking lot of the still, dark station, traffic signals flicker quickly and silently between their colors at the empty intersections.

"Be in touch," I say to Genzen. "When you come home we'll climb a mountain together."

He hurries back towards the temple to ring the wake-up bell, his daily job. My eyes follow him as he crosses the long lot towards the staircase that leads to the walkway over the tracks, towards the road back to the temple. By the time he reaches it he is scarcely a shadow, his outline dissolving in night.

It is done. I am alone, on my own way. I sit under the light of the *koban* sign of a deserted police stall at the edge of the station lot, to pass the couple of hours until the first bus will depart. I feel more or less safe—I will never really ever be scared to be out in Japan—but somehow the prospect of police warms the light of the sign. As though the invisible police in the closed office will charge out and save me, if the monks of Gendoji run to the station with sickles and shovels to keep me from leaving.

Dawn comes slowly, the glass *eki* walls reflecting the morning sun's first rays. A delivery truck painted with a rosy-cheeked, blond boy and a slice of white bread comes to a stop in the empty parking lot. Over the idling engine and through the open door that the driver climbs out from, exuberant talk radio chatter seeps into the stillness. *Yamazakipan*, reads the side of the truck. The driver unloads some crates and carries them to the door.

The woman from the kiosk unlocks the doors to receive the delivery. I recognize her from Gendoji—we have been eating, or trying to eat, the expired bread treats that she started to bring us a few weeks ago, after the station remodeling and kiosk expansion. She hasn't quite figured out the new sales patterns, so three or four times already she has come to the temple offering crates and crates of unsellable, expired bread. There is only so much we can eat of the pre-packaged melon *pan*s, cream *pan*s, chocolate *pan*s, and weird meat *pan*s like hamburger or crab. The novelty quickly wore off.

I go into the bathroom, which runs alongside the outer wall of the station, and I wash my face. Yesterday was a shikunichi bath day and I carefully shaved, but looking into the mirror I feel freakish—my bulging eyes contrast insanely with the deep bags beneath them. Smooth head, tense jaw, gaunt face and enormous Western nose. I draw in a long breath: "I'm ready," I say out loud to myself in the neon light of the abandoned bathroom. I go back outside and sit upright on top of my backpack.

Just after the main station lights come on and the doors open, the newly ordained, quirky, and reputedly kensho-attained monk Sesso-san arrives at the eki. No sickle or shovel, I gratefully note. I check my watch—it is just after five am, so he is in *taiso*, the communal exercise period between the first and second rounds of zazen. From across the station lot, I watch him go inside, buy a can of coffee from a vending machine, and stand outside the big glass doors smoking a cigarette. I had no idea that communal exercise could include such stretches—another Gendoji revelation.

Sesso-san looks at me for a moment from across the station plaza, then returns his attention to his cigarette and coffee. I can't tell if his disregard of me comes from non-recognition, disbelief, equanimity, or a mysterious Japanese-ness of simply not seeing what is not meant to be seen; perhaps it's just his eccentricity. He doesn't approach me, or even look again in my direction until he is about to leave, when he tosses one more puzzled glance back at me before heading towards the stairs that lead up to the walkway over the train tracks, stretching his arms behind him with an elastic rope as he walks—it is exercise time, after all.

As I slipped out of the temple this morning, trying to remain unnoticed, straining with Genzen under the weight of my baggage and my departure, Ankai-san met me with the same indifference. He walked by as I laced on my shoes outside the Kannondo, my luggage heaped in the entranceway and Genzen already trying to strap some of it on. He was walking towards the graveyard in samue and sneakers, probably to practice his forbidden martial arts routine before ringing the four a.m. bell, the last call for zazen. He bowed at the center of the courtyard, as we always do upon crossing in front of the altars: bowed once to the hondo and once to the Kannondo. He bowed directly to the doorway we sat in, towards the image of Kannon behind us, but he did not look up, and though he could not have possibly missed seeing us, no acknowledgement at all crossed his face.

As we descended the stairs outside the main gate, we saw Ankai-san again, stretching his leg high against a gate pillar. The light that hung in front of the main gate lit the scene, but still we all acted as though nothing out of the ordinary was transpiring. He neither spoke nor looked up; I looked up, at least, rested my eyes on him for a moment, but could not bring myself to say any words, and just continued on with an inner "Goodbye."

"He'll be disappointed to see me in zazen," Genzen said as we got out of earshot, turning a corner in the little neighborhood we walked through towards the station. "I bet he thinks it's me leaving, that he'll finally be free of me."

I surmised to Genzen that his behavior had been somehow typically Japanese, but for Genzen it had just been a function of their relationship. Though they had been warm with each other in the past, more recently Ankai-san has not made eye contact with Genzen at all. He avoids him at all costs—when Genzen enters a room, Ankai-san leaves. If Genzen speaks, Ankai-san does not hear.

"I even tried buying him ice cream," Genzen told me. "He didn't even touch it."

Is this what I've been learning here, how to despise and push away the people I live closest to?

In the early morning light, I regret again that my leaving is in this context of my battered faith. On one hand I wish that I had not succumbed to it, left within it; on the other hand, it seems that staying at Gendoji would only have damaged it further—I feel myself moving forward towards Dharma situations that I hope can start to heal it. I don't know what they might be. I certainly won't be returning to my American temple—after touching single-minded practice I can't imagine returning to "Zen resort" life. Maybe some strict, but somehow balanced, American monastery... maybe a mountaintop hermitage, like Shogan-san...

A bus, just like the one that brought me on my first clumsy days in Japan, pulls into the lot and idles at its stop. I glance a confirmation at the kanji indicating its destination, the station where I will catch the train that will deliver me to Kyoto, to the hostel at which I've already made my reservations. I collect my bags and waddle under their weight to the bus door.

On a payphone in the Kyoto Eki I talk to my ex-girlfriend who is sick and sad. I am sick, and sad. I tell her happy birthday, and I'm coming home. She says it's stupid to even talk about our intimacy—it's so obvious. I ride the bus and almost spend the day with an American girl who says that she is planning to return to Okayama tonight, but that in fact she does have tomorrow off as well.... She could be late, her pretty green eyes flash. I wear black samue. She asks if I am a martial artist and I try to say about the way that nothing is really reached by our minds nor quite outside them, I mean that no, I'm just a charming Zen guy. I just wear this stuff to get into the tourist temples free.

I have three days until my flight home, and I'm planning to go to Nara but am basically just killing time. She tells me she is going on a palace tour. I wouldn't mind seeing a palace, maybe dinner... It seems too much to just invite myself, though, and it's suddenly weird. I don't know what to do. We split up abruptly at the terminal. I'm expecting her to come with me into the train station at least, but I look up and she is walking away.

Just as well.

In Nara people feed deer. Sick of seeing temples, I sit on a park bench, hear traffic, and think about the faces on the bellies of the statues in the temples of the Buddha's wrathful friends. One I just saw at Todaiji holds a brush and a scroll—his weapons. His face is in a Zen frown, and his scroll and brush make me think of the line in a critical essay I'm reading in an English book I picked up in a Kyoto bookstore: *"Accepted proof of so-called enlightenment is actually a set of literary skills, developed over twenty years."* What have I been doing? Where am I going? What am I looking for anymore?

On the train, I try to help an English woman in white with her luggage. She is kind, but we don't spend the day together either, much less the night. We're just foreigners, floating imperviously through Japan. I have a headache—tired, tired of traveling. It is more than badly-dosed caffeine; I am ill. I take a nap on the park bench, which helps. These flailing days before my flight are surreal—who am I anymore? A monk? A lost kid? An exile? I've been dragging my strung-out, exhausted body and mind to the most revered and ancient Zen sites in the world. What else would I do in Kyoto? But I can't help remembering a time, outside a South of Market drag show with a gorgeous boy in silver lamé (or was it me in silver?), that I woke up to something. What does our effort do for us, exactly? It seems I've been this strung-out, this tired, everyday since I arrived in Japan.

"Another year in the dream," I said on the phone, as close as I could come to the meaning of "happy birthday." In another dream there are no years. Breath, color, sound. Light glitters through the trees, dancing in this dirty Nara park.

She said she loves me—*why does she always say she loves me?*—I said I haven't given up on the idea of the strict American monastery up north, and that when you're in the real discipline for a while you get to where you don't want to be doing anything else… you know, pretty much. I didn't tell her that I have no idea who I am, or what time is, or where I'm going, or who the wrathful faces are carved in those wooden Buddha *hara*s. I didn't mention that I self-consciously but necessarily offered incense to the enormous Vairochana Buddha at the *Kegon* sect's ancient Todaiji temple. The girl on the bus told me you could climb into that Buddha's nose, if you wanted to. Maybe she didn't know, or just didn't say about how it could possibly be otherwise. She didn't know to say that Buddha was each smell, each tinge of head pain, passing traffic, burp and light play. Baby deer in shade.

# 13   Homecoming

Not long after returning to my home temple in the U.S., I am charged with driving a visiting Japanese dignitary and his retinue back over the long dirt road after a visit. They have spent a night, observed sanctioned and unsanctioned ceremonies, and tried to come to terms with this strange community, made up mostly of laypeople, that seems to consider itself a monastery. I've been admittedly a little self-conscious watching them watch us—I've been back a few weeks now, but it would be too much to say that I'm completely at ease with our way of life.

The lectures still bug me—the psychologizing and philosophizing, the endless irrelevant questions as the lectures roll on and on and the people listening start to relax their postures, uncross their legs, and chime in like it was a self-help seminar or a college philosophy class. The food still makes me cringe: the peanut butter, the soymilk, the half-and-half. What possible need is there for half-and-half? I still sigh each time I see the professionally-prepared stipend checks sticking out from the mailbox slots. I can't help but to roll my eyes at the short-term students, flirting, flaunting, posturing. And I'm just as annoyed as always at the senior teachers, who are of course as busy as ever tending to their families, their travels, their engagements, and finding just scrapings of time to serve their vital functions for the students who rely on them.

Watching the group of Japanese clergy notice all of these same idiosyncrasies makes me a little extra sensitive, but even so, it's different for me now, being back. I see what I see, and I react how I react, but I don't fundamentally believe anymore that something is wrong with our practice. I don't feel like we need fixing, and I'm not stuck on an idea of how that fixing that we don't need would happen. It's not that I now think American Zen is perfect, but I seem to have lost all of my better ideas about how it should be. I understand and appreciate how we got to be the way we are: decades of struggling to hold the weight of a twenty-five hundred year old tradition alongside the needs and expectations of young, radical seekers in a young, culturally unmoored country. Above all, and though I have no idea where this strange American road will take me, I am overwhelmed with gratitude.

I am happy to drive the Japanese monks, and I sincerely bring forth my Japanese Zen mind to meet them. I take the chance to inquire about some still-obscure details of Japanese monastic forms.

"At what point, precisely, in the *nenju* ceremony should the assembly go into *gassho*?"

"Should the wake-up bell be handled bowl up or bowl down, and what *doanryo* officer is to ring it in the absence of a *shuso*?"

"Under what circumstances should someone other than the *ino* serve as *kokyo*?"

Even as I ask, though, I notice a lightness, a freedom from this monk and his retinue and the tradition he embodies. I notice that I'm curious, but not fixated; that I'd like to refine our practice, but I really don't feel anymore like we need to become something else. I feel, in fact, some confidence in my temple, in my Sangha, in our Buddhism, no matter how this visiting monk sees it. I've maybe finally come to believe what my teacher suggested long ago: our practice is good.

The dignitary is cordial, even jovial, and helpful. He agrees that these are important questions, and he acknowledges that certain monastic forms may well need to change to accommodate the American circumstances. Still, he is relieved that someone is asking, and he indicates that our "lifestyle" might in fact someday develop into a genuine form of Zen if these questions continue to be asked. He confesses to being moved, despite some reservations, by our mountain practice. He sees promise here, though the lack of discipline strikes him as a real lack of dedication. If we are patient and sincere, he suggests, True Zen might yet arrive in the West.

I agree, nodding and grunting affirmations as I drive.

I drop them off on the other side of the mountain, bowing deeply and repeatedly, fussing and refusing to go back until they have disappeared in the car that will carry them to the airport. Once they are gone, I drive back over the long dirt road to my temple.

Cresting the ridge, the ocean a glimmer on the western horizon, the deep valleys arrayed far below to the east, I feel again a wide open vastness, a deep appreciation. We are just a group of people diligently studying ourselves, sincerely meeting our lives, and that is enough. In fact it is more than enough—it is overflowing abundance. We may not have true Zen, whatever that is, and whoever could say. But we do have a practice and a way of life that has given me, and continues to give me, my own life. We may not be doing real Zen, but we are making Zen real.

The universe contacts to the size of a tear, which in turn expands to include all things, and then pours down itself: gratitude.

A week later, I meet an American Zen nun recently returned from several months at a women's monastery in Japan. Over a meal—not a grain of rice in sight, and a mere ten minutes of mandatory silence—we get to talking. I tell her about how I am feeling. Feelings are tolerated in American Zen, and she has no choice but to indulge me. I describe my sense of a pendulum swinging back, a pendulum that has from the start kept the beat of my practice, oscillating from formal to informal, intensive to relaxed, exclusive to inclusive. I seem to be swinging back away from the austerities and excesses of Japanese temple life; swinging back, though not without some kicking and screaming, into the excesses of American temple life.

I tell this sincere American nun I've just met that my view is shifting, that some of what has previously frustrated me about American Zen as I know it—the lack of single-mindedness, the couples, the children, the food, the corporate model—is striking me now not as laziness or misunderstanding of the tradition but rather as a vital renewal of an archaic and foreign paradigm that won't ever quite work for Americans. I tell her that practice for me lately seems to be about maturation, and that maturation seems to be about the whole being maturing, and civilization maturing, the whole earth and oceans maturing, and that the whole maturation by definition involves more tools than one, more approaches than one. American Zen realizes that, I tell her, so it includes more than just orthodox Zen, allows more influence than just the single Zen teacher, more life than just the monastic schedule, more contacts than merely the faithful. I have a deeper faith in that inclusiveness than I do in the idea that full maturity can somehow blossom from narrowly defined "spiritual" practice or insight, no matter how drastic or dramatic, no matter how orthodox or ancestral. It may well be that Japanese Zen rigor can catalyze insight experiences, or force the surrender of the grasping self, more efficiently than the less structured American Zen, but I don't trust that strict and single-minded style to bring about a holistic maturation, especially in Westerners. On the contrary, it seems to be a one size fits all, and one practice resolves all, reductionism.

I don't mean, I tell her, that awareness, concentration, surrender, and real presence aren't intensely activated in the Japanese style: indeed, that's the paradox or the point. In the face of the adversity, the mind becomes very alert, the practice becomes the lifeline. But even though my moment-by-moment refuge in Buddha was spurred and supported in the strict monastic system, the overall experience, with its austerity, negativity, and tension, felt more damaging than helpful. Samadhi at what cost? I ask her. "Encountering the ego" at what cost? And what about the side effects: treating people harshly, fusing "practice" with "pain"? Not that anger and unhappiness, pain of all kinds, can't be used in Dharma practice, but isn't it obvious that an environment saturated with those afflictions is harmful? I ask the American nun if she worried, like me, about what the life was really doing to us, from the seniors down to the juniors who seemed far too quick to learn the brutal joys of seniority.

She tells me that she did doubt whether she would in the long term thrive in that environment, but she hesitates to take a stand on whether or not it is the "true path." For her, we miss the point as much by explaining away our difficulties with Japanese Zen as merely insurmountable cultural differences, as we do by taking the difficulties personally as our own failures of practice and enlightenment. For both of us, we realize, a more useful framework is *go-en*, or "karmic affinity." What if we understand all of our attractions, aversions, and reactions to something not as reflecting the truth of the thing, but simply as expressions of our own affinities? Japanese Zen produces great beings, kind sages; American Zen too can mold clear, compassionate, and awake people. The Buddhist question has always been not "what is true?" but "what works?" It is not to ask "Where is the true way?" but rather to ask, "Where is my heart drawn?"

She and I agree, then, that we won't say we just lacked the strength to make it in Japan, but we will also resist suggesting that "true practice wasn't there anyway." We won't say that we've returned to our respective American Zen temples, because they offer the best path, or the truest path, or the strongest path. In fact, from now on we commit to not claiming that anything we do is the "right thing," much less the "best thing," but only that it *is* that thing which we are doing. It is by definition where our karmic affinity lies, and as such it's beyond good and bad. It's a question of go-en. It means to live our lives with confidence in the actual ground of our lives, not based on our ideals or our analyses of how a life should be lived. We will strive wholeheartedly to fulfill our own right path, but with a kind of clarity and confidence that doesn't need our "right" to make anyone else "wrong."

This humility includes knowing that wherever we find ourselves, wherever we are drawn, there will be a light and there will be a shadow. This shouldn't surprise us. Wherever Buddhism has gone, my friend offers, it has picked up the light of the culture and it has picked up the shadow of the culture. In Japan, then, it is no surprise that the temples are like the army—militarism is a shadow of Japan. And it should be no surprise either when we find that the temples in the U.S. seem as much like corporations—what else would be shadow of this culture?

That said, she tells me the stories of her own failures in Japan, her own struggles, her own lack of affinity. She describes the same harshness that I experienced, the same approach of degrading, hammering away at "small self" in order to weaken and overcome it. She wonders with me whether for her that process was weakening or just finally reinforcing ego-attachment. She tells me about the ritual of bedtime at her temple: at the end of each grueling, non-stop day, the nuns would all lay out their bedding, lay down, and a few minutes later hear the bell for after-hours work. They would get up and work for another hour or two, sometimes more, tying up the day's loose ends before going back finally to bed. Night after night this occurred, until she realized that she shouldn't expect any particular bedtime at all. When she let herself believe that the "bedtime" was the actual bedtime, she was sunk.

"Sounds awful," I say, shaking my head. Over my plate of leftovers, the rich and varied, if slightly aged, summer practitioner's fare, her description of Japan strikes me as nothing other than awful, incites in me some festering bitterness. What were we thinking in Japan? Chasing something so that we could stop seeking? Hurting ourselves to improve ourselves? Starving ourselves and hardening ourselves to achieve some idea of the Way of Compassion? Where did we think that could lead? Isn't it just more of that same delusional habit of taking the self way too seriously? Why try to bash down and tear apart the self, considering that the teaching is that it has never from the first existed at all? Why not instead just gently, persistently seek the self, and abide in the natural purity of the impossibility of grasping it? Why make it such a body-breaking event? My gut is clenching again, my jaw clamping down against everything, every awful moment I lived in Japan.

"Awful," I say again, this time genuinely bitter.

"Yes! It was awful!" she agrees, laughing. "But there is something else there."

I remember too that there is something else. She tells me a story about helping with a temple tea ceremony. After she worked for several hours, obsessing with a toothless old nun over the elaborate preparations, the old nun dismissed her and worked alone on the final details. My new American friend describes lingering at the edges of the hall and watching as the old nun patiently sculpted a perfect mound of ash to support the charcoal beneath the tea kettle. When the mound was perfected, she painstakingly carved a Chinese character into it, her whole frail body folded over it, absorbed. When she finally finished, she set the kettle on the hearth. It obscured the ash completely, and with it, all of her fine work.

The American nun's eyes dampen.

"You could hardly see any of the ash anymore."

I nod slowly. I remember with suddenly overwhelming fondness the rainy streets of takuhatsu, the chant of "ho" rising up as the single voice of a dozen brothers. I see in a flash twenty teacups rippling like a wave down a long table of still, seated monks, as each waits just an instant for his senior to drink first. I hear the low, still rumble of morning chanting. I smell the musty grassiness of straw tatami mats. I taste the sour jolt of umeboshi plum against the bland morning rice.

"The kettle covered the ash," she repeats, absorbed in her image. "None of the guests were ever meant to see it; it was like she had done it for nothing."

Zen students come and go in the hot bustle of the dining area. The nun I've just met looks down at her food on the table, and then looks up out the window towards the mountains that surround us.

"No one but her ever saw it," she says, repeating herself, her shiny eyes still fixed on the distant slopes.

And I see it too, for the first time, the ten-thousandth time—that immaculate gift of Japan.

# Epilogue

Where are we left, then?

How, five years later and willingly reimmersed in American Zen, has my own understanding developed to resolve the many problems this story has raised? More generally, and more importantly, where are we left as Western Buddhists as a whole? Can we admit now that we have sold out the vital monastic core of our tradition by compromising with our individualistic, egalitarian, and materialistic culture? Or will we assert that we are in fact propelling the Buddhadharma forward, skilfully adapting to keep it alive in our actual, day-to-day world? No one can ultimately answer, of course, though perhaps too many would claim to. Nonetheless, towards tying up the dangling ends of this story, I offer a few reflections.

Soto Zen has long emphasized the monastic life and its details, and equally long has struggled with how monasticism can relate to the spiritual needs of ordinary people living worldly lives. In the first centuries of Soto Zen in Japan, while other Japanese Buddhist schools offered spiritual practices that were in themselves accessible and edifying to masses of laypeople, Soto Zen could rarely lift zazen out from its monastic context. In that sense Dogen's zazen was markedly unlike the universal single practices of his contemporaries Shinran and Nichiren. Instead of offering zazen meditation as a universal practice, medieval Soto

Zen teachers offered monastic rituals tailored to the wider society. By performing monastic-style ceremonies for laypeople, the power of the monks and their monasteries was shared by the culture at large. That is, Soto Zen spread through Japan by the power and mass appeal of ritual, not by a movement of lay people taking up zazen practice.

We in Soto Zen like to think that Dogen's zazen can be universally recommended, and yet as we study his zazen we cannot avoid his monastic centrism. As scholars develop their understanding of Dogen, his monastic bias becomes more and more clear, and the universal teachings he seems sometimes to propound are increasingly understood as fundamentally inextricable from the monastic system that he experienced in China. It is not simply "sitting without striving" or "zazen-only" shikantaza, it is just sitting, non-striving, within a monastic architecture and liturgical schedule replete with esoteric and exoteric supports and meanings. It is quite possible that for Dogen the basic point was not, as we sometimes imagine, simply that daily activity with the proper attitude is precisely the Buddha Way, but rather that ritualized daily activity, when situated in the sacred context of the ancestral monastic order and orthodox monastic life, is the Buddha Way. Can zazen, then, be taken out of the monastery? And even if it can, what is lost in the process?

I was struck in Japan that what seemed the only word for what we in the States call "practice" was *shugyou*, "ascetic discipline," a word implying formal monastic training. The awe and respect I was often accorded by laypeople in Japan surprised me, as did their genuine concern and sympathy for me as I undertook what they related to primarily as austerities. The presumed difficulty of the monastic life has long been at the core of Japanese laypeople's respect for Zen monks, and only rarely do laypeople regard zazen as something they themselves might practice. There are, to be sure, as I have indicated in this story, a very few devoted laypeople who frequent training centers and engage in zazen, even sesshin and dokusan, living creative and sporadic versions of monastic life much like the majority of Zen practitioners in the West. But in my understanding and experience, the general attitude about lay Soto Zen practice in Japan, the fulfillment of Dogen's supposed universal recommendation, is and has since medieval times been little more than a vicarious connection to an elite monastic order. The monks' ascetic discipline, renunciation, awakening, and ritual services generate spiritual merit which the laity absorb by proximity.

In the West, obviously, our problem is different. We lack the thousand year history of culturally integrated Buddhist monasticism by which we can relate to and understand our own spiritual lives and practice. Most of us practitioners of meditation, helplessly democratic and self-centered, expect that we all should have equal access to the pure essence of the tradition. If "just doing" in a monastery is precisely the enlightened activity of all Buddhas throughout and beyond time, then too our own "just doings"—just driving, just soccer practice, just googling—should be equally ordained enlightenment in the one mind of the cosmic Buddha.

We recognize that we are making a stretch here, that the overwhelmingly monastic-centered Buddhist tradition is straining to accommodate this preconception, but we will not relent: we are entitled to enlightenment, whatever our lifestyle. Carefully selected traditional Zen texts, translated into English by people with the same assumptions we have, seem to offer abundant support for the view that we can find the Buddha Way within our lives just as they are. We see no need to abandon our home lives, to enter the monastery, or to change much of anything about the conditions of our lives, apart, perhaps, from our inner orientation. We see Zen not as an external way of life, but as an attitude or inner posture, a way of relating to whatever conditions are before us. We insist that this is the essence of Zen, and we resist or ignore the fact that it is by no means the Zen of the Japanese and Chinese Buddhist ancestors we venerate, or of "Gendoji," or even of lay-centered Japanese parish temples like "Komyoji."

The American Zen teacher Norman Fischer has called this entitled, egalitarian Western reality "plan B." Ideally, perhaps, we would all live in the tradition of Chinese, Japanese, or Indian monastic ascetics, and perhaps in fact that would be the best way to live, the most Buddhist, the most conducive to enlightenment. Such a lifestyle Fischer calls "plan A," the traditional model of Buddhist practice. Unwilling or unable to renounce or to turn away from the attachments and excitements of our worldly lives, however, even the most devoted of Western Buddhists tend to find themselves in the midst of "plan B."

American monasticism, if the term can be properly applied in the absence of a culture that supports and maintains such an institution, is accordingly already tilted towards this "plan B" orientation. This is not in itself a problem—the vaunted "Chinese" monasticism that Dogen and his earliest disciples practiced already included profound accommodations to Japanese cultural norms, just as the authentic Chinese monasticism that Dogen had previously practiced under Master Rujing was already a startling, nearly unrecognizable, leap from the Indian monasticism it in turn claimed to represent. Problem or not, though, this cultural complexity does undermine to some extent my reflections in this book. I have been unfair in setting out to draw comparisons that basically cannot be drawn, as it already too late, the terms are already too different, the values already too deeply divergent—American Zen has already created its own terms. The new shoots cannot perhaps be so meaningfully compared to the standing tree.

The question is thus less about authenticity than practicality: what have we lost, and what have we gained? As I've said, I can find myself nostalgic for clarity and power of Japanese monastic life: the rainy brotherhood of takuhatsu, the peace and joy of takuhatsu lunch, the way that the teacups ripple every morning across the low, long, somber table, as each monk waits just an instant for his senior to drink first. I occasionally miss the focused intensity of monthly sesshins, the late night sitting and the pounding slap of the kyosaku. And I struggle, still, to find the meaning of Zen in my busy, albeit quasi-monastic, life. The simplicity of Japanese Zen training is invaluable to the spiritual path. It allows for no division of the person: there is exactly one life and exactly one goal, privately and communally, and every single aspect of a monk's life is explicitly in service of that.

Here in the U.S., even as a full-time resident priest in one of the most formal and established Zen temples in the Western world, my life remains at some level divided. "Jiryu" at my seat in the zendo, in my various formal and priestly roles, but "Mark" at Home Depot, at DMV, to my in-laws. I wear samue and koromo on temple grounds, but increasingly on excursions from the temple I find myself disguised in lay clothes to avoid the novelty or aversion that I feel reflected back to me by a culture that has no context but karate for medieval Japanese dress. I maintain that my inner orientation is undivided, or strives at least to be, that each mundane thing I meet I endeavor to regard as though it were the offering tray, the lineage papers, the oryoki bowls. In the temple I am fully supported to do so, and naturally it's harder to find outside, but the effort is continuous. Each meeting, each moment, wherever it is, is no different from zazen, chanting, and kinhin. Each day, wherever I am and whatever I am doing, is fundamentally just a ritual meditation round in the ongoing, all-pervading, and endless sesshin.

But my understanding of that continual practice, and, insofar as I can, my access to it, is inseparable from my monastic background. When I am able to see each day as sesshin, it is only because I have sat so many sesshins; when I succeed in lifting a deli sandwich as though it were an oryoki bowl, it is only on the strength of the countless oryoki meals that I've eaten. So how can I recommend this to others, as though they to could simply dive into the practice? Is Zen practice truly universal, or is it only available as the fruit of monastic training?

There is no easy answer to this; it is a question that gets to the very heart of Zen. Since the foundations of Chinese Ch'an in the Sixth

Ancestor's so called "sudden enlightenment," and reinforced irreversibly with the development of the Tendai school's "original enlightenment" doctrine in Japan, this has been the central problem of Zen. Complete enlightenment is the basis, the all-pervading, fundamental fact of everything. This original enlightenment is perfect and complete from the start, and as such there is no approaching it and no turning away from it. It is simply *thus*, that each and every experience or object, however confused or deluded, clear or awake, violent or peaceful, is exactly the fulfillment of great enlightenment, is exactly the substance, body, and mind of the Buddha. If everything is already perfect, though, what could "practice" possibly mean? How could there be any meaningful path to walk at all? This original awakeness cannot be measured or obstructed, so how could we take any steps towards it? It is not dependent in the slightest upon our appreciating it or not, so why would we break our bones in a monastic effort to appreciate it? It could be argued that this development of extreme universalist Mahayana Buddhism marked the beginning of the end of the monastic orders, and of a progressive, staged, comprehensible Buddhist practice at all. But what does it mean for our ordinary lives, monastic or otherwise?

This problem of whether Zen is universally available or only accessible under special conditions can be studied directly in our own seated meditation. To strictly practice Dogen's shikantaza, just sitting zazen, we are instructed to simply sit in the midst of this original awakening. We just sit. But when we do so we notice that there is an undeniable relationship between our concentrated, concerted effort and our feeling of natural clarity. Surely we all find in meditation those moments of ease and effortless presence—but are those moments not bought, even if indirectly, through the struggle of applying our mind, through the disciplined physical and mental toil of still, upright sitting? Our shikantaza is vast and wide open, but its depth and breadth seem related to a core effort, a core concentration from which we extend out, a gross effort which we gradually release and purify into an ever more subtle effort. To just dive into shikantaza, as critics of Soto Zen have always insisted and as our own meditation experience likely confirms, overlooks basic truths about how our minds and our meditation work. It is, in short, impractically idealistic.

It may surprise us then, that it is we American Zen students, not our Japanese and Chinese forbearers, who are idealists; it is we who claim to plunge directly into the mind of Buddha without recourse to the provisional stages of monastic and meditative discipline. It is not the arrogant and strict Soto Zen masters, maintaining monastic forms at the cost of all comfort, ease, and joy, nor the young monks in their wide hats, ringing their bells in earnest blessing as they walk the streets on alms rounds, who are naïve idealists. It is instead we American Zen practitioners, too often foolishly idealistic in our insistence that the Way is right here, right now, wherever we are and whatever we are doing.

My concerted breath practice enables and matures, in each period of meditation, a more open shikantaza, a less effortful, more present way of being that goes far beyond breath attention. Likewise, as I have admitted, my appreciation and access to the lay Zen of "plan B" is based on and develops out from my "plan A" monastic forays; neither would be as meaningful without the other. My practice of marriage is an unfolding of the intimacy of monastic training. Occasional moments of clear meditation while sitting on the bus are enabled and encouraged by long hours of sitting in the zendo. But how far can one go before needing to re-connect with that spiritual source; and how available is this "universal practice" to those for whom monastic training, or even extended periods of meditation, has not and will never be an option?

American Zen, vague and problematic as it is, affirms this need to reconnect with the source of our practice, but always situates it in service of a wider, further-reaching practice. A sesshin here and there, a Dharma talk now and again, an occasional sitting or simple incense offering at home: each of these are upheld as sources of energy for formless practice, rather than as ends in themselves. Monastic practice, we say here, is easy—a view quite unlike Japanese assumptions about the ascetic struggles of monastics. Most of us in American Zen see lay practice, practice in the world wherever we are, as the most difficult path. We don't turn away from this difficulty, and perhaps unwisely we don't consider it insurmountable, but we go straight towards it, seeing it completely as our practice and encouraging one another that we indeed have no other life, no other place to find the Dharma than here. And when it becomes too difficult, we are perhaps able take a break from the rigor of lay life, and in contrast to the Japanese model in which monks might hop the monastery wall for a break from the rigor of the monastery, we go to the monastery for a little practice R&R, some relief from the struggle of practice within lay life. But however long we are able to stay, we tend to value the easy, clear monastic practice only insofar as it supports us in the more difficult and higher stakes project of practicing within our worldly lives.

Whichever path is better, or more traditional, or more conducive to real spiritual understanding and compassion, the basic fact that I'm left with is that I simply am a Western Buddhist, and that try as I might, my "plan B" Western Buddhist values underlie my practice. I have tried, and failed, to force myself to think that monastic practice is better than, or even finally necessary at all for meaningful, everyday, worldly practice.

Have I lost something in that? Yes. Have I gained something?—indeed, my whole life, just as it is, reclaimed and renewed as precisely the territory of unsurpassed enlightenment.

Made in United States
Orlando, FL
08 July 2025